iOS Auto Layout
Demystified

 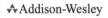

iOS Auto Layout Demystified

Second Edition

Erica Sadun

♦♦Addison-Wesley

Upper Saddle River, NJ • Boston • Indianapolis • San Francisco
New York • Toronto • Montreal • London • Munich • Paris • Madrid
Cape Town • Sydney • Tokyo • Singapore • Mexico City

Visit us on the Web: informit.com/aw

Library of Congress Control Number: 2013948434

Copyright © 2014 Pearson Education, Inc.

ISBN-13: 978-0-321-96719-0
ISBN-10: 0-321-96719-4

Text printed in the United States on recycled paper at RR Donnelley in Crawfordsville, Indiana.

First printing: October 2013

Editor-in-Chief
Mark Taub

Senior Acquisitions Editor
Trina MacDonald

Senior Development Editor
Chris Zahn

Managing Editor
Kristy Hart

Senior Project Editor
Betsy Gratner

Copy Editor
Kitty Wilson

Indexer
Joy Dean Lee

Proofreader
Anne Goebel

Technical Reviewers
Mike Shields
Ashley Ward

Editorial Assistant
Olivia Basegio

Cover Designer
Chuti Prasertsith

Compositor
Nonie Ratcliff

❖

Hop. Hop. THOOM.

❖

Table of Contents

Preface

Auto Layout reimagines the way developers create user interfaces. It creates a flexible and powerful system that describes how views and their content relate to each other and to the windows and superviews they occupy. In contrast with older design approaches, this technology offers incredible control over layout, with a wider range of customization than frames, springs, and struts allow. Somewhat maligned by exasperated developers, Auto Layout has gained a reputation for difficulty and frustration, particularly when used through Interface Builder (IB).

That's why this book exists. You're about to discover Auto Layout mastery by example, with plenty of explanations and tips. Instead of struggling with class documentation, you'll learn in simple steps how the system works and why it's far more powerful than you first imagined. You'll read about common design scenarios and discover best practices that make Auto Layout a pleasure rather than a chore to use.

You'll explore many of the strengths of Auto Layout as well. It's a technology that has a lot going for it:

- **Auto Layout is declarative.** You express the interface behavior without worrying about *how* those rules get implemented. Just describe the layout; let Auto Layout calculate the frames.

- **Auto Layout is descriptive and relational.** You describe how items relate to each other onscreen. Forget about sizes and positions. What matters is the relationships.

- **Auto Layout is centralized.** Whether in IB or a layout section in your own code, Auto Layout rules tend to migrate to a single nexus, making it easier to inspect and debug.

- **Auto Layout is dynamic.** Your interface updates as needed to respond to user- and application-sourced changes.

- **Auto Layout is localizable.** Conquer the world with Auto Layout. It's built to adapt to varying word and phrase lengths while maintaining interface integrity.

- **Auto Layout is expressive.** You can describe many more relationships than you could in the older springs-and-struts system. Go beyond "hug this edge" or "resize along this axis" and express the way a view relates to other views, not just its superview.

- **Auto Layout is incremental.** Adopt it on your own timescale. Add it to just parts of your apps and parts of your interfaces, or jump in feet first for a full Auto Layout experience. Auto Layout offers backward compatibility, enabling you to build your interfaces using all springs-and-struts, all constraints, or a bit of both.

This book aims to be inspirational. I've tried to show examples of nonobvious ways to use Auto Layout to build interactive elements, animations, and other features beyond what you might normally encounter in IB. These chapters provide a launch pad for Auto Layout work and introduce unfamiliar features that expand your design possibilities.

As the title suggests, this book is primarily targeted at iOS developers. I have included OS X coverage where possible. So, if you're an OS X developer, you're not left out completely in the cold. I live primarily in the iOS world. Please keep that in mind as you read.

Auto Layout has made a profound difference in my day-to-day development. I wrote this book hoping it will do the same for you. It's my intention that you walk away from this book with a solid grounding in Auto Layout. And, if I'm lucky, the book will provide you with a "Eureka!" moment or two to lead you forward.

—Erica Sadun, July 2013

How This Book Is Organized

This book offers practical Auto Layout tutorials and how-tos. Here's a rundown of what you'll find in this book's chapters:

- Chapter 1, "Introducing Auto Layout"—Ready to get started? This chapter explains the basic concepts that lie behind Auto Layout. You'll read about why you should be using Auto Layout in your apps and why it's essentially a constraint satisfaction system.

- Chapter 2, "Constraints"—With Auto Layout, you build interfaces by declaring rules about views. Each layout rule you add creates a requirement about how part of the interface should be laid out. These rules are ranked based on a numeric priority that you supply to the system, and Auto Layout builds your interface's visual presentation accordingly. This chapter introduces constraints and the rules of layout, and it explains why your rules must be unambiguous and satisfiable.

- Chapter 3, "Interface Builder Layout"—Working with constraint-based design in Interface Builder can sometimes be a frustrating experience for developers new to Auto Layout. Fully updated for iOS 7 and Xcode 5, this chapter teaches you the tricks you need for making IB create exactly the interface you want.

- Chapter 4, "Visual Formats"—This chapter explores what visual constraints look like, how you build them, and how to use them in your projects. You'll read how metrics dictionaries and constraint options extend visual formats for more flexibility. And you'll see numerous examples that demonstrate these formats and explore the results they create.

- Chapter 5, "Debugging Constraints"—Constraints can be maddeningly opaque. The code and interface files you create them with don't lend themselves to easy perusal. It takes only a few "helpful" Xcode log messages to make some developers start tearing out their hair. This chapter is dedicated to shining light on the lowly constraint and helping you debug your work.

- Chapter 6, "Building with Auto Layout"—Designing for Auto Layout changes the way you build interfaces. It's a descriptive system that steps away from exact metrics such as frames and centers. You focus on expressing relationships between views, describing how items follow one another onscreen. You uncover the natural relationships in your design and detail them through constraint-based rules. This chapter introduces the expressiveness of Auto Layout design, spotlighting its underlying philosophy and offering examples that showcase its features.

- **Chapter 7, "Layout Solutions"**—The chapters leading up to this one focus on know-how and philosophy. This chapter introduces solutions. You'll read about a variety of real-world challenges and how Auto Layout provides practical answers for day-to-day development work. The topics are grab bag, showcasing requests developers commonly ask about.

- **Appendix A, "Answers to Exercises"**—This appendix provides the answers to all the chapter-ending exercises.

About the Sample Code

This book follows the trend I started in my *iOS Developer's Cookbook* series. This book's iOS sample code always starts off from a single main.m file, where you'll find the heart of the application powering the example. This is not how people normally develop iOS or Cocoa applications or how they should be developing them, but it provides a great way of presenting a single big idea. It's hard to tell a story when readers must search through many files and try to find out what is relevant and what is not. Offering a single launching point concentrates the story, allowing access to an idea in a single chunk.

The presentation in this book does not produce code in a standard day-to-day best-practices approach. Instead, it offers concise solutions that you can incorporate into your work as needed. For the most part, the examples for this book use a single application identifier: com.sadun.helloworld. This avoids clogging up your iOS devices with dozens of examples at once. Each example replaces the preceding one, ensuring that your home screen remains relatively uncluttered. If you want to install several examples simultaneously, you can simply edit the identifier, adding a unique suffix, such as com.sadun.helloworld.table-edits.

You can also edit the custom display name to make the apps visually distinct. Your iOS Team Provisioning Profile matches every application identifier, including com.sadun.helloworld. This allows you to install compiled code to devices without having to change the identifier; just make sure to update your signing identity in each project's build settings.

There is a smattering of OS X code in this book as well. This is not an OS X–centered book (as you can guess from the title), but I've covered OS X topics where it makes sense to do so. I spend the majority of my time in iOS, so please forgive any OS X faux pas I make along the way and do drop me notes to help me correct whatever I've gotten wrong.

Getting the Sample Code

You'll find the source code for this book at http://github.com/erica/Auto-Layout-Demystified on the open-source GitHub hosting site. There, you'll find a chapter-by-chapter collection of source code that provides working examples of the material covered in this book.

As explained later, you can get the sample code either by using git directly or by clicking GitHub's download button. It was at the right center of the page when I wrote this book. It enables you to retrieve the entire repository as a ZIP archive or tarball.

Getting Git

You can download this book's source code by using the git version control system. An OS X implementation of git is available at http://code.google.com/p/git-osx-installer. OS X git implementations include both command-line and GUI solutions, so hunt around for the version that best suits your development needs.

Getting GitHub

GitHub (http://github.com) is the largest git-hosting site, with more than 150,000 public repositories. It provides both free hosting for public projects and paid options for private projects. With a custom Web interface that includes wiki hosting, issue tracking, and an emphasis on social networking of project developers, it's a great place to find new code or collaborate on existing libraries. You can sign up for a free account at the GitHub Web site, which then allows you to copy and modify this repository or create your own open-source iOS projects to share with others.

Contribute!

Sample code is never a fixed target. It continues to evolve as Apple updates its SDK and the Cocoa Touch libraries. Get involved. You can pitch in by suggesting bug fixes and corrections and by expanding the code that's on offer. GitHub allows you to fork repositories and grow them with your own tweaks and features and then share them back to the main repository. If you come up with a new idea or approach, let me know. My team and I are happy to include great suggestions both at the repository and in the next edition of this book.

Contacting the Author

If you have any comments or questions about this book, please drop me an e-mail message at erica@ericasadun.com or stop by the GitHub repository and contact me there.

Editor's Note: We Want to Hear from You!

As the reader of this book, you are our most important critic and commentator. We value your opinion and want to know what we're doing right, what we could do better, what areas you'd like to see us publish in, and any other words of wisdom you're willing to pass our way.

You can e-mail or write me directly to let me know what you did or didn't like about this book—as well as what we can do to make our books stronger.

Please note that I cannot help you with technical problems related to the topic of this book, and that due to the high volume of mail I receive, I might not be able to reply to every message.

When you write, please be sure to include this book's title and author as well as your name and phone or e-mail address. I will carefully review your comments and share them with the author and editors who worked on the book.

E-mail: trina.macdonald@pearson.com

Mail: Trina MacDonald
        Senior Acquisitions Editor
        Addison-Wesley/Pearson Education, Inc.
        75 Arlington St., Ste. 300
        Boston, MA 02116

Acknowledgments

No book is the work of one person. I want to thank my team who made this possible. The lovely Trina MacDonald gave me the green light on this title, thus ultimately providing the opportunity you now have to read it. Chris Zahn is my wonderful development editor, and Olivia Basegio makes everything work even when things go wrong.

I send my thanks to the entire Addison-Wesley/Pearson production team, specifically Kristy Hart, Betsy Gratner, Kitty Wilson, Nonie Ratcliff, and Chuti Prasertsith.

Thanks go as well to Neil Salkind, my agent for many years, and Stacey Czarnowski, my new Neil; to Rich Wardwell, my technical editor on the first edition, and Mike Shields and Ashley Ward, my tech editors on the second; and to my colleagues, both present and former, at TUAW and the other blogs I've worked at.

I am deeply indebted to the wide community of iOS developers who supported me in IRC and who helped by reading drafts of this book and offering feedback. Particular thanks go to Oliver Drobnik, Aaron Basil (of Ethervision), Harsh Trivedi, Alfonso Urdaneta, Michael Prenez-Isbell, Alex Hertzog, Neil Taylor, Maurice Sharp, Mike Greiner, Rod Strougo, Chris Samuels, Hamish Allan, Jeremy Tregunna, Lutz Bendlin, Diederik Hoogenboom, Matt Yohe, Mahipal Raythattha, Neil Ticktin, Robert Jen, Greg Hartstein, Jonathan Thompson, Ajay Gautam, Shane Zatezalo, Wil Macaulay, Douglas Drumond, Bill DeMuro, Evan Stone, Alex Mault, David Smith, Duncan Champney, Jeremy Sinclair, August Joki, Mike Vosseller, Remy "psy" Demarest, Joshua Weinburg, Emanuele Vulcano, and Charles Choi. Their techniques, suggestions, and feedback helped make this book possible. If I have overlooked anyone who contributed to this effort, please accept my apologies for the oversight.

Special thanks also go to my husband and kids. You are wonderful.

About the Author

Erica Sadun is the bestselling author, coauthor, and contributor to several dozen books on programming, digital video and photography, and Web design, including the widely popular *The Core iOS 6 Developer's Cookbook*, fourth edition. She currently blogs at TUAW.com and has blogged in the past at O'Reilly's Mac Devcenter, Lifehacker, and Ars Technica. In addition to being the author of dozens of iOS-native applications, Erica holds a Ph.D. in computer science from Georgia Tech's Graphics, Visualization and Usability Center. A geek, a programmer, and an author, she's never met a gadget she didn't love. When not writing, she and her geek husband parent three geeks-in-training, who regard their parents with restrained bemusement when they're not busy rewiring the house or plotting global domination.

1

Introducing Auto Layout

Auto Layout re-imagines the way developers create user interfaces. It provides a flexible and power-ful system that describes how views and their content relate to each other and to the superviews they occupy. In contrast to older design approaches, this technology offers incredible control over layout, with a wider range of customization than you can get with frames, springs, and struts.

Auto Layout has garnered both a loyal user base and fanatical detractors. Its reputation for diffi-culty and frustration, particularly when used through Interface Builder (IB), are occasionally merited. Although Xcode 5 vastly improves that situation (by doing away with several baffling and alienating features), this is a technology that continues to evolve toward full maturity.

Auto Layout is a fantastic tool. It does things that earlier technologies could never dream of. From edge case handling to creation of reciprocal relationships between views, Auto Layout introduces immense power. What's more, Auto Layout is compatible with many of Apple's most exciting application programming interfaces (APIs), including animations, motion effects, and sprites.

That's why this book exists. You're about to learn Auto Layout mastery by example, with plenty of explanations and tips. Instead of struggling with class documentation, you'll read, in simple steps, how the system works, how to tweak it to make it work better, and why Auto Layout is far more powerful than many developers realize. You'll discover common design scenarios and discover best practices that make Auto Layout a pleasure rather than a chore to use.

Origins

Auto Layout first debuted on iOS in 2012, as part of the iOS 6 release. It also appeared about a year earlier in OS X 10.7 Lion. Intended to replace the older springs-and-struts-based Autosizing, Auto Layout is a new system that builds relationships between views, specifying how views relate to their superviews and to each other.

Auto Layout is based on the Cassowary constraint-solving toolkit. Cassowary was developed at the University of Washington by Greg J. Badros and Alan Borning to address user interface layout challenges. Here's what the Cassowary SourceForge project page (http://sourceforge.net/p/cassowary/wiki/Home/) says about it:

> Cassowary is an incremental constraint solving toolkit that efficiently solves systems of linear equalities and inequalities. Constraints may be either requirements or preferences. Re-solving the system happens rapidly, supporting UI applications.

Cassowary was developed around an important interface phenomenon: that inequality and equality relationships occur naturally in user interfaces. Cassowary developed a rule-based system that enabled developers to describe these relationships between views. These relationships were described through constraints. *Constraints* are rules that describe how one view's layout is limited with respect to another. For example, a view might occupy only the left half of the screen, or two views might always need to be aligned at their bottoms.

Cassowary offers an automatic solver that transforms its system of constraint-based layout rules (essentially a set of simultaneous linear equations, if you're a math geek) into view geometries that express those rules. Cassowary's constraint system is powerful and nuanced. Since its debut, Cassowary has been ported to JavaScript, .NET/Java, Python, Smalltalk, C++, and, via Auto Layout, to Cocoa and Cocoa Touch.

In iOS and OS X, the constraint-powered Auto Layout efficiently arranges the views in your interface. You provide rules, whether through IB or through code, and the Auto Layout system transforms those rules into view frames.

Saying "Yes" to Auto Layout

There are many reasons developers want to say "No" to Auto Layout. Maybe it's too new, too strange, or requires a bit of work to update interfaces. But you *should* say "Yes." Auto Layout revolutionizes view layout with something wonderful, fresh, and new. Apple's layout features make your life easier and your interfaces more consistent, and they add resolution-independent placement for free. You get all this, regardless of device geometry, orientation, and window size.

Auto Layout works by creating relationships between onscreen objects. It specifies the way the runtime system automatically arranges your views. The outcome is a set of robust rules that adapt to screen and window geometry. With Auto Layout, you describe constraints that specify how views relate to one another, and you set view properties that describe a view's relationship to its content. With Auto Layout, you can make requests such as the following:

- Match one view's size to another view's size so that they always remain the same width.

- Center a view (or even a group of views) in a superview, no matter how much the superview reshapes.

- Align the bottoms of several views while laying out a row of items.

- Offset a pair of items by some constant distance (for example, adding a standard 8-point padding space between views).

- Tie the bottom of one view to another view's top so that when you move one, you move them both.

- Prevent an image view from shrinking to the point where the image cannot be fully seen at its natural size. (That is, don't compress or clip the view's content.)

- Keep a button from showing too much padding around its text.

The first five items in this list describe constraints that define view geometry and layout, establishing visual relationships between views. The last two items relate a view to the content it presents. When working with Auto Layout, you negotiate both these kinds of tasks.

Here are some of the strengths that Auto Layout brings to your development.

Geometric Relationships

Auto Layout excels at building relationships. Figure 1-1 shows a custom iOS control built entirely with Auto Layout. This picker enables users to select a color. Each pencil consists of a fixed-size tip view placed directly above a stretchable bottom view. As users make selections, items move up and down together to indicate their current choice. Auto Layout constraints ensure that each tip stays exactly on top of its base, that each "pencil" is sized to match its fellows, and that the paired tip and base items are laid out in a bottom-aligned row.

Figure 1-1   This pencil-picker custom control was built entirely with Auto Layout.

This particular pencil picker is built programmatically; that is, a data source supplies the number of pencils and the art for each tip. By describing the relationships between the items, Auto Layout simplifies the process of extending this control. You need only say "place each new item to the right, match its width to the existing pencils, and align its bottom" to grow this picker from 10 items to 11, 12, or more. Best of all, constraint changes can be animated. The pencil tip animates up and down as the base reshapes to new constraint offsets.

The following code shows how these items were laid out in my project:

```
// This sample extensively uses custom macros to minimize the
// repetition and wordiness of this code, while giving a sense of the
// design choices and layout vocabulary offered by Auto Layout.
// Read more about similar custom macros in Chapter 6.
```

```objc
- (void) layoutPicker
{
    for (int i = 0; i < segmentCount; i++)
    {
        // Add base
        UIImageView *base = [[UIImageView alloc] initWithImage:baseArt];
        base.tag = i + 1;
        [self addSubview:base];
        PREPCONSTRAINTS(base);

        // Load tip
        UIImageView *tip = [[UIImageView alloc] initWithImage:segmentArt[@(i)]];
        tip.tag = i + 1001;
        [self addSubview:tip];
        PREPCONSTRAINTS(tip);

        // Constrain tips on top of base
        CONSTRAIN_VIEWS(@"V:[tip][base]|", tip, base);

        // Left align tip and base
        ALIGN_LEFT(tip, base);

        // Tips and base have same width so
        // match the tip width to the base width
        MATCH_WIDTH(tip, base);
    }

    // Set up leftmost base
    UIView *view1 = [self viewWithTag:1];
    ALIGN_LEFT(view1, 0);

    // Line up the bases
    for (int i = 2; i <= segmentCount; i++)
    {
        // Each base to the right of the previous one
        UIView *view1 = [self viewWithTag:i-1];
        UIView *view2 = [self viewWithTag:i];
        CONSTRAIN_VIEWS(@"H:[view1][view2]", view1, view2);
    }

    for (int i = 1; i <= segmentCount; i++)
    {
        // Create base height constraint so the
        // base's height (the pencil without the tip) is
        // fixed to the value of baseHeight
        UIImageView *base = (UIImageView *)[self viewWithTag:i];
        baseHeight = base.image.size.height;
```

```
CONSTRAIN_HEIGHT(base, baseHeight);

        // Create tip size constraints fixing the
        // tip's width and height to these values
        UIImageView *tip = (UIImageView *)[self viewWithTag:i + 1000];
        CONSTRAIN_WIDTH(tip, targetWidth);
        CONSTRAIN_HEIGHT(tip, targetHeight);
    }
}
```

Content-Driven Layout

Auto Layout is content driven. That is, it considers a view's content during layout. For example, imagine a resizable content view with several subviews, like the one shown in Figure 1-2. Suppose that you want to be able to resize this view but don't want to clip any subview content while doing so. Auto Layout helps you express these desires and rank them so that the system makes sure not to clip when resizing.

Figure 1-2 shows a small OS X application whose primary window protects the content of its two subviews. (Throughout this book, I try to add a few OS X examples where possible. Auto Layout is virtually identical on iOS and OS X.) These subviews include a label whose content is the string Label and a resizable button whose content is, similarly, the string Button. The left side of the figure shows the original content view as the application launches; the right side shows the same window after it's been resized to its minimum extent.

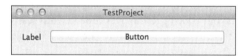

Figure 1-2 Auto Layout can ensure that the stretchable button shown in the original view (left) won't clip while resizing. The window cannot resize any smaller than the small view (right) because doing so would cause either the label or button to clip.

At the right of Figure 1-2, you see the smallest possible version of this view. Because its Auto Layout rules resist clipping (these rules are called *compression resistance*), the window cannot resize any further. The only way to allow it to shrink beyond this size is to demote or remove one or both of its "do not clip" subview rules. A similar rule, called *content hugging*, allows a view to resist padding and stretching, keeping the frame of each view close to the natural size of the content it presents.

Keep content in mind and adapt your rules as your views change the data they present. For example, if you were switching from one language to another, you might need the width of each label and button to adapt to different word lengths. For example, localizing English text to Spanish or Portuguese might cause a 20%–25% expansion in word size. Localizing to Hebrew or Arabic can shrink English text by a third.

Prioritized Rules

With prioritized rules, Auto Layout weighs the importance of layout choices and adapts to challenging edge conditions and special cases. Rule balancing is an important part of Auto Layout design work. You not only specify the layout qualities of each view but also prioritize them. When rules come into conflict—and they do quite regularly—the system uses your rankings to select the most important layout qualities to preserve.

In the example of Figure 1-2, the integrity of the label and of the button contents have priority over any request for a smaller window. This forces a natural minimum on the window size and prevents the window from resizing any further than that.

Inspection and Modularization

One of the great things about Auto Layout is how well it can be centralized and inspected. This is, however, a benefit only if you create your layouts in code. While you can browse constraints in IB, and even visualize them with the proper tools, recovering the *intent* of each layout choice is an intractable issue.

In code, you can compartmentalize your rules to common methods (such as `loadView` and `updateViewConstraints`) and freely annotate them. Code trades off review against visualization. You can inspect your layouts with ease to ensure that your logic is properly expressed. You cannot preview those rules, however, except by running the application.

You can easily modularize constraints. Once you've built a routine that centers a view in its superview, you can re-use that routine indefinitely. By building a library of common constraint requests (for example, "align this view to the bottom" or "create a row of these views with center-Y alignment"), you cause your layout code to refine over time in both real-world readability and overall reliability. You can see this modularization in the code example that accompanies Figure 1-1.

Incremental Adoption

Auto Layout is backward compatible. Interfaces and nib files built using older Autosizing technology still work in Auto Layout. You are welcome to mix and match autoresizing views with constraint-based layout. For example, you can load a nib whose subviews are laid out using struts and springs and allow that view, in turn, to operate as a first-class member of the Auto Layout world. The key is encapsulation.

As long as rules do not directly conflict (for example, you can't say "stretch using Autosizing" *and* "stretch using Auto Layout" at the same time on a single view), you can reuse complex views you have already established in your projects. You can, for example, load Autosizing nibs and seamlessly place them into your Auto Layout scenes.

Constraints

Now that you've read about the *why* of Auto Layout, this section introduces the *what*. Here's the basic vocabulary you need to start talking about this technology.

Constraints, as you learned earlier, are rules that allow you to describe view layout. They limit how things relate to each other and specify how they can be laid out. With constraints, you can say "these items are always lined up in a horizontal row" or "this item resizes itself to match the height of that item." Constraints provide a layout language that you add to views to describe geometric relationships.

The constraints you work with belong to the `NSLayoutConstraint` class. This Objective-C class specifies relationships between view attributes, such as heights, widths, positions, and centers. What's more, constraints are not limited to equalities. They can describe views using greater-than-or-equal and less-than-or-equal relations so that you can say that one view must be at least as big as or no bigger than another. Auto Layout development is built around creating and adjusting these relationship rules in a way that fully defines your interfaces.

Together, an interface's constraints describe the ways views can be laid out to dynamically fit any screen or window geometry. In Cocoa and Cocoa Touch, a well-defined interface layout consists of constraints that are *satisfiable* and *sufficient*.

> **Note**
>
> Each individual constraint refers to either one or two views. Constraints relate one view's attributes either to itself or to another view.

Satisfiability

Cocoa/Cocoa Touch takes charge of meeting layout demands through its constraint satisfaction system. The rules must make sense both individually and as a whole. That is, a rule must be created in a valid manner, and it also must play a role in the greater whole. In logic systems, this is called *satisfiability*, or *validity*. A view cannot be both to the left *and* to the right of another view. So, the key challenge when working with constraints is to ensure that the rules are rigorously consistent.

Any views you lay out in IB can be guaranteed to be satisfiable, as IB offers a system that optionally checks and validates your layouts. It can even fix conflicting constraints. This is not true in code. You can easily build views and tell them to be exactly 360 points wide and 140 points wide at the same time. This can be mildly amusing if you're trying to make things fail, but it is more often utterly frustrating when you're trying to make things work, which is what most developers spend their time doing.

When rules fail, they fail loudly. At compile time, Xcode issues warnings for conflicting IB constraints and other IB-based layout issues. At runtime, the Xcode console provides verbose updates whenever the solver hits a rough patch. That output explains what might have gone wrong and offers debugging assistance.

In some cases, your code will raise exceptions. Your app terminates if you haven't implemented handlers. In other cases (such as the example that follows), Auto Layout keeps your app running by deleting conflicting constraint rules for you. This produces interfaces that can be somewhat unexpected.

Regardless of the situation, it's up to you to start debugging your code and your IB layouts to try to track down why things have broken and the source of the conflicting rules. This is never fun.

Consider the following console output, which refers to the view I mentioned that attempts to be both 360 points and 140 points wide at the same time:

> **Note**
>
> The boldface in this code is mine. I've used it to highlight the sizes for each constraint, plus the reason for the error. In this example, both rules have the same priority and are inconsistent with each other.

```
2013-01-14 09:02:48.590 HelloWorld[69291:c07]
    Unable to simultaneously satisfy constraints.
Probably at least one of the constraints in the following list is one you
don't want. Try this: (1) look at each constraint and try to figure out which
you don't expect; (2) find the code that added the unwanted constraint or
constraints and fix it.
(Note: If you're seeing NSAutoresizingMaskLayoutConstraints that you don't
understand, refer to the documentation for the UIView property
translatesAutoresizingMaskIntoConstraints)
(
    "<NSLayoutConstraint:0x7147d40 H:[TestView:0x7147c50(360)]>",
    "<NSLayoutConstraint:0x7147e70 H:[TestView:0x7147c50(140)]>"
)

Will attempt to recover by breaking constraint
    <NSLayoutConstraint:0x7147d40 H:[TestView:0x7147c50(360)]>

Break on objc_exception_throw to catch this in the debugger.
The methods in the UIConstraintBasedLayoutDebugging category on
    UIView listed in <UIKit/UIView.h> may also be helpful.
```

This unsatisfiable conflict cannot be resolved except by breaking one of the constraints, which the Auto Layout system does. It arbitrarily discards one of the two size requests (in this case, the 360 size) and logs the results.

Sufficiency

Another key challenge is making sure that your rules are specific enough. An underconstrained interface (one that is *insufficient* or *ambiguous*) creates random results when faced with many possible layout solutions (see the top portion of Figure 1-3). You might request that one view lies to the right of the other, but unless you tell the system otherwise, you might end up with the left view at the top of the screen and the right view at the bottom. That one rule doesn't say anything about vertical orientation.

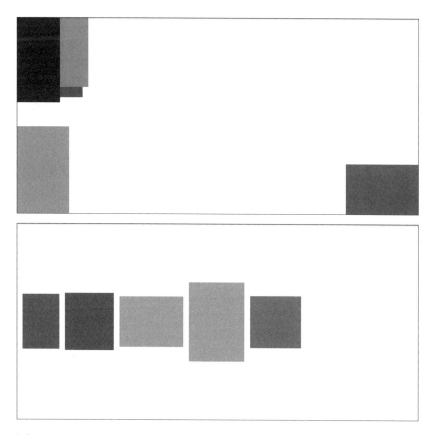

Figure 1-3   Odd layout positions (top) are the hallmark of an underconstrained layout. Although these particular views are constrained to show up onscreen, their near-random layout indicates insufficient rules describing their positions. By default, views might not show up at all, especially when they are underconstrained. Chapter 4, "Visual Formats," discusses fallback rules, which ensure that views are both visibly sized and onscreen. A sufficient layout (bottom) provides layout rules for each of its views.

A sufficient set of constraints fully expresses a view's layout, as in the bottom portion of Figure 1-3. In this case, each view has a well-defined size and position.

Sufficiency does not mean "hard coded." In the layout shown at the bottom of Figure 1-3, none of these positions are specified exactly. The Auto Layout rules say to place the views in a horizontal row, center-aligned vertically to each other. The first view is pinned off of the super-view's left-center. These constraints are sufficient because every view's position can be determined from its relationships to other views.

A sufficient, or *unambiguous*, layout has at least two geometric rules per axis, or a minimum of four rules in all. For example, a view might have an origin and a size—as you would use with frames—to specify where it is and how big it is. But you can express much more with Auto Layout. The following sufficient rule examples define a view's position and extent along one axis, as illustrated in Figure 1-4:

- You could pin the horizontal edges (A) of a view to exact positions in its superview. (The two properties defined in this example are the view's minimum X and maximum X positions.)

- You could match the width of one view to another subview (B) and then center it horizontally to its superview (width and center X).

- You could declare a view's width to match its intrinsic content, such as the length of text drawn on it (C), and then pin its right (*trailing*) edge to the left (*leading*) edge of another view (width and maximum X).

- You could pin the top and bottom of a view to the superview (D) so that the view stretches vertically along with its superview (minimum Y and maximum Y).

- You could specify a view's vertical center and its maximum extent (E) and let Auto Layout calculate the height from that offset (center Y and maximum Y).

- You could specify a view's height and its offset from the top of the view (F) and then hang the view off the top of the superview (minimum Y and height.).

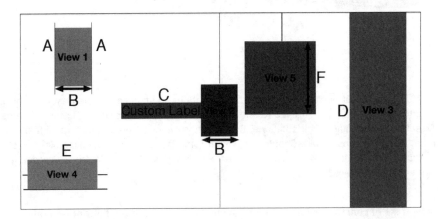

Figure 1-4   Sufficient layout requires at least two rules per axis.

Each of these rules provides enough information along one axis to avoid ambiguity. That's because each one represents a specific declaration about how the view fits into the overall layout.

When rules fail, they lack this exactness. For example, if you supply only the width, where should the system place the item along the X-axis? At the left? Or the right? Somewhere in the middle? Or maybe entirely offscreen? Or if you only specify a Y position, how tall should the view be? 50 points? 50,000 points? 0 points? Missing information leads to ambiguous layouts.

You often encounter ambiguity when working with inequalities, as in the top image in Figure 1-3. The rules for these views say to stay within the bounds of the superview—but where? If their minimum X value is greater than or equal to their superview's minimum X value, what should that X value be? The rules are insufficient, and the layout is therefore ambiguous.

Constraint Attributes

Constraints use a limited geometric vocabulary. Attributes are the "nouns" of the constraint system, describing positions within a view's alignment rectangle. Relations are "verbs," specifying how the attributes compare to each other.

The attribute nouns (see Figure 1-5) speak to physical geometry. Constraints offer the following view attribute vocabulary:

- **Left, right, top, and bottom**—The edges of a view's alignment rectangle on the left (A in Figure 1-5), right (B), top (C), and bottom (D) of the view. These correspond to a view's minimum X, maximum X, minimum Y, and maximum Y values. (The coordinate system used by UIKit and Auto Layout has its origin at the top-left.)

- **Leading and trailing**—The leading and trailing edges of the view's alignment rectangle. In left-to-right (English-like) systems, these correspond to "left" (leading, A) and "right" (trailing, B). In right-to-left linguistic environments like Arabic or Hebrew, these roles flip; right is leading (B), and left is trailing (A).

> **Tip**
>
> When internationalizing your applications, always prefer leading and trailing over left and right. This allows your interfaces to flip properly when using right-to-left languages, like Arabic and Hebrew.

- **Width and height**—The width (E) and height (F) of the view's alignment rectangle.

- **CenterX and CenterY**—The X-axis (H) and Y-axis (G) centers of the view's alignment rectangle.

- **Baseline**—The alignment rectangle's baseline (I), typically a fixed offset above its bottom attribute.

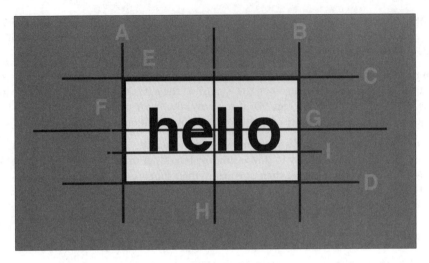

Figure 1-5   Attributes specify geometric elements of a view.

Relations compare values. Constraint math is limited to three relations: setting equality or setting lower and upper bounds for comparison. You can use the following layout relations:

- **NSLayoutRelationLessThanOrEqual**—For less-than-or-equal inequality
- **NSLayoutRelationEqual**—For equality
- **NSLayoutRelationGreaterThanOrEqual**—For greater-than-or-equal-to inequality

You might not think that these three relations would give you much to work with. However, these three relations cover all the ground needed for user interface layout. They offer ways to set specific values and apply maximum and minimum limits.

About Those Missing Views

It's common for developers new to Auto Layout to "lose" views. They discover that views they have added end up offscreen or that they have a zero size due to constraints. (Incidentally, Auto Layout works with positive sizes, zero or larger. You cannot create views with negative widths or heights.) The missing views problem catches many devs. This problem happens with both underconstrained views and views with inconsistent rules.

In this section, you'll see a little bit of constraint code, even before you've read about the details of the constraint class and how instances work. Please bear with me. I've added highlights to help explain ambiguous and underconstrained scenarios to make a point. If you work with Auto Layout, you should be aware of these situations *before* you start using the technology.

Underconstrained Missing Views

Underconstrained views don't give Auto Layout enough information to build from, so it often defaults to a size of zero. Consider the following example. This code creates a new view, prepares it for Auto Layout, and then adds two sets of constraints, which I've highlighted in boldface:

```
// Create a new view and add it into the Auto Layout system
// This view goes missing despite the initWithFrame: size
UIView *view = [[UIView alloc]
    initWithFrame:CGRectMake(0.0f, 0.0f, 30.0f, 30.0f)];
[self.view addSubview:view];
view.translatesAutoresizingMaskIntoConstraints = NO;

// Add two sets of rules, pinning the view and setting height
[self.view addConstraints:[NSLayoutConstraint
    constraintsWithVisualFormat:@"V:|[view(==80)]" // 80 height
    options:0 metrics:nil
    views:NSDictionaryOfVariableBindings(view)]];
[self.view addConstraints:[NSLayoutConstraint
    constraintsWithVisualFormat:@"H:|[view]"
    options:0 metrics:nil
    views:NSDictionaryOfVariableBindings(view)]];
```

The first set of constraints pins the view to the top of its superview and sets the height to 80. The second set pins the view to the superview's leading edge. (This is the left side in the United States, with English's left-to-right writing system.) I deliberately did not specify a width. The view's size is, therefore, underconstrained.

You might expect Auto Layout to default to the initial frame size, which was set to 30 by 30 points. It does not. When this snippet sets `translatesAutoresizingMaskIntoConstraints` to `NO`, that initialization is essentially thrown away. As the view appears onscreen, the ambiguous rules passed to Auto Layout result in a width that falls to zero, creating a view that's not visible:

```
2013-01-14 10:47:40.460 HelloWorld[73891:c07]
    <UIView: 0x884dfc0; frame = (0 0; 0 80); layer = <CALayer: 0x884e020>>
```

> ### Note
> When adding and removing constraints at runtime, order matters. Auto Layout validates its rules at each step. When updating constraints—such as when a device reorients—remove invalid constraints *first* before adding new rules to avoid raising exceptions.

Missing Views with Inconsistent Rules

Inconsistent rules may also produce views that are missing in action. For example, imagine a pair of rules that say "View A is three times the width of View B" and "View B is twice the width of View A." The following code snippets implement these rules. I've boldfaced the parts of the code that tell the rule story:

```
NSLayoutConstraint *constraint;
constraint = [NSLayoutConstraint
    constraintWithItem:viewA
    attribute:NSLayoutAttributeWidth
    relatedBy:NSLayoutRelationEqual
    toItem:viewB
    attribute:NSLayoutAttributeWidth
    multiplier:3.0f constant:0.0f];
[self.view addConstraint:constraint];

constraint = [NSLayoutConstraint
    constraintWithItem:viewA
    attribute:NSLayoutAttributeWidth
    relatedBy:NSLayoutRelationEqual
    toItem:viewB
    attribute:NSLayoutAttributeWidth
    multiplier:2.0f constant:0.0f];
[self.view addConstraint:constraint];
```

Surprisingly, these two rules are neither unsatisfiable nor ambiguous, even though common sense suggests otherwise. That's because both rules are satisfied when View A and View B have zero width. At zero, View A's width can be three times the width of View B, and View B twice the width of View A:

$0 = 0 * 3$ and $0 = 0 * 2$

When this code is run and the rules are applied, the views present the zero-width frames expected from this scenario:

```
2013-01-14 11:02:38.005 HelloWorld[74460:c07]
    <TestView: 0x8b30910; frame = (320 454; 0 50); layer = <CALayer: 0x8b309d0>>
2013-01-14 11:02:38.006 HelloWorld[74460:c07]
    <TestView: 0x8b32570; frame = (320 436; 0 68); layer = <CALayer: 0x8b32450>>
```

Tracking Missing Views

You can track down "missing" views with the debugger by inspecting their geometry after you expect them to appear (for example, in viewDidAppear: and awakeFromNib). You may want to add NSAssert statements about their expected size and positions. Some will be, as discussed, zero sized.

The following view, for example, had a zero-sized frame because it was underconstrained in the Auto Layout system:

```
2013-01-09 14:31:41.869 HelloWorld[29921:c07] View: <UIView: 0x71bb390;
frame = (30 430; 0 0); layer = <CALayer: 0x71bb3f0>>
```

Other views may simply be offscreen because you haven't told Auto Layout that the views must appear onscreen. For example, this view had a positive size (20 points by 20 points), but its frame with its (–20, –20) origin lay outside its view controller's presentation:

```
2013-01-09 14:33:37.546 HelloWorld[29975:c07] View: <UIView: 0x7125f70;
frame = (-20 -20; 20 20); layer = <CALayer: 0x7125fd0>>
```

In other cases, you might load a view from a storyboard or nib file and see only part of it onscreen, or it may occupy the entire screen at once. These are hallmarks of an underlying Auto Layout issue.

Ambiguous Layout

During development, you can test whether a view's constraints are sufficient by calling hasAmbiguousLayout. This returns a Boolean value of YES for a view that could have occupied a different frame or NO for a view whose constraints are fully specified.

These results are view specific. For example, imagine a fully constrained view whose child is underconstrained. The view itself does not have ambiguous layout, even though its child does. You can and should test the layout individually for each view in your hierarchy, as follows:

```
@implementation VIEW_CLASS (AmbiguityTests)
// Debug only. Do not ship with this code
- (void) testAmbiguity
{
    NSLog(@"<%@:0x%0x>: %@",
        self.class.description, (int)self,
        self.hasAmbiguousLayout ? @"Ambiguous" : @"Unambiguous");

    for (VIEW_CLASS *view in self.subviews)
        [view testAmbiguity];
}
@end
```

Note

In this code snippet, and throughout this book, VIEW_CLASS is defined as either UIView or NSView, depending on the deployment system.

This code descends through a view hierarchy and lists the results for each level. Here's what a simple layout with two subviews returned for the underconstrained layout code originally shown in Figure 1-3 (top):

```
HelloWorld[76351:c07]  <UIView:0x715a9a0>:  Unambiguous
HelloWorld[76351:c07]  <TestView:0x715add0>:  Ambiguous
HelloWorld[76351:c07]  <TestView:0x715c9e0>:  Ambiguous
```

The superview does not express ambiguous layout, but its child views do.

You can run tests for ambiguous layout as soon as you like—in `loadView` or wherever you set up new views and add constraints. It's generally a good first step to take any time you're adding new views to your system as well. It ensures that your constraints really are as fully specified as you *think* they are.

Use these tests during development but *do not* ship them in App Store code. They help you check your layouts as you incrementally build interfaces.

Exercising Ambiguity

Apple offers a curious tool in the form of its `exerciseAmbiguityInLayout` view method. This method automatically tweaks view frames that express ambiguous layouts. This is a view method (`UIView` and `NSView`) that checks for ambiguous layout and attempts to randomly change a view's frame.

Figure 1-6 shows this call in action. Here, you see an OS X window with three underconstrained subviews. Their positions have not been set programmatically, so they end up wherever Auto Layout places them. In this example, after you exercise ambiguity (see Figure 1-6, right), the light-colored view, initially at the bottom right, moves to the bottom left.

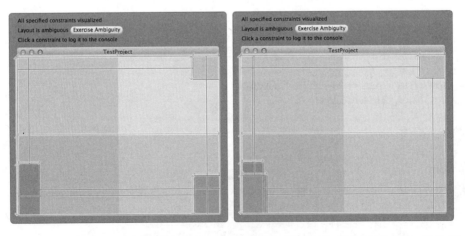

Figure 1-6   Exercising ambiguity allows you to change view frames to other legal values that are allowed under your current set of Auto Layout constraints.

This tells you that (1) this is one of the affected underconstrained views and (2) you can see some of the range that might apply to this view due to its lack of positioning constraints.

Exercising ambiguity is a blunt and limited weapon. In this example, some views are unchanged, even though they also had ambiguous layout. You shouldn't rely on exercising ambiguity to exhaustively find issues in your project, although it can be a useful tool for the right audience. Exercising ambiguity won't cure cancer or create world peace, but it *has* helped me out of a (rare) pickle or two.

Visualizing Constraints

The purple outline that surrounds the window in Figure 1-6 is an OS X–only feature. On OS X, you can visualize constraints by calling `visualizeConstraints:` on any NSWindow instance. You pass it an array of constraint instances that you want to view.

Here is a simple way to exhaustively grab the constraints from a view and all its subviews, by using simple class extension:

```
@implementation VIEW_CLASS (GeneralConstraintSupport)
// Return all constraints from self and subviews
- (NSArray *) allConstraints
{
    NSMutableArray *array = [NSMutableArray array];
    [array addObjectsFromArray:self.constraints];
    for (VIEW_CLASS *view in self.subviews)
        [array addObjectsFromArray:[view allConstraints]];
    return array;
}
@end
```

> **Note**
>
> Apple can and does regularly extend classes. When creating categories for production code, do *not* use obvious names (like `allConstraints`) that may conflict with Apple's own development. Adding custom prefixes, typically company or personal initials, guards your code against conflicts with potential future updates. This book does not follow this advice in the interest of making the code more readable.

The purple backdrop that appears tells you whether the window's layout is ambiguous. It tests from the window down its view hierarchy, all the way to its leaves. If it finds any ambiguity, it makes the Exercise Ambiguity button available, which means you don't have to call the option from your own code.

This visualization option also shows you the constraints you passed as clickable blue lines, helping you locate those constraints in a live application. You can click any item to log it to the Xcode debugging console.

> **Tip**
>
> All these methods—testing for ambiguous layout, exercising layout ambiguity, and visualizing constraints—are meant for development builds only. Don't ship production code that calls them.

Intrinsic Content Size

With Auto Layout, a view's content plays as important a role in its layout as its constraints. This is expressed through each view's `intrinsicContentSize`, which describes the minimum space needed to express the full view content without squeezing or clipping that data. It derives from the natural properties of the content that each view presents.

For an image view, for example, the intrinsic content size corresponds to the size of the image it presents. A larger image requires a larger intrinsic content size. Consider the following code snippet. It loads an iOS 7 standard `Icon.png` image into an image view and reports the view's intrinsic content size. As you'd expect, this size is 60 by 60 points, the size of the image supplied to the view (see Figure 1-7, top):

```
UIImageView *iv = [[UIImageView alloc]
    initWithImage:[UIImage imageNamed:@"Icon-60.png"]];
NSLog(@"%@", NSStringFromCGSize(iv.intrinsicContentSize));
```

For a button, the intrinsic content size varies with its title (see the button images in Figure 1-7). As a title grows or shrinks, the button's intrinsic content size adjusts to match. This snippet creates a button and assigns it a pair of titles, and it reports the intrinsic content size after each assignment:

```
UIButton *button =
    [UIButton buttonWithType:UIButtonTypeSystem];

// Longer title, Figure 1-7, middle image
[button setTitle:@"Hello World" forState:UIControlStateNormal];
NSLog(@"%@: %@", [button titleForState:UIControlStateNormal],
    NSStringFromCGSize(button.intrinsicContentSize));

// Shorter title, Figure 1-7, bottom image
[button setTitle:@"On" forState:UIControlStateNormal];
NSLog(@"%@: %@", [button titleForState:UIControlStateNormal],
    NSStringFromCGSize(button.intrinsicContentSize));
```

When run, this snippet outputs the following sizes:

```
2013-07-02 12:16:46.576 HelloWorld[69749:a0b] Hello World: {78, 30}
2013-07-02 12:16:46.577 HelloWorld[69749:a0b] On: {30, 30}
```

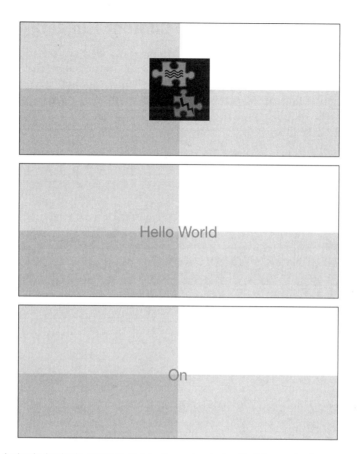

Figure 1-7   A view's intrinsic content size is the natural size that its contents occupy.

The Hello World version of the button expresses a wider intrinsic content size than the On version, and both use the same height. These values can vary further as you customize a font face and font size and title text.

A view's intrinsic size allows Auto Layout to best match a view's frame to its natural content. Earlier, you read that unambiguous layout generally requires setting two attributes in each axis. When a view has an intrinsic content size, that size accounts for one of the two attributes. You can, for example, place a text-based control or an image view in the center of its superview, and its layout will not be ambiguous. The intrinsic content size plus the location combine for a fully specified placement.

When you change a view's intrinsic contents, you need to call `invalidateIntrinsicContent Size` to let Auto Layout know to recalculate at its next layout pass.

Compression Resistance and Content Hugging

As the name suggests, *compression resistance* refers to the way a view protects its content. A view with a high compression resistance fights against shrinking. It won't allow that content to clip. Consider the buttons on the toolbar in Figure 1-8. Both screenshots show an application responding to a constraint that wants to set that button width to 40 points.

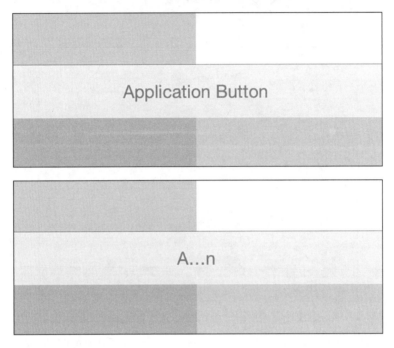

Figure 1-8   Compression resistance describes how a view attempts to maintain its minimum intrinsic content size. The button at the top of this figure has a high compression resistance.

In Figure 1-8, the top version of the button uses a high compression resistance priority value, and the bottom version uses a low value. As you can see, the higher priority ensures that the top button succeeds in preserving its intrinsic content. The resistance of the bottom button is too low. The resizing succeeds, and the button compresses, clipping the text.

The bottom button's "don't clip" request (that is, the compression resistance priority) is still there, but it's not important enough to prevent the "please set the width to 40" constraint from resizing the view to the button's detriment. Auto Layout often comes across two conflicting requests. When only one of those requests can win, it satisfies the one with the higher priority.

You specify a view's compression resistance through IB's Size Inspector (which you open by selecting View > Utilities > Show Size Inspector > View > Content Compression Resistance

Priority), as shown in Figure 1-9, or by setting a value in code. Set the value separately for each axis, horizontal and vertical. Values may range from 1 (lowest priority) to 1,000 (required priority), and the default is 750:

```
[button setContentCompressionResistancePriority:500
    forAxis:UILayoutConstraintAxisHorizontal];
```

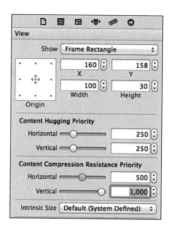

Figure 1-9   Adjust a view's Content Compression Resistance Priority and Content Hugging Priority settings in IB's Size Inspector or through code. Although these numbers are presented as a scale of positive integers in IB, they're actually typed as floats: typedef float UILayoutPriority (iOS) and NSLayoutPriority (OS X). The new Intrinsic Size pop-up enables you to override sizes for placeholder items, so you can test your layout with varied configurations. Compression resistance defaults to 750.

In IB, this is also where you set a view's *content hugging* priority. This refers to the way a view prefers to avoid extra padding around its core content (as shown here) or stretching of that core content (as with an image view that uses a scaled content mode). The buttons in Figure 1-10 are being told to stretch. The button at the top has a high content hugging priority, so it resists that stretching. It hugs to the content (in this case, the words *Application Button*). The button at the bottom has a lower content hugging priority, and the request to stretch wins out. The button pads its contents and produces the wide result you see.

As with compression resistance, you set a view's hugging priority in IB's Size Inspector (refer to Figure 1-9) or in code, like this:

```
[button setContentHuggingPriority:501
    forAxis:UILayoutConstraintAxisHorizontal]
```

Content hugging defaults to 250.

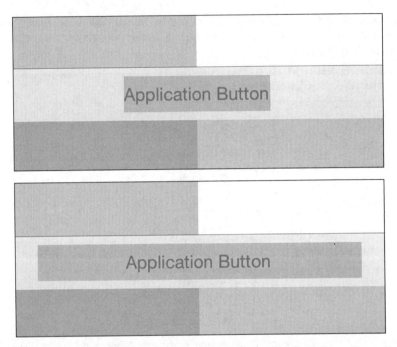

Figure 1-10   Content hugging describes a view's desire to match its frame to the natural size of its content. A strong hugging priority limits the view from growing much larger than the content it presents. A weak priority may allow a view to stretch and isolate its content among a sea of padding. Because of iOS 7's borderless buttons, I've added a light background tint to the button to highlight extents.

Image Embellishments

When you include embellishments in your pictures such as shadows, sparkles, badges, and other items that extend beyond the image's core content, an image's natural size may no longer reflect the way you want Auto Layout to handle layout. In Auto Layout, constraints determine view size and placement, using a geometric element called an *alignment rectangle*. The UIKit API calls help you control that placement.

Alignment Rectangles

As developers create complex views, they may introduce visual ornamentation such as shadows, exterior highlights, reflections, and engraving lines. As they do, these features are often drawn onto image art rather than being added through layers or subviews. Unlike frames, a view's alignment rectangle should be limited to a core visual element. Its size should remain unaffected as new items are drawn onto the view. Consider the left side of Figure 1-11. It shows a view drawn with a shadow and a badge. When laying out this view, you want Auto Layout to focus on aligning just the core element—the blue rectangle—and not the ornamentation.

Figure 1-11   A view's alignment rectangle (center) refers strictly to the core visual element to be aligned, without embellishments.

The center image in Figure 1-11 highlights the view's alignment rectangle. This rectangle excludes all ornamentation, such as the drop shadow and badge. It's the part of the view you want Auto Layout to consider when it does its work. Contrast this with the rectangle shown in the right image. This version includes all the visual ornamentation, extending the view's frame beyond the area that should be considered for alignment.

The right-hand rectangle in Figure 1-11 encompasses all the view's visual elements. It encompasses the shadow and badge. These ornaments could potentially throw off a view's alignment features (for example, its center, bottom, and right) if they were considered during layout.

By working with alignment rectangles instead of frames, Auto Layout ensures that key information like a view's edges and center are properly considered during layout. In Figure 1-12, the adorned view is perfectly aligned on the background grid. Its badge and shadow are not considered during placement.

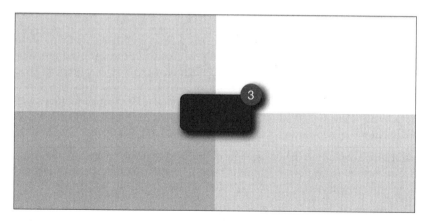

Figure 1-12   Auto Layout only considers this view's alignment rectangle when laying it out as centered in its superview. The shadow and badge don't affect its placement.

Visualizing Alignment Rectangles

Both iOS and OS X enable you to overlay views with their alignment rectangles in your running application. You set a simple launch argument from your app's scheme: `UIViewShowAlignmentRects` for iOS and `NSViewShowAlignmentRects` for OS X. Set the argument value to `YES` and make sure to prefix it with a dash, as shown in Figure 1-13.

When the app runs, rectangles show over each view. The resulting rectangles are light and can be difficult to see. You will need to look closely at times.

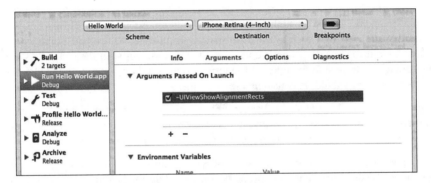

Figure 1-13   Set launch arguments in the scheme editor.

Alignment Insets

Drawn art often contains hard-coded embellishments such as highlights, shadows, and so forth. These items take up little memory and run efficiently. Because of the low overhead, many developers predraw effects to art assets. Figure 1-14 demonstrates a typical problem encountered when using image-based ornamentation with Auto Layout. The left image shows a basic image view, whose art I created in Photoshop. I used a standard drop shadow effect. When added to the image view, the 20-point by 20-point area I left for the shadow throws off the view's alignment rectangle, causing it to appear slightly too high and left.

In its default implementation, the image view has no idea that the image contains ornamental elements. You have to tell it how to adjust its intrinsic content so that the alignment rectangle considers just that core material.

To accommodate the shadow, you load and then rebuild the image. This is a two-step process. First, you load the image as you normally would (for example, with `imageNamed:`). Then you call `imageWithAlignmentRectInsets:` on that image to produce a new version that supports the specified insets. The following snippet accommodates a 20-point shadow by insetting the alignment `rect` on the bottom and right:

```
UIImage *image = [[UIImage imageNamed:@"Shadowed.png"]
    imageWithAlignmentRectInsets:UIEdgeInsetsMake(0, 0, 20, 20)];
UIImageView *imageView = [[UIImageView alloc] initWithImage:image];
```

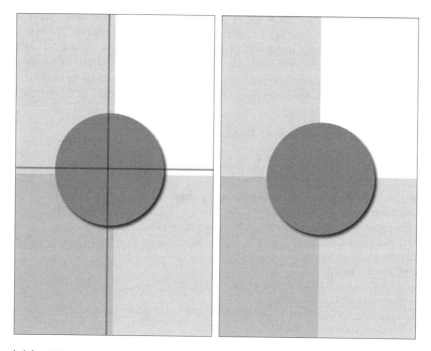

Figure 1-14   Adjust your images to account for alignment when using Auto Layout. At the left, the image view was created with an unadjusted image. It displays slightly too far left and up, which you can see by looking at the points where the circle crosses the background grid. I added lines over the image on the left to emphasize where the centering should have occurred. The image on the right shows the adjusted image view. It centers exactly onto its parent view.

Insets define offsets from the top, left, bottom, and right of some rectangles. You use them to describe how far to move in (using positive values) or out (using negative values) from rectangle edges. These insets ensure that the alignment rectangle is correct, even when there are drawn embellishments placed within the image. The fields are defined as follows:

```
typedef struct {
    CGFloat top, left, bottom, right;
} UIEdgeInsets;
```

After specifying the alignment `rect` insets, the updated version now properly aligns, as you see on the right in Figure 1-14. I logged the pertinent details so that you can compare the view details. Here's what the view frame looks like (it shows the full 200×200 image size), the intrinsic content size built from the image's alignment insets (180×180), and the resulting alignment rectangle used to center the image view's frame:

```
HelloWorld[53122:c07] Frame: {{70, 162}, {200, 200}}
HelloWorld[53122:c07] Intrinsic Content Size: {180, 180}
HelloWorld[53122:c07] Alignment Rect: {{70, 162}, {180, 180}}
```

It's a bit of a pain to construct these insets by hand, especially if you may later update your graphics. When you know the alignment rect and the overall image bounds, you can, instead, automatically calculate the edge insets you need to pass to this method. Listing 1-1 defines a simple inset builder. It determines how far the alignment rectangle lies from each edge of the parent rectangle, and it returns a UIEdgeInset structure that represents those values. Use this function to build insets from the intrinsic geometry of your core visuals.

Listing 1-1   **Building Edge Insets from Alignment Rectangles**

```
UIEdgeInsets BuildInsets(
    CGRect alignmentRect, CGRect imageBounds)
{

    // Ensure alignment rect is fully within source
    CGRect targetRect =
        CGRectIntersection(alignmentRect, imageBounds);

    // Calculate insets
    UIEdgeInsets insets;
    insets.left = CGRectGetMinX(targetRect) -
        CGRectGetMinX(imageBounds);
    insets.right = CGRectGetMaxX(imageBounds) -
        CGRectGetMaxX(targetRect);
    insets.top = CGRectGetMinY(targetRect) -
        CGRectGetMinY(imageBounds);
    insets.bottom = CGRectGetMaxY(imageBounds) -
        CGRectGetMaxY(targetRect);

    return insets;
}
```

Declaring Alignment Rectangles

Cocoa and Cocoa Touch offer several additional ways to report alignment geometry. You may implement alignmentRectForFrame:, frameForAlignmentRect:, baselineOffsetFromBottom, and alignmentRectInsets. These methods allow your views to declare and translate alignment rectangles from code.

For the most part, thankfully, you can ignore alignment rectangles and insets. Things just, for the most part, work. The edge cases you encounter usually happen when Auto Layout comes into conflict with transforms (and other circumstances when the actual frame doesn't match the visual frame, as with buttons).

A few notes on these items:

- alignmentRectForFrame: and frameForAlignmentRect: must always be mathematical inverses of each other.

- Most custom views only need to override `alignmentRectInsets` to report content location within their frame.

- `baselineOffsetFromBottom` is available only for `NSView` and refers to the distance between the bottom of a view's alignment rectangle and the view's content baseline, such as that used for laying out text. This is important when you want to align views to text baselines and not to the lowest point reached by typographic descenders, like *j* and *q*.

Here's some information about `alignmentRectForFrame:` and `frameForAlignmentRect:` from the `UIView.h` documentation:

> These two methods should be inverses of each other. UIKit will call both as part of layout computation. They may be overridden to provide arbitrary transforms between frame and alignment rect, though the two methods must be inverses of each other. However, the default implementation uses `alignmentRectInsets`, so just override that if it's applicable. It's easier to get right.

> A view that displayed an image with some ornament would typically override these, because the ornamental part of an image would scale up with the size of the frame. Set the `NSUserDefault` `UIViewShowAlignmentRects` to `YES` to see alignment rects drawn.

`NSLayoutConstraint.h` on OS X adds the following comment:

> If you do override these, be sure to account for the top of your frame being either `minY` or `maxY` depending on the superview's flippedness.

You can see this flippedness adjustment made in Listing 1-2, in the next section.

Implementing Alignment Rectangles

Listing 1-2 provides a trivial example of code-based alignment geometry. This OS X app builds a fixed-size view and draws a shadowed rounded rectangle into it. When USE_ALIGNMENT_ RECTS is set to 1, its `alignmentRectForFrame:` and `frameForAlignmentRect:` methods convert to and from frames and alignment rects. As Figure 1-15 shows, these reporting methods allow the view to display with proper alignment.

Listing 1-2   **Using Code-Based Alignment Frames**

```
@interface CustomView : NSView
@end

@implementation CustomView
- (void) drawRect:(NSRect)dirtyRect
{
    NSBezierPath *path;
```

```
    // Calculate offset from frame for 170x170 art
    CGFloat dx = (self.frame.size.width - 170) / 2.0f;
    CGFloat dy = (self.frame.size.height - 170);

    // Draw a shadow
    NSRect rect = NSMakeRect(8 + dx, -8 + dy, 160, 160);
    path = [NSBezierPath
        bezierPathWithRoundedRect:rect xRadius:32 yRadius:32];
    [[[NSColor blackColor] colorWithAlphaComponent:0.3f] set];
    [path fill];

    // Draw fixed-size shape with outline
    rect.origin = CGPointMake(dx, dy);
    path = [NSBezierPath
        bezierPathWithRoundedRect:rect xRadius:32 yRadius:32];
    [[NSColor blackColor] set];
    path.lineWidth = 6;
    [path stroke];
    [ORANGE_COLOR set];
    [path fill];
}


- (NSSize)intrinsicContentSize
{
    // Fixed content size - base + frame
    return NSMakeSize(170, 170);
}


#define USE_ALIGNMENT_RECTS 1
#if USE_ALIGNMENT_RECTS
- (NSRect)frameForAlignmentRect:(NSRect)alignmentRect
{
    // 1 + 10 / 160 = 1.0625
    NSRect rect = (NSRect){.origin = alignmentRect.origin};
    rect.size.width = alignmentRect.size.width * 1.06250;
    rect.size.height = alignmentRect.size.height * 1.06250;
    return rect;
}


- (NSRect)alignmentRectForFrame:(NSRect)frame
{
    // Account for vertical flippage
    CGFloat dy = (frame.size.height - 170.0) / 2.0;
    rect.origin = CGPointMake(frame.origin.x, frame.origin.y + dy);

    rect.size.width = frame.size.width * (160.0 / 170.0);
    rect.size.height = frame.size.height * (160.0 / 170.0);
```

```
    return rect;
}
#endif
@end
```

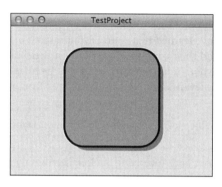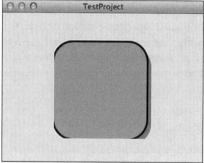

Figure 1-15 Implementing intrinsic content size and frame/alignment `rect` conversion methods ensures that your view will align and display correctly (as shown on the left) rather than be mis-aligned and possibly clipped (as shown on the right).

Exercises

After reading this chapter, test your knowledge with these exercises:

1. A label is constrained with 8-point offsets from its superview's leading and trailing edges. It is 22 points high. Is this label's layout ambiguous? If so, how can you remove the ambiguity?

2. You create a system-style button and assign it the title Continue. The button's center is constrained to a point (150, 150) from its superview's top and leading edges. Is this view's layout ambiguous? If so, how can you remove the ambiguity?

3. In `viewWillAppear:` you create a new test view and add it to your view controller:

```
UIView *testView = [[UIView alloc]
    initWithFrame:CGRectMake(50, 50, 100, 30)];
view.backgroundColor = [UIColor blueColor];
[self.view addSubview:view];
view.translatesAutoresizingMaskIntoConstraints = NO;
```

   After these lines, you add constraints that center the test view within its superview. What size will the view be when the app runs? Why?

4. A 54-by-54-point image consists of a 50-by-50-point square, with a drop shadow offset 4 points to the right and 4 points down. (a) Show code that assigns alignment insets to this image. (b) When the image is added to an image view and center-aligned to its superview on both axes, what geometric point within the image lies at the center of the superview?

5. You add a button to your view and constrain it to stretch from side to side at a priority of 500. Will it stretch? Why or why not?

Conclusions

This chapter introduces the core concepts that underpin Auto Layout, Cocoa's declarative constraint-based descriptive layout system. You have learned that Auto Layout focuses on the relationships between views and between views and their content—instead of on their frames. A logical priority-based framework drives Auto Layout. You have discovered that its rules must be satisfiable, consistent, and sufficient. Here are a few final thoughts to take away from this chapter:

- Constraints are fun and powerful. They provide elegant solutions to common layout situations.

- Don't be afraid to mix and match Auto Layout and Autosizing. As long as rules do not conflict, you can port existing layouts to the new Auto Layout world.

- Auto Layout is more than just constraints. Its content-protecting features provide a key component that helps specify what to show—and not just where to show it. For example, compression resistance and content hugging adapt graphical user interfaces (GUIs) during internationalization, allowing you to easily accommodate differing label sizes when languages change.

- Auto Layout is essentially a linear equation solver that attempts to find a satisfiable geometric expression of its rules. When its equations produce too many solutions, you end up with underconstrained ambiguous layout. When its equations cannot produce any solution, you know that constraints are in conflict.

2

Constraints

Auto Layout is a constraint satisfaction system. The word constraint *means "limitation" or "restriction." Each rule you build creates a requirement about how one part of the interface relates with another. You rank these rules using a numeric priority, and Auto Layout builds your interface's visual presentation based on your rules and ranking. In this chapter, you will read about constraints in depth—what they are and how to specify them. You will learn about the kinds of constraints used in Auto Layout, how to install constraints in the system, and how priorities affect your results.*

Constraint Types

Auto Layout centers on several core constraint classes:

- **Layout constraints** (NSLayoutConstraint class, *public*)—These rules specify view geometry. They restrict a view's position and size by relating a view to other views and/or to constant values.

- **Content size constraints** (NSContentSizeLayoutConstraint class, *private*)—Content size rules specify how a view's size should relate to its content. For example, content hugging rules avoid adding padding, and content compression rules prevent clipping.

- **Autosizing constraints** (NSAutoresizingMaskLayoutConstraint class, *private*)— Autosizing constraints translate the older autoresizing masks into the Auto Layout system.

- **Layout support constraints** (_UILayoutSupportConstraint class, *private*)—Introduced in iOS 7, layout support constraints establish practical boundaries for the tops and bottoms of your view controller instances. These constraints restrict content from overlapping with obstacles such as status bars.

- **Prototyping constraints** (NSIBPrototypingLayoutConstraint class, *private*)—Also new to iOS 7, prototyping constraints are constraints that Interface Builder (IB) adds for you. They enable you to build interfaces incrementally yet still have a working interface to test. When you ship apps, your code should not use, reference, or otherwise include prototyping constraints.

Although all but one of these classes are private, you can and do create all of them through
public application programming interfaces (APIs) and IB. You may see instances of each class
mentioned in Xcode output logs, like this, during normal application development and debugging sessions:

```
2013-07-17 09:56:26.788 HelloWorld[14733:c07]
    <NSAutoresizingMaskLayoutConstraint:0x767ae50
    h=&-& v=&-& H:[UIView:0x7668030(30)]>
2013-07-17 09:56:26.789 HelloWorld[14733:c07]
    <NSLayoutConstraint:0x766bfc0
    H:[UIImageView:0x766aac0(>=0)]>
2013-07-17 09:56:26.790 HelloWorld[14733:c07]
    <NSContentSizeLayoutConstraint:0x7674b00
    H:[UIImageView:0x766aac0(512)] Hug:250 CompressionResistance:1>
2013-07-17 09:56:26.792 HelloWorld[14733:c07]
    <_UILayoutSupportConstraint:0x8e14e80
    V:[_UILayoutGuide:0x8e1f260(0)]>
2013-07-17 09:56:26.793 HelloWorld[14733:c07]
    <NSIBPrototypingLayoutConstraint:0x895e390
    'IB auto generated at build time for view with ambiguity'
    H:|-(137@251)-[UIButton:0x895b750](LTR) priority:251
    (Names: '|':UIView:0x895b570 )>
```

Although developer-created `NSLayoutConstraint` instances are by far the most common items
you work with, you'll encounter these other classes as well. The circumstances under which
Auto Layout generates these items are specific to the roles the constraints play:

- Autosizing constraints (`NSAutoresizingMaskLayoutConstraint`) pop up when you
  work with hybrid systems that mix and match old-style layout with Auto Layout views.
  The Auto Layout system translates masks into equivalent constraints, allowing struts-and-
  springs-style layout to coexist with Auto Layout rules.

- Content size constraints (`NSContentSizeLayoutConstraint`) appear most commonly
  when you work with labels, image views, and controls, many of which are built with
  embedded image views. These constraints are tied to the intrinsic content size feature
  that text and images naturally express. You may see them as well with any other custom
  view class that can express a natural size.

- In IB, you create layout support constraints (`_UILayoutSupportConstraint`) by
  constraining views to top or bottom layout guide proxies. In code, your constraints may
  refer to a view controller's `topLayoutGuide` or `bottomLayoutGuide` properties. These
  store references to `_UILayoutGuide` objects, which are (invisible) placement views used
  during layout.

  Here's an example of how these guides work in iOS 7:

  ```
  UIView *topLayoutGuide = (UIView *) self.topLayoutGuide;
  CONSTRAIN(@"V:[topLayoutGuide][textView]|", topLayoutGuide, textView);
  ```

In this example, a text view stretches between the top guide, which defines the top of the application content space, and the bottom of the parent.

- IB adds prototyping constraints (NSIBPrototypingLayoutConstraint) on your behalf when working with underconstrained storyboard and xib files. These constraints, which are meant to allow incremental development, offer a way for IB to project view frames into temporary constraints.

What all constraint types, regardless of class, have in common is that (1) they express the way items should be laid out onscreen and (2) they have an intrinsic priority that ranks the strength of each request in the Auto Layout system.

Note

There are, in fact, other internal constraint classes, particularly on the UIKit side of things. You won't normally encounter instances of window-anchoring constraints, window-autoresizing constraints, or scroll view automatic content-size constraints in your day-to-day work, and they don't affect the way you build with Auto Layout.

Priorities

Constraint priorities are numbers that express how strongly Auto Layout considers each layout request. Auto Layout uses priorities to resolve constraint conflicts and decide which rule takes precedence.

A constraint's priority is exposed as a readable and sometimes settable property on the instance. The priority ranges from 1 (lowest priority) to 1,000 (required priority). Strictly speaking, priorities are floats:

```
typedef float UILayoutPriority;
typedef float NSLayoutPriority;
```

It's easier to think of them and treat them as unsigned integers, which is how they're presented in IB. Follow Apple's IB example. I cannot conceive of any reason you'd ever need—or want—to use fractional priorities.

Conflicting Priorities

Any rule with a priority of 501 always wins out over a rule with a priority of 500. If you tell a view to be both 30 points and 40 points high at the same time, but assign the latter rule a higher priority, the 40-point height prevails. The following example implements these two rules using these priorities:

```
NSLayoutConstraint *heightConstraint = [NSLayoutConstraint
    constraintWithItem:view
    attribute:NSLayoutAttributeHeight
```

```
    relatedBy:NSLayoutRelationEqual
    toItem:nil
    attribute:NSLayoutAttributeHeight
    multiplier:1.0 constant:30];
    heightConstraint.priority = 500;
[view addConstraint:heightConstraint];

heightConstraint = [NSLayoutConstraint
    constraintWithItem:view
    attribute:NSLayoutAttributeHeight
    relatedBy:NSLayoutRelationEqual
    toItem:nil
    attribute:NSLayoutAttributeHeight
    multiplier:1.0 constant:40];
    heightConstraint.priority = 501;
[view addConstraint:heightConstraint];
```

As you'd expect, when you run this code, the result is a 40-point-high view. The rule that is prioritized at a level of 501 overrules the request prioritized at 500. The constraints are not in conflict due to the different priorities even though they attempt to control the same value. They do *not* generate any warnings in the console:

```
2013-01-16 10:05:53.638 HelloWorld[97799:c07]
    <TestView: 0xfe38a80; frame = (254 464; 66 40);
    layer = <CALayer: 0xfe38af0>>
```

Enumerated Priorities

Apple offers platform-specific priority enumerations, which you see in Table 2-1. The items are roughly the same across both UIKit and AppKit, although AppKit includes window-specific priorities, which appear around the 500 mark.

The AppKit-only priorities enable you to rank constraints related to the way users resize a window. Your constraints, when ranked higher than window-resizing defaults, can prevent users from shrinking or expanding windows beyond certain points.

While priority numbers basically mean the same thing across OS X and iOS, the separate enumerations affect any cross-platform code. For that reason, I ended up building custom enumerations for my cross-platform development, adding a few tweaks along the way.

For example, my personal enumeration includes a "mild suggestion" priority with a rank of 1. It allows me to assign fallback layouts that rank far below my common presentation rules. The most common use-case ensures that a view is both onscreen and visible when I need it to be. This enables me to iteratively develop view content without running into the zero-sized missing views problem.

Table 2-1   **Priority Enumerations for UIKit and AppKit**

UIKit `UIView` Priorities

```
enum {
    UILayoutPriorityRequired = 1000, // Required
    UILayoutPriorityDefaultHigh = 750, // Compression resistance default
    UILayoutPriorityDefaultLow = 250, // Compression hugging default
    UILayoutPriorityFittingSizeLevel = 50, // System layout fitting size
};
typedef float UILayoutPriority;
```

AppKit `NSView` Priorities

```
enum {
    NSLayoutPriorityRequired = 1000, // Required
    NSLayoutPriorityDefaultHigh = 750, // Compression resistance default
    NSLayoutPriorityDragThatCanResizeWindow = 510, // Window can resize
    NSLayoutPriorityWindowSizeStayPut = 500, // Window keeps size
    NSLayoutPriorityDragThatCannotResizeWindow = 490, // SplitView divider
    NSLayoutPriorityDefaultLow = 250, // Compression hugging default
    NSLayoutPriorityFittingSizeCompression = 50, // Fitting size
};
typedef float NSLayoutPriority;
```

Apple recommends that you work around but not at fixed priority levels such as window sizing and fitting sizes. As a good citizen of the view layout system, you should tweak your priorities slightly higher or lower. These adjustments express the priority's *relative* rank compared to the fixed system values.

That isn't to say that you cannot set a button's compression resistance priority to the default value of 750. Instead, when you create constraints that involve that button, a priority of 751 says "more important than default compression resistance" and a priority of 749 says "less important."

> **Note**
>
> Be very careful when updating constraint priorities at runtime, especially if the priority value changes from required to not required or vice versa. When an updated priority's role changes the effect of an installed constraint, it can raise an exception at runtime, as shown here:
>
> ```
> 2013-01-17 10:31:50.820 HelloWorld[16232:c07] *** Assertion
>     failure in -[NSLayoutConstraint setPriority:],
>     /SourceCache/Foundation_Sim/Foundation-992/
>     Layout.subproj/NSLayoutConstraint.m:155
> 2013-01-17 10:31:50.821 HelloWorld[16232:c07] *** Terminating app due
>     to uncaught exception 'NSInternalInconsistencyException',
>     reason: 'Mutating a priority from required to not on an
>     installed constraint (or vice-versa) is not supported.
>     You passed priority 1000 and the existing priority was 502.'
> ```

Content Size Constraints

Every view's frame consists of an origin (the location at which the view sits) and a size (the width and height of that view within its parent). Although you can express exact rules for both position and size, sometimes you want Auto Layout to infer sizing from a view's content. You work with two kinds of constraints related to content size: content hugging and compression resistance. These rules specify how easily Auto Layout can stretch, squash, or pad a view in relation to that intrinsic size.

Intrinsic Content Size

As you read in Chapter 1, "Introducing Auto Layout," the sizes of labels, image views, and controls often depend on the content they present. For example, a button labeled Go! can be narrower than a Share Link or Send Feedback button. An image is sized both by its underlying art and a natural screen scale. Whenever a view's bounds vary in this way, content size enables Auto Layout to automatically fit that material into its rules.

Views without natural content report an intrinsic content size of (–1, –1). UIKit declares this "no content" size as `UIViewNoIntrinsicMetric`. AppKit on OS X offers no equivalent. Apple writes:

> Note that not all views have an `intrinsicContentSize`. UIView's default implementation is to return (`UIViewNoIntrinsicMetric`, `UIViewNoIntrinsicMetric`). The _intrinsic_ content size is concerned only with data that is in the view itself, not in other views. Remember that you can also set constant width or height constraints on any view, and you don't need to override `instrinsicContentSize` if these dimensions won't be changing with changing view content.

Content Hugging

Content hugging constraints restrict the amount of stretching and padding a view allows itself to experience. A high-content hugging priority matches a view's frame to its intrinsic content size. If that content size is small, you will want the frame to be small as well. The lines of force pull inward to the view's natural edges to resist padding (see Figure 2-1).

Consider Figure 2-2. It shows an image view displaying an application icon. Layout constraints tell this view to center itself and to stretch out to fill as much screen as possible.

The top part of Figure 2-2 shows this view using a very high (required) content hugging priority. The view's bounds constrict to the base size, producing a small centered result. The middle and bottom parts of the figure use a low content hugging priority. As a result, the view fills up a much larger portion of the screen.

Content modes account for the other difference between the middle and bottom screenshots. In iOS, content mode defines how content reshapes with respect to the view frame.

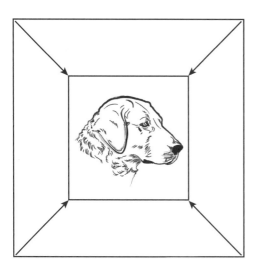

Figure 2-1   Content hugging squeezes a view inward, toward its content, to match that content's natural size and avoid padding or stretching.

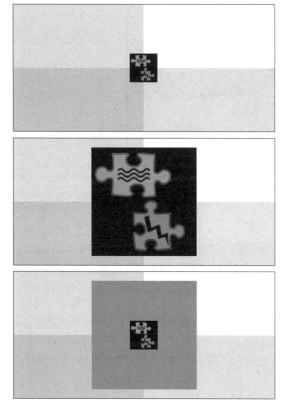

Figure 2-2   Views with low content hugging priorities may stretch to large sizes.

The view in the middle image in Figure 2-2 uses `UIViewContentModeScaleAspectFill`. The art zooms to fill up the view. The bottom image uses `UIViewContentModeCenter`, so its art is centered and unscaled. The colored background behind the image shows the view's full extent, which is the same size as in the middle image.

Compression Resistance

Compression resistance constraints prevent a view from clipping its content. A high resistance priority ensures that a view's intrinsic content is fully displayed. With compression resistance, the lines of force originate from within the content, pushing outward to ensure that the entire intrinsic content is seen (see Figure 2-3).

Figure 2-3   Compression resistance keeps views from clipping their content by matching their size to their intrinsic content.

This is demonstrated in Figure 2-4, where the widths in both images have been constrained to half their natural size (256 points instead of 512 points), using a medium (500) priority.

The left image uses a required (1,000) resistance priority; the right one uses a very low (1) priority. In the first case, the resistance wins out over the width constraint. In the second case, it loses to it. The view resizes below its natural content extent, and the image clips accordingly.

To create these images, I used a center content mode so that the image would display at its natural size, and I enabled `clipsToBounds` to ensure that the view's image would not extend beyond its bounds.

Figure 2-4   When a view's compression resistance priority is lowered, the view may end up clipping its content. These views use a center content mode.

Setting Content Size Constraints in Code

For each view, you can assign content hugging and compression resistance priorities in code. The default hugging priority is 250, and the default resistance priority is 750. Table 2-2 shows the UIKit and AppKit APIs. As you see, these differ slightly by platform. The main difference is nomenclature. UIKit refers to axes, and AppKit talks about orientations. They are, otherwise, functionally equivalent. Both axes and orientations are enumerated values. Each enumeration defines horizontal as 0 and vertical as 1.

The priorities you assign to these methods are also equivalent. You assign a value from 1 (lowest priority) to 1,000 (required priority). In turn, these values produce the behaviors shown in Figures 2-1 through 2-4.

Table 2-2   **Content Size APIs for UIKit and AppKit**

UIKit

- (void) setContentHuggingPriority: (UILayoutPriority) priority
    forAxis: (UILayoutConstraintAxis) axis
- (UILayoutPriority) contentHuggingPriorityForAxis:
    (UILayoutConstraintAxis) axis
- (void) setContentCompressionResistancePriority: (UILayoutPriority) priority
    forAxis: (UILayoutConstraintAxis) axis
- (UILayoutPriority) contentCompressionResistancePriorityForAxis:
    (UILayoutConstraintAxis) axis

```
enum {
   UILayoutConstraintAxisHorizontal = 0,
   UILayoutConstraintAxisVertical = 1
};
typedef NSInteger UILayoutConstraintAxis;
```

AppKit

```
- (void) setContentHuggingPriority:(NSLayoutPriority)priority
      forOrientation:(NSLayoutConstraintOrientation)orientation
- (NSLayoutPriority) contentHuggingPriorityForOrientation:
      (NSLayoutConstraintOrientation)orientation
- (void) setContentCompressionResistancePriority:(NSLayoutPriority)priority
      forOrientation:(NSLayoutConstraintOrientation)orientation
- (NSLayoutPriority) contentCompressionResistancePriorityForOrientation:
      (NSLayoutConstraintOrientation)orientation
```

```
enum {
   NSLayoutConstraintOrientationHorizontal = 0,
   NSLayoutConstraintOrientationVertical = 1
};
typedef NSInteger NSLayoutConstraintOrientation;
```

Setting Content Size Constraints in IB

The interactive setting pane shown in Figure 2-5 appears for some (but not all) views in Xcode 5. In IB, select a view and open the Size Inspector (by selecting View > Utilities > Show Size Inspector). If the priority sliders appear, adjust values in the View > Content Hugging Priority or View > Content Compression Resistance Priority. The sliders and stepper text fields limit those values between 1 and 1,000.

As Figure 2-5 shows, IB offers interactive tips as you adjust priorities. These tips describe the level you're setting. For the most part, I find it easiest to skip the explanation and enter a value in the text field to the right, especially since the manual control over values while dragging is coarse.

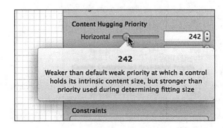

Figure 2-5   IB provides pop-up tips that describe what each priority means.

Building Layout Constraints

Layout constraints (instances of NSLayoutConstraint) define rules about a view's physical geometry. They specify how a view should be laid out and how a view relates to other views in the same hierarchy.

To express these rules, you use the simple mathematical vocabulary shown in Table 2-3. This vocabulary consists of view attributes, relations, and the basic operations of addition and multiplication.

Table 2-3 **Elements of Constraints**

Type	Description	Values
Attribute	The **left**, **right**, **top**, and **bottom** of a view.	NSLayoutAttributeLeft NSLayoutAttributeRight NSLayoutAttributeTop NSLayoutAttributeBottom
Attribute	The **leading** and **trailing** edges of a view, which are correspondingly left and right for English-like locales, and right and left for right-to-left locales, specifically Arabic and Hebrew deployment.	NSLayoutAttributeLeading NSLayoutAttributeTrailing
Attribute	The **width** and **height** of a view.	NSLayoutAttributeWidth NSLayoutAttributeHeight
Attribute	The center point of a view, which is expressed along axes as **centerX** and **centerY**.	NSLayoutAttributeCenterX NSLayoutAttributeCenterY
Attribute	A view's **baseline**, which usually describes the point above a view's bottom along which text is set.	NSLayoutAttributeBaseline
Attribute	A placeholder when an attribute is not used in relation to another constraint, such as when setting width or height.	NSLayoutAttributeNotAnAttribute
Relation	Constraints allow you to relate attributes to each other through equalities (==) and inequalities (<= and >=).	NSLayoutRelationLessThanOrEqual NSLayoutRelationEqual NSLayoutRelationGreaterThanOrEqual
Math	A **multiplier** and an additive **constant** for each constraint.	CGFloat values that you supply

The Layout Constraint Class

You create mathematical rules by building instances of the NSLayoutConstraint class and adding them to your views. Instances offer the following base properties:

- **priority**—This attribute stores a constraint's priority value. Priorities allow the Auto Layout system to rank constraints to choose which requests to honor. You read about priorities and their values earlier in this chapter.

- **firstItem** and **secondItem**—These properties point to views. A constraint may talk about the properties of one view or the relation between two views. A valid constraint always has a non-nil first item. The second item may or may not be nil.

- **firstAttribute** and **secondAttribute**—Attributes are the "nouns" of the constraint system, describing features of a view's alignment rectangle, such as left, right, center, and height. These properties are set to any of the 12 enumerated attributes in Table 2-3. If you don't have a second item, you set the second attribute to NSLayoutAttributeNotAnAttribute.

- **relation**—Relations are the "verbs" of the constraint system, specifying how attributes compare to each other: the same (==), greater than or equal to (>=), or less than or equal to (<=). A constraint's relation constant must be set to one of the three enumerated values listed in Table 2-3.

- **multiplier** and **constant**—These properties provide the algebra that gives the constraint system its power and flexibility. They allow you to say one view is half the size of another or that a view is offset from its superview by a set distance. These properties are both floating-point values. They correspond to the *m* (multiplier) and *b* (constant) elements used to form the constraint equation. You can ignore any multiplier of 1 or constant of 0; they are identity operations.

Constraint Math

All constraints, regardless of how they are created, are essentially equations or inequalities with the following form:

$$y \text{ (relation) } m * x + b$$

If you have a math background, you may have seen a form more like this, with *R* referring to the relation between *y* and the computed value on the right side:

$$y \, R \, m * x + b$$

y and *x* are view attributes of the kind listed in Table 2-3, such as width or centerY or top. Here, *m* is a constant scaling factor, and *b* is a constant offset. For example, you might say, "View B's left side should be placed 15 points to the right of View A's right side." The relation equation that results is something like this:

View B's left = View A's right + 15

Here, the relation is equality, the constant offset (*b*) is 15, and the scaling factor or multiplier (*m*) is 1. I've taken care here to keep the preceding equation from looking like code because, as you'll see, you do not use code to declare your constraints in Objective-C.

Constraints do not have to use strict equalities. They can use inequality relations as well. For example, you might say, "View B's left side should be placed *at least* 15 points to the right of View A's right side," or

> View B's left >= View A's right + 15

Offsets let you place fixed gaps between items, and the multipliers let you scale. Scaling proves especially useful when you're laying out grid patterns, letting you multiply by the height of a view, not just add a fixed distance to the next view.

First and Second Items

Every relation equation you build looks like this, with the multiplier (*m*) and constant (*b*) always applying to the second item:

`firstItem.firstAttribute` (*R*) `secondItem.secondAttribute` * *m* + *b*

There are no hard-and-fast rules about which view must be the first item and which must be second. You assign them however you like. For example, you can do this:

> View B's left = View A's right + 10

Or you can do this:

> View A's right = View B's left – 10

These are essentially identical statements.

In the first example, View B is `firstItem`; in the second, it's `secondItem`. They both describe a layout where View B appears 10 points to the right of View A. Here's another, more visual, way of showing the relationship described by *both* of these two identical constraints:

> [viewA]-10-[viewB]

This visual format is discussed in detail in Chapter 4, "Visual Formats." There's a trick to keeping math positive, as in the first example (the one with + 10 rather than – 10.) To accomplish this, you make the leading, left, or top item the `firstItem`, and the trailing, right, or bottom item the `secondItem`. This is somewhat counterintuitive, as many people think of the request as "viewA.trailing followed by 10 points followed by viewB.leading." But, since you can't legally say this using `NSLayoutConstraint`:

> View A's trailing + 10 = View B's leading

you have to settle either for keeping the views in order (and using a negative value that describes how much to move to get back from the `secondItem` to the `firstItem`) or flipping the view order you're trying to produce and keeping the number positive.

As you'll discover in Chapter 4, working with visual format strings *does* allow you to build this rule using a more intuitive "[viewA]-10-[viewB]"-style layout.

Creating Layout Constraints

You build layout constraints in any of three ways:

- You can use IB to design your interfaces. IB can generate constraints that support your layout. You can further customize the set of constraints from within the visual editor.

- You can use a visual formatting language to describe your constraints and allow the NSLayoutConstraint class to generate individual instances from your request (constraintsWithVisualFormat:options:metrics:views:).

- You can build instances of the NSLayoutConstraint class by supplying each component of a base relation (constraintWithItem:attribute: relatedBy:toItem:attribute: multiplier:constant:).

Officially, the order of these three approaches matches the way Apple expects you to build your constraints, from most preferred to least preferred. The overall "safety" of the technology and guarantees of valid layout decrease as you go down the list.

Unofficially, my experiences go the opposite direction. I find that building constraints from the ground up offers the greatest level of developer control and the best expression of the *Principle of Least Astonishment*. If you want your interfaces to match your expectations and design, you're generally best off building your constraints manually in code, using either of the latter two methods.

Unfortunately, while vastly improved in Xcode 5, IB may fail at several levels. It scatters constraint references around the interface. It offers no way to group and document functionally related constraints. It provides no editor that enables you to express edge conditions, which is a primary concern in working with Auto Layout design. (You explore these conditions in Chapter 6, "Building with Auto Layout.")

At the same time, there are things that IB does *really* well. It provides a design tool that works in the same visual space as the result you're creating. That's important when you're working on teams with nonprogrammers. It enables you to lay out items and test applications without having to write your own constraints. (It generates some of them for you.) It helps you test constraints and suggests fixes for problems in your layouts. For simple layouts, it provides fast and workable solutions.

I find that coupling IB-based storyboards and nib files with code-based constraint management provides a smooth solution for these issues. Another solution that has worked well for me involves building self-contained interface sections using Autosizing and then importing them into apps as modular Auto Layout components.

I'm not saying you can't set up expressive constraints in IB. You can. However, inspecting the constraints you build is hard to do, and it's impossible to do it rigorously. Plus your layout vocabulary is limited.

All three design approaches eventually end up as NSLayoutConstraint instances. No matter how you specify your Auto Layout rules, they all factor down to a set of layout constraints that are added to views in your interface.

Building NSLayoutConstraint Instances

The NSLayoutConstraint's class method constraintWithItem:attribute: relatedBy: toItem:attribute:multiplier:constant: (*gesundheit!*) creates a single constraint at a time. Each layout constraint defines a rule about either one or two views.

With two views, the creation method produces a strict *view.attribute R view.attribute * multiplier + constant* relation, where *R* is one of equal-to (==), greater-than-or-equal-to (>=), or less-than-or-equal-to (<=) relations.

Consider the following example:

```
[self.view addConstraint:
    [NSLayoutConstraint
        constraintWithItem:self.view
        attribute:NSLayoutAttributeCenterX
        relatedBy:NSLayoutRelationEqual
        toItem:textfield
        attribute:NSLayoutAttributeCenterX
        multiplier:1
        constant:0]];
```

This call adds a new constraint to a view controller's view (self.view) that horizontally center-aligns a text field. It does this by setting an equality relation (NSLayoutRelationEqual) between the two views' horizontal centers (NSLayoutAttributeCenterX attributes). The multiplier here is 1, and the offset constant is 0. This represents the following equation:

*[self.view]'s centerX = ([textfield]'s centerX * 1) + 0*

It basically says, "Please ensure that my view's center and the text field's center are co-aligned at their *X* positions."

The addConstraint: method adds that constraint to the view, where it is stored with any other constraints in the view's constraints property.

Unary Constraints

Not all constraints reference two views. Some constraints, particularly those dealing with view sizing, operate on only a single view. For example, a constraint stating that a view's width is 50 points doesn't reference any other item.

These kinds of constraints are *unary* and do not involve a second item. In this case, the
`secondItem` property will be `nil`, which you can easily test by examining the constraint:

```
if (constraint.secondItem == nil)
    NSLog(@"Constraint is unary");
```

For example, you might establish a unary constraint that sets a view's minimum width to 100
points:

```
NSLayoutConstraint *constraint = [NSLayoutConstraint
    constraintWithItem:view
    attribute:NSLayoutAttributeWidth
    relatedBy:NSLayoutRelationGreaterThanOrEqual
    toItem:nil
    attribute:NSLayoutAttributeNotAnAttribute
    multiplier:1
    constant:100];
[view addConstraint:constraint];
```

This constraint corresponds to the following rule:

> *[view]'s width >= 100*

The second item in this constraint is `nil`, and the attribute is set to "not an attribute." You can
actually set the second attribute to any attribute you like if you don't particularly care about
readability. The constraint will still work as described here because there's no second item to
refer to.

Zero-Item Constraints Are Illegal

Each constraint references either one or, more commonly, two views. You cannot create a valid
constraint with no items. Consider the following code, which attempts to add a constraint with
no items:

```
[self.view addConstraint:
    [NSLayoutConstraint
        constraintWithItem:nil
        attribute:NSLayoutAttributeNotAnAttribute
        relatedBy:NSLayoutRelationEqual
        toItem:nil
        attribute:NSLayoutAttributeNotAnAttribute
        multiplier:1 constant:0]]
```

It compiles properly, without warnings. When run, however, it raises an exception:

```
2013-01-17 12:14:37.653 HelloWorld[17700:c07] *** Terminating app
    due to uncaught exception 'NSInvalidArgumentException', reason:
    '*** +[NSLayoutConstraint constraintWithItem:attribute:relatedBy:
    toItem:attribute:multiplier:constant:]:
    Constraint must contain a first layout item'
```

View Items

A constraint points to the views it affects by using the `firstItem` and `secondItem` properties. These properties are read-only and can be set only during constraint creation.

These two properties are typed as `id`, a fact that, frankly, irritates me. There is no circumstance I have encountered where the first and second items legally point to any other class other than views. (I suspect this is done to allow the same class to be used in both iOS and OS X.)

To address this issue, I created a trivial class category (see Listing 2-1) that provides the typed `firstView` and `secondView` properties I prefer to deal with. As with all other class categories, you want to add namespace prefixes in your own code that ensure that category methods and properties will not conflict with any future development done on Apple's end. You have been warned.

To allow this category to work across platforms, I established a `VIEW_CLASS` constant that refers to the proper base class on the software development kit (SDK) I'm working with. Here's how that's defined across all my constraint work:

```
#pragma mark - Cross Platform
#if TARGET_OS_IPHONE
    #define VIEW_CLASS UIView
#elif TARGET_OS_MAC
    #define VIEW_CLASS NSView
#endif
```

This definition is used throughout the book wherever code may be applicable to both iOS and OS X. Alternatively, you can define it with this:

```
#if TARGET_OS_IPHONE
    @compatibility_alias VIEW_CLASS UIView;
#elif TARGET_OS_MAC
    @compatibility_alias VIEW_CLASS NSView;
#endif
```

Note

Always add namespace prefixes to class extensions so they don't conflict with Apple's potential expansions. I do not follow this practice in this book, in the interest of keeping my code samples readable. Not using namespace prefixes in your production code can cause future compatibility problems.

Listing 2-1   **Extending `NSLayoutConstraint` to Return View-Specific Properties**

```
@interface NSLayoutConstraint (ViewHierarchy)
@property (nonatomic, readonly) VIEW_CLASS *firstView;
@property (nonatomic, readonly) VIEW_CLASS *secondView;
@end
```

```
@implementation NSLayoutConstraint (ViewHierarchy)
// Cast the first item to a view
- (VIEW_CLASS *) firstView
{
    return self.firstItem;
}

// Cast the second item to a view
- (VIEW_CLASS *) secondView
{
    return self.secondItem;
}
@end
```

Constraints, Hierarchies, and Bounds Systems

When constraints reference two views, these views must always belong to the same view hierarchy. You encounter only two legal scenarios for two-view constraints. Either one view has a superview relationship to the other (that is, firstItem is an ancestor of secondItem or vice versa) or the two views must be siblings of some sort (that is, they must have a non-nil common view ancestor [belong to the same window]). If you attempt to do otherwise, you will encounter a nasty crash.

Consider Figure 2-6, where View 3 and its children exist in one window and View 4 in another:

- You can establish a constraint between View 1 and View 3 because View 1 is a subview of View 3.

- You can also build a constraint between View 2 and View 3 even though View 2 is an indirect subview. It's still legal.

- You cannot establish a constraint between any of Views 1 through 3 and View 4. View 4 does not belong to the same hierarchy as the other three.

These checks crop up a lot when you're using constraints. While NSView offers the ancestorSharedWithView: method, UIView does not. To address this, I created the cross-platform view class extension shown in Listing 2-2. This class implements two common tests. It checks whether one view is an ancestor of another view, and it returns two views' nearest common ancestor.

Be aware of bounds systems. You should not relate a button on some view, for example, with a text field inside a separate collection view. If there's some sort of content view with its own bounds system (such as collection views, scroll views, and table views), don't hop out of that to an entirely different bounds system. Listing 2-2 does not check for this, although if you'd like to add that in, you certainly can.

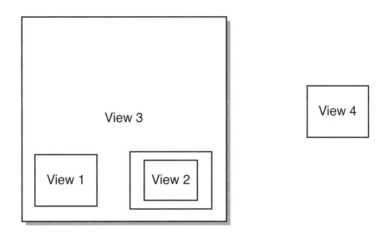

Figure 2-6   You cannot establish a constraint between View 4 in its own window and any of the other views.

Listing 2-2   **Supporting the View Hierarchy**

```
@implementation VIEW_CLASS (HierarchySupport)
// Return an array of all superviews
- (NSArray *) superviews
{
    NSMutableArray *array = [NSMutableArray array];
    VIEW_CLASS *view = self.superview;
    while (view)
    {
        [array addObject:view];
        view = view.superview;
    }

    return array;
}


// Test if the current view has a superview relationship to a view
- (BOOL) isAncestorOfView: (VIEW_CLASS *) aView
{
    return [[aView superviews] containsObject:self];
}


// Return the nearest common ancestor between self and another view
- (VIEW_CLASS *) nearestCommonAncestorToView: (VIEW_CLASS *) aView
```

```
{
    // Check for same view
    if ([self isEqual:aView])
        return self;

    // Check for direct superview relationship
    if ([self isAncestorOfView:aView])
        return self;
    if ([aView isAncestorOfView:self])
        return aView;

    // Search for indirect common ancestor
    NSArray *ancestors = self.superviews;
    for (VIEW_CLASS *view in aView.superviews)
        if ([ancestors containsObject:view])
            return view;

    // No common ancestor
    return nil;
}
@end
```

Installing Constraints

To get constraints to enter the Auto Layout system, you add them to views. Here's an example:

```
[myView addConstraint: aConstraintInstance];
```

Because the visual format system returns arrays of constraints rather than single constraints, the NSLayoutConstraint class also offers a way to add a collection of constraints simultaneously:

```
[myView addConstraints: myArrayOfConstraints];
```

Constraints always have a natural home, in the nearest common ancestor of their firstItem and the secondItem properties. For example, consider the views you saw in Figure 2-6:

- A constraint between View 1 and View 3 should be added to View 3, the superview.
- Similarly, a constraint between View 2 and View 3 belongs with View 3. Although View 3 is not View 2's superview, it is its ancestor.
- When working with View 1 and View 2, View 3 is the nearest common ancestor. You add the constraint there even though it's not mentioned as either the first or second item.

IB follows this rule, and you should, too. If you're trying to track down where each constraint lives in the IB hierarchy, you'll find them in the storyboard outline, added to the nearest common ancestor of the first and second items.

Here's what Apple says on the matter in the `UIView.h` (iOS) and `NSLayoutConstraint.h` (OS X) header files:

> A constraint is typically installed on the closest common ancestor of the views involved in the constraint. It is required that a constraint be installed on a common ancestor of every view involved. The numbers in a constraint are interpreted in the coordinate system of the view it is installed on. A view is considered to be an ancestor of itself.

Every constraint, in fact, can and should self-install itself to a natural and correct view destination. Listing 2-3 shows an `NSLayoutConstraint` class category that does this. It looks for the nearest common ancestor between its two items and adds itself to that view. If the constraint is unary, it installs onto the first item.

With this category, you call `install` (and `remove`) on the constraint itself. The information you need in order to know where to install already exists within every (legally defined) constraint. And, if your constraints are consistently installed to consistent destinations, removing constraints becomes a trivial problem as well.

Auto Layout also offers a blunt-trauma approach to removing constraints. It automatically disposes of constraints when a view is removed from its hierarchy:

`[view removeFromSuperview]`

Then, any constraint referencing that view is automatically removed from Auto Layout. Suppose, for instance, that you have a constraint that describes the relationship between Figure 2-6's View 1 and View 2. View 3 owns the constraint because it is View 1 and View 2's nearest common ancestor. When you remove View 2 from its superview, Auto Layout automatically removes the constraint from View 3. This removal happens on your behalf, without explicit requests.

Listing 2-3 **Self-Installing Constraints**

```
@implementation NSLayoutConstraint (SelfInstall)
- (BOOL) install
{
    // Handle Unary constraint
    if (self.isUnary)
    {
        [self.firstView addConstraint:self];
        return YES;
    }

    // Find nearest common ancestor
    VIEW_CLASS *view =
        [self.firstView nearestCommonAncestor:self.secondView];
    if (!view)
    {
        NSLog(@"Error: No common ancestor between items.");
```

```
        return NO;
    }

    // Install to nearest common ancestor
    [view addConstraint:self];
    return YES;
}

// You may want to rename this to installWithPriority:, which in
// retrospect would have been a far better method name.
- (BOOL) install: (float) priority
{
    // Set priority and install
    self.priority = priority;
    return [self install];
}

// Discussed further in the section that follows
- (void) remove
{
    if (self.isUnary)
    {
        VIEW_CLASS *view = self.firstView;
        [view removeConstraint:self];
        return;
    }

    // Remove from preferred recipient
    VIEW_CLASS *view =
        [self.firstView nearestCommonAncestor:self.secondView];
    if (!view) return;

    // This is safe. If the constraint isn't on the view, this is a no-op
    [view removeConstraint:self];
}
@end
```

Removing Constraints

You can add and remove constraints from views at any time. The two built-in methods
removeConstraint: and removeConstraints: enable you to remove one or an array of
constraints from a given view. Because these methods work on object pointers, they might not
do what you expect when you attempt to remove constraints.

Suppose, for instance, that you build a center-matching constraint and add it to your view. You
cannot then build a second version of the constraint with the same rules and expect to remove

it using the `removeConstraint:` call. They are equivalent constraints, but they are not the *same* constraint. Here's an example of this conundrum:

```
// Build and add the constraint
[self.view addConstraint:
    [NSLayoutConstraint constraintWithItem:textField
        attribute:NSLayoutAttributeCenterX
        relatedBy:NSLayoutRelationEqual
        toItem:self.view
        attribute:NSLayoutAttributeCenterX
        multiplier:1.0f constant:0.0f]];

// Attempt to remove the constraint
[self.view removeConstraint:
    [NSLayoutConstraint constraintWithItem:textField
        attribute:NSLayoutAttributeCenterX
        relatedBy:NSLayoutRelationEqual
        toItem:self.view
        attribute:NSLayoutAttributeCenterX
        multiplier:1.0f constant:0.0f]];
```

Executing these two method calls ends up as follows: The `self.view` instance contains the original constraint, and the attempt to remove the second constraint is ignored. Removing a constraint not held by the view has no effect.

You have two choices for resolving this. First, you can hold on to the constraint when it's first added by storing it in a local variable. Here's what this looks like:

```
NSLayoutConstraint *myConstraint =
    NSLayoutConstraint constraintWithItem:textField
        attribute:NSLayoutAttributeCenterX
        relatedBy:NSLayoutRelationEqual
        toItem:self.view
        attribute:NSLayoutAttributeCenterX
        multiplier:1.0f constant:0.0f]];
[self.view addConstraint:myConstraint];

// later
[self.view removeConstraint:myConstraint];
```

To remove an equivalent constraint, you can use a method that compares constraints and removes one that mathematically matches the one you pass. Alternatively, you can tag constraints (using a class category) so you can find them and remove them at a future time. Removing constraints plays a major role in Auto Layout. Whenever you refresh a layout—most commonly when a device rotates—you need to remove invalid constraints and replace them with fresh rules.

Knowing whether your constraints will be static (used for the lifetime of your view) or dynamic (updated as needed) helps you decide which approach you need. If you think you might need to remove a constraint in the future, either hold on to it via a local variable so that you can later remove it from your view or implement workarounds that let you search for the constraint at a later time.

Comparing Constraints

All constraints use a fixed structure of the following form, along with an associated priority:

*view1.attribute (relation) view2.attribute * multiplier + constant*

Each element in this equation is exposed through a constraint's object properties, namely `priority`, `firstItem`, `firstAttribute`, `relation`, `secondItem`, `secondAttribute`, `multiplier`, and `constant`. These properties make it easy to compare two constraints.

Views store and remove constraints as objects. If two constraints are stored in separate memory locations, they're considered unequal, *even if they describe the same conditions*. To allow your code to add and remove constraints on-the-fly without storing those items locally, you use comparisons.

Listing 2-4 creates an `NSLayoutConstraint` category that compares the properties between two constraints and determines whether they match. The `isEqualToLayoutConstraint:` method considers the equation but not the priority. Two constraints describing the same conditions are essentially equivalent, regardless of the priority a developer has currently assigned.

Listing 2-4   Constraint-to-Constraint Attribute Comparison

```
@implementation NSLayoutConstraint (ConstraintMatching)

// This ignores any priority, looking only at y (R) mx + b
- (BOOL) isEqualToLayoutConstraint: (NSLayoutConstraint *) constraint
{
    if (self.firstItem != constraint.firstItem) return NO;
    if (self.secondItem != constraint.secondItem) return NO;
    if (self.firstAttribute != constraint.firstAttribute) return NO;
    if (self.secondAttribute != constraint.secondAttribute) return NO;
    if (self.relation != constraint.relation) return NO;
    if (self.multiplier != constraint.multiplier) return NO;
    if (self.constant != constraint.constant) return NO;

    return YES;
}
@end
```

Matching Constraints

Once a constraint is installed, you can do two important things with it. You can either remove it (and likely replace it with a new rule) or modify its constant (usually to animate a view). These tasks are both often used in Auto Layout work to create lively interfaces that respond to user interaction.

Although you can create instance variables and outlets that point to specific constraints, a highly interactive GUI can create numerous constraints that are added, modified, and removed on-the-fly. Lightweight and short-lived constraints may not hang around long enough to make it worth your while to point to them directly.

I ended up building a view category dedicated to retrieving installed constraints. Listing 2-5 presents a number of constraint-matching methods that search through views to find constraints that match a single constraint, that match an array of constraints (useful for constraint arrays built via visual formats), and that reference a specific view (handy for animation). It also provides a pair of methods that remove the constraints thus matched.

Listing 2-5   **Finding Matching Constraints and Removing Them**

```
@implementation VIEW_CLASS (ConstraintMatching)

// Find the first matching constraint
- (NSLayoutConstraint *) constraintMatchingConstraint:
    (NSLayoutConstraint *) aConstraint
{
    // Try to find a matching constraint in the view's
    // installed constraints
    for (NSLayoutConstraint *constraint in self.constraints)
    {
        if ([constraint isEqualToLayoutConstraint:aConstraint])
            return constraint;
    }

    // Search superviews as well
    for (VIEW_CLASS *view in self.superviews)
        for (NSLayoutConstraint *constraint in view.constraints)
        {
            if ([constraint isEqualToLayoutConstraint:aConstraint])
                return constraint;
        }

    return nil;
}


// Find all matching constraints. Use this to pull out
// installed constraints matching a set generated from
```

```objc
// a visual pattern.
- (NSArray *) constraintsMatchingConstraints: (NSArray *) constraints
{
    NSMutableArray *array = [NSMutableArray array];
    for (NSLayoutConstraint *constraint in constraints)
    {
        NSLayoutConstraint *match =
            [self constraintMatchingConstraint:constraint];
        if (match)
            [array addObject:match];
    }
    return array;
}

// All constraints matching that view
// This method is *insanely* useful.
- (NSArray *) constraintsReferencingView: (VIEW_CLASS *) view
{
    NSMutableArray *array = [NSMutableArray array];
    for (NSLayoutConstraint *constraint in self.constraints)
        if (([constraint.firstItem isEqual:view]) ||
            ([constraint.secondItem isEqual:view]))
            [array addObject:constraint];
    return array;
}

// Remove matching constraint
- (void) removeMatchingConstraint:
    (NSLayoutConstraint *) aConstraint
{
    NSLayoutConstraint *match =
        [self constraintMatchingConstraint:aConstraint];
    if (match)
    {
        [self removeConstraint:match];
        [self.superview removeConstraint:match];
    }
}

// Remove matching constraints
- (void) removeMatchingConstraints: (NSArray *) anArray
{
    for (NSLayoutConstraint *constraint in anArray)
        [self removeMatchingConstraint:constraint];
}
@end
```

Laws of Layout Constraints

Here are a few basic facts about layout constraints that you should keep in mind:

- **Layout constraints have priorities.** Priorities range numerically from 1 to 1,000. Higher priorities are always satisfied before lower priorities. The highest priority you can assign is "required" (value: 1,000), which is also the default. During layout, the system iterates through any constraints you have added, attempting to satisfy them all. Priorities come into play when deciding which constraint has less sway. A 99 priority constraint is broken in favor of a 100 priority constraint when the two come into conflict.

- **Layout constraints don't have any natural "order" outside of priorities.** All constraints of the same priority are considered at the same time. If you need some constraint to take precedence, assign it a higher priority.

- **Layout constraints are relationships and are not directional.** You don't have to solve the right side to calculate the left side.

- **Layout constraints can be approximated.** Optional constraints try to optimize their results. Consider the constraint "View 2's top edge should be at the same position as View 1's bottom edge." The constraint system attempts to squeeze these two together by minimizing their distance. If other constraints prevent them from touching, the system places them as close as it can, minimizing the absolute distance between the two attributes.

- **Layout constraints can have cycles.** As long as all items are satisfied, it doesn't matter which elements refer to which. Don't sweat the cross-references. In this declarative system, circular references are okay, and you will not encounter infinite looping issues.

- **Layout constraints can be redundant.** If constraints do not contradict each other, you may safely install multiple items that implement the same layout logic.

- **Layout constraints can refer to view siblings.** You can align the center point of one view's subview with the center point of an entirely different view as long as both views have a common view ancestor. For example, you might create a complex text entry view and align its rightmost button's right attribute with the right attribute of an embedded image view below it. Or you might attach a "handle" to a "drawer," as in Chapter 6, where both items move together, but neither is the parent of the other.

- **Auto Layout may not play nicely with transforms.** Exercise care when mixing transforms with Auto Layout, especially those that include rotation:
    - Auto Layout doesn't support transforms that don't preserve rectangles.
    - Auto Layout doesn't support nonzero alignment insets on views with bounds transforms that don't preserve rectangles.

- **Auto Layout does not work with the new iOS 7 view dynamics.** You can use Auto Layout *inside* any view that's affected by dynamic behaviors, but you cannot combine Auto Layout view placement with dynamic animator management.

- **Auto Layout does work with motion effects.** The visual changes applied by UIMotionEffect instances won't disturb your underlying layout as they only affect the view's layer.

- **Layout constraints should not cross bounds systems.** Don't cross into and out of scroll views, collection views, and table views for alignment. If there's some sort of content view with its own bounds system, avoid hopping out of that to an entirely different bounds system in another view. Doing so may not crash your app, but it's not a good idea, and it's not well supported by Auto Layout. Here are a few further points about bounds:

  - Auto Layout doesn't support crossing bounds transforms that don't preserve rectangles.

  - Auto Layout doesn't support crossing rotational bounds transforms with edge layout constraints, such as right, left, top, and bottom.

  - Auto Layout doesn't support crossing rotational bounds transforms with dimensional layout constraints, such as width and height.

- **Layout constraints can fail at runtime.** If your constraints cannot be resolved and come into conflict, the runtime system chooses which constraints to disregard so it can present whatever view layout it can. This is usually ugly and nearly always not the visual presentation you intended. Auto Layout sends exhaustive descriptions of what went wrong to your Xcode console. Use these reports to fix your constraints and bring them into harmony with each other.

  Custom views that directly set view frames (for example, in layoutSubviews) are especially vulnerable to runtime failure. Frame updates that contradict existing constraint rules can cause crashes.

- **Badly formed layout constraints will interrupt application execution.** Although you have not read about visual formats in detail (see Chapter 4), it's important to note that some constraint calls may crash your application through unhandled exceptions. For example, if you pass a constraint format string such as @"V[view1]-|" (which is missing a colon after the letter V) to a constraint creation method, you'll encounter a runtime exception:

  ```
  Terminating app due to uncaught exception 'NSInvalidArgumentException',
  reason: 'Unable to parse constraint format'
  ```

  This error cannot be detected during compilation; you must carefully check your format strings by hand. Designing constraints in IB helps avoid bad-typo scenarios.

- **A constraint must refer to at least one view.** You can create a constraint without any items and compile that code without warnings, as you saw earlier in this chapter, but it will raise an exception at runtime. Consider this to be "not a good thing."

- **Beware of invalid attribute pairings.** You cannot legally match a view's left edge to another view's height. Invalid pairings raise runtime exceptions. Specifically, you shouldn't mix size attributes with edge attributes. You can generally guess which pairs are problematic because they make no sense.

- **Take care of Auto Layout.** Don't get constraints wet. Don't expose constraints to bright light. And, no matter how much constraints cry, no matter how much constraints beg, don't feed constraints after midnight.[1]

Exercises

After reading this chapter, test your knowledge with these exercises:

1. Can you build an `NSContentSizeLayoutConstraint` by hand? How and why do these constraints appear in Auto Layout?

2. What happens at runtime when two conflicting rules have exactly the same priority?

3. Why use layout priorities like 251 and 249 in preference to ones like 257 and 243?

4. Why might you use views without intrinsic content size?

5. What happens if you install a constraint between a view and its superview on the child view?

6. What is the difference between constraining View A's width to twice the size of View B's width and constraining View B's width to half of View A's width? What happens if you install both constraints?

7. In Figure 2-6, where would you install a constraint between View 1 and View 3? Between View 1 and View 2? Between View 2 and View 3? Between View 2 and View 4? If you add a button as a subview to View 2, where do you install a constraint between that button and View 1? Between that button and View 4?

8. You create View A and add a subview, View B. You add constraints that center View B in its superview and size View B to 100 points by 100 points. (a) Is View B's layout ambiguous? (b) How many items are stored in View A's `constraints` array? (c) How many items are stored in View B's `constraints` array?

   You remove View B from its superview. (d) After this, how many constraints are stored in View A's constraints array? (e) How many constraints are stored in View B's array?

Conclusions

This chapter rather exhaustively introduces constraints, discussing what they are, where they come from, and how they are represented in the Auto Layout system. You have read about the kinds of constraints you might deal with and how you add and remove them from views. Before you move on to the next chapter, here are a few thoughts to take with you:

---

1. *Gremlins*, Joe Dante, 1984.

- Priorities play an important role in adding nuance to your interfaces. They help you manage edge conditions, allowing Auto Layout to decide which rules should win out in an otherwise conflicting design. If you find yourself creating only required constraints, you're missing out on a powerful part of Auto Layout.

- Although Apple recommends using IB as the primary avenue for creating constraints, you may find that code-level constraints offer tighter control and better solutions for achieving reliable interface design. Most importantly, code helps you document your design choices and inspect your implementation—which IB rather fails at.

- Compression resistance and content hugging become especially important when internationalizing text in your interface. As labels and buttons resize, these constraints allow you to adjust interface layout so your apps will look as good in German and Japanese as they do in English.

- Although $y \mathrel{R} m * x + b$ looks like an absolutely minimal way to lay out an interface, it provides a surprising robustness in its expressive reach. (The tl;dr of this was explained to me as follows: "*If you describe a linear inequality as a shaded region on the number line, you can describe a system of linear inequalities as an* N *dimensional polytope with optimal solutions at the vertices.*"—*Anonymous Engineer*) You'll discover in the following chapters that simple constraints can be flexible and powerful.

3

Interface Builder Layout

Compared to earlier Xcode releases, Xcode 5 with its redesigned Interface Builder (IB) vastly enhances Auto Layout. Even so, learning constraint-based design in IB can be a frustrating experience for many new developers. This chapter will help reduce that frustration and introduce the tools that IB provides. You'll read about how Auto Layout integrates with IB and how you can best explore, construct, test, and validate your interfaces.

This is a hands-on chapter. You will gain the most from it by launching Xcode, creating new projects, and following along with these examples in live IB documents. The more you play with the tools, the more the mystery will dissipate, as IB constraints become part of your design workflow.

> **Note**
>
> IB is a constantly evolving product. Details described in this chapter may change as Apple updates Xcode.

Designing in IB

For decades, IB and its antecedents have offered a customizable interface editor. Designers and developers collaborate with tools built around the concept that interface expression is inherently a visual problem. IB enables teams to design interfaces using the same language and expressive space as the product they end up building.

IB's power and flexibility have grown over time. Until 2011, IB focused on Autosizing, a system that used struts (fixed offsets from a superview) and springs (flexible sizing allowances) to establish placement rules. Although this older system remains part of IB, the new constraint-based Auto Layout greatly enhances visual layout.

With Auto Layout, you express a view's relationships to itself, to its parent, and to view siblings within the layout hierarchy. These relationships can include both equalities and inequalities and may refer to view attributes such as position, extent, and (for text) baseline offsets. These features enable Auto Layout to implement nuanced boundary conditions in a way that

Autosizing never could. For example, you might say, "I want these views to lay out in a line with equal sizing, but they should never come any closer than 20 points to the edges of the superview" or "If there's a shortage of horizontal space, I want the text in my left-hand labels to clip before any right-hand buttons are affected."

In Xcode 5, IB lets you establish, tweak, prioritize, and test layout rules in new ways. Constraint settings pop-ups appear with a simple double-click, so you don't have to keep moving between multiple inspector panes. Preview panes enable you to test how your constraints will look in any orientation. You can validate your rules with just a few clicks using new menu choices, and Auto Layout offers suggestions on how to complete your constraints.

If you've been using constraints for a while, you'll find Xcode 5's approach to Auto Layout a happy surprise. If you're new to the technology, you'll find plenty of assistance for evaluating, verifying, and improving your GUI designs.

Disabling Auto Layout

At times, you may need to disable Auto Layout and use Autosizing in IB instead. Perhaps you have investments in proprietary designs that you're not ready to migrate. Perhaps you want to stick with familiar and tested tools for production. Perhaps you're incrementally migrating existing projects and need to keep some portions in the Autosizing world. Fortunately, you can easily switch off Auto Layout on an individual storyboard and nib file basis.

Here's what you do:

1. In Xcode, select any user interface document (a storyboard or a nib file) from the Project Navigator (View > Navigators > Show Project Navigator).

2. Open the File Inspector (View > Utilities > Show File Inspector).

3. In the File Inspector, locate the Interface Builder Document section. Just below the View As dropdown, uncheck the Use Autolayout check box, which you see in Figure 3-1, to return IB to using Autosizing.

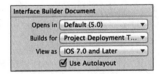

Figure 3-1   Disable Auto Layout by unchecking the Use Autolayout box in Xcode's File Inspector. This option appears for both iOS and OS X projects.

> **Note**
>
> Although Apple documentation now universally refers to the technology as Auto Layout, some older references still use *Autolayout* as a single word. Apple encourages you to file bug reports or submit a Feedback form for any out-of-spec use of the older Autolayout name.

Under Autosizing, views use the `autoresizingMask` property to ensure that they resize correctly, such as when a device reorients or a user resizes a window. With Auto Layout disabled, you work with struts, springs, and `autoresizingMasks`. Figure 3-2 shows the Size Inspector (View > Utilities > Show Size Inspector) for a view with Auto Layout disabled (right) and enabled (left).

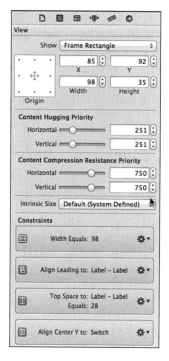 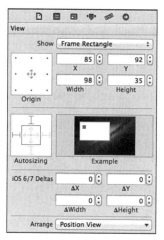

Figure 3-2   When Auto Layout is enabled (left), IB's Size Inspector offers controls to adjust a view's layout priorities and provides a list of constraints that mention the view. When Auto Layout is disabled (right), the inspector reverts to the Autosizing struts and springs editor that correspond to a view's `autoresizingMask` property.

Opting Out of Auto Layout in Code

Autosizing is the default in code. You opt views *out* of Autosizing to participate in the new Auto Layout system. All views default to the older behavior, even when modern runtimes use constraint-based layout. That's because the runtime invisibly handles the translation between your old-style code and the new-style constraint system on your behalf.

When a view's `translatesAutoresizingMaskIntoConstraints` property is set to `YES` (the default), the runtime uses that view's autoresizing mask to produce matching constraints in the new Auto Layout system. The rules apply like they always did, even though the implementation details have been modernized. Here you create and opt a view into Auto Layout:

```
// Create a new view. It defaults to autosizing.
UIView *view = [[UIView alloc] initWithFrame:frame];

// Opt view into Auto Layout
view.translatesAutoresizingMaskIntoConstraints = NO;
```

Here's what Apple has to say on the matter. This comment is from the `UIView.h` header file. It's essentially identical to the text in `NSLayoutConstraint.h` on OS X:

> By default, the autoresizing mask on a view gives rise to constraints that fully determine the view's position. Any constraints you set on the view are likely to conflict with autoresizing constraints, so you must turn off this property first. IB will turn it off for you.

Autoresizing translation is performed, invisibly, on your behalf. The runtime creates constraints that implement Autosizing rules and adds them to the Auto Layout system.

Combining Autosizing with Auto Layout

You are welcome to mix and match autoresizing views with constraint-based layout as long as their rules don't clash. For example, you can load a nib whose subviews are laid out using struts and springs and allow that view, in turn, to operate as a first-class member of the Auto Layout world. The key is encapsulation. As long as rules do not conflict, you can reuse complex views you have already established in your projects.

Basic Layout and Auto-Generated Constraints

Constraint-based layout is cooked right into modern versions of IB. Just as IB assists you in creating aligned, centered, and indented object placement, it can create constraints that represent the layout you've built. Figure 3-3 shows a switch being added to a new iOS view controller's layout. Guides ensure that this switch is centered vertically and horizontally within its parent.

Inferred Constraints

As of Xcode 5 and iOS 7, IB *infers* constraints on your behalf. This means you can build interfaces incrementally yet still have a working interface to test. Create a new single view project with a switch, as in Figure 3-3. IB creates two constraints for you that position the switch away from the top and left of the parent view.

Figure 3-3   Adding a switch in IB.

On a 4-inch iPhone, this switch lies 268 points from the top and 136 points from the left. As you can see in Figure 3-4, the button is centered in portrait orientation but not in landscape.

You can confirm these inferred items by logging the constraints attached to the view controller's view at runtime. To do so, save your interface and add the following code to your primary view controller:

```
- (void) viewDidAppear:(BOOL)animated
{
    for (NSLayoutConstraint *constraint in self.view.constraints)
        NSLog(@"%@", constraint);
}
```

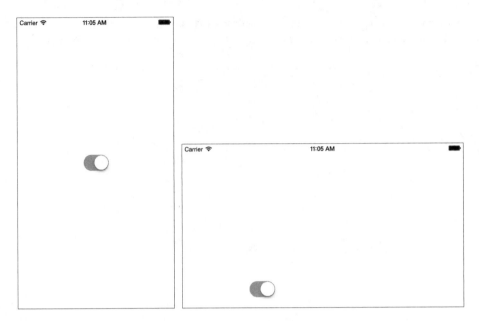

Figure 3-4   IB infers constraints from fixed positions.

When you run this app, the `viewDidAppear:` message logs all constraints attached to the primary view. Under iOS, you'll discover constraints that set the left and top edges with respect to the parent view:

```
2013-08-14 16:09:49.751 test[31487:a0b]  <NSIBPrototypingLayoutConstraint:0x8993900
'IB auto generated at build time for view with fixed frame' H:|-(136)-
[UISwitch:0x898fe50](LTR)    (Names: '|':UIView:0x898fc70 )>
2013-08-14 16:09:49.753 test[31487:a0b]  <NSIBPrototypingLayoutConstraint:0x8993be0
'IB auto generated at build time for view with fixed frame' V:|-(268)-
[UISwitch:0x898fe50]    (Names: '|':UIView:0x898fc70 )>
```

I boldfaced the key text in these log messages to indicate the rationale behind the IB-generated constraints. This example shows what happens when you place views and then save your work without adding constraints. Whenever Xcode detects constraint-less views, it assumes that you're just starting development. It adds courtesy constraints built from the view frames to provide minimum fallback behavior for interface elements.

In addition to these constraints, you'll see placeholder constraints for the view controller's top and bottom layout guides. Under iOS 7, the `UIViewController` class introduces built-in spacing views at the top and bottom of the scene. Each spacer has an associated length that describes where the controller's main content begins and ends vertically. These help align your content, ensuring the material you need to remain visible does so without overlapping status bars, navigation bars, tab bars, and other UI features.

In the following debug output, the top guide is 20 points high and the bottom is 0 points high:

```
2013-08-14 16:09:49.753 test[31487:a0b]  <_UILayoutSupportConstraint:0x8993c90
V:[_UILayoutGuide:0x8992ee0(20)]>
2013-08-14 16:09:49.754 test[31487:a0b]  <_UILayoutSupportConstraint:0x898f5e0
V:|-(0)-[_UILayoutGuide:0x8992ee0]    (Names: '|':UIView:0x898fc70 )>
2013-08-14 16:09:49.754 test[31487:a0b]  <_UILayoutSupportConstraint:0x8990cd0
V:[_UILayoutGuide:0x89933f0(0)]>
2013-08-14 16:09:49.754 test[31487:a0b]  <_UILayoutSupportConstraint:0x8990ac0
_UILayoutGuide:0x89933f0.bottom == UIView:0x898fc70.bottom>
```

These lengths vary depending on the container layout you use. Tab bars and navigation bars may raise the bottom or lower the top of the core application space used by a view controller.

IB displays guide proxies associated with the view controller scene, as you see in Figure 3-5. You connect constraints directly to these guides, ensuring that your user interface items lay out with respect to the top and the bottom of the *scene* rather than the top and the bottom of the *screen*. In iOS 7's new edge-to-edge design, your view controller's frame may extend beyond and under navigation bars, toolbars, tab bars, and so forth. Using layout guides keeps your buttons, labels, and so forth from inadvertently floating up under those items and out of view.

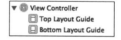

Figure 3-5   New to Xcode 5, top and bottom layout guides enable you to constrain content to your active application space.

Ambiguity Resolution Constraints

As you start building constraints, you may run across another kind of IB-supplied constraint. To discover this type of IB-generated constraints, you add *insufficient* constraints to your view:

1. Add and center a switch if you have not done so already. Then select the switch.

2. Ctrl+drag (or hold down the right mouse button and drag) from the switch toward the left and release within the superview. The direction you drag influences the choices IB presents.

3. Select Leading Space to Container from the contextual pop-up (see Figure 3-6). IB adds a new constraint, colored orange. This color tells you that the constraints attached to the view are ambiguous. Blue constraints are unambiguous, and red constraints involve conflicted rules.

4. Save and run the updated interface.

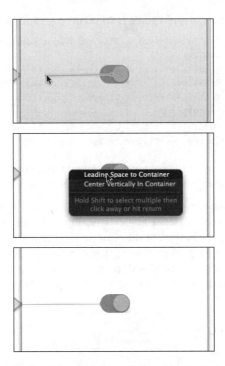

Figure 3-6   Add a leading space constraint by Ctrl+dragging (or holding down the right mouse button and dragging) from the switch to the left.

This time, the first few log messages from your custom `viewDidAppear:` method look like this:

```
2013-08-15 12:25:58.398 test[38829:a0b] <NSLayoutConstraint:0x8c806a0 H:|-(136)-
[UISwitch:0x8c7cc90]   (Names: '|':UIView:0x8c7cab0 )>
2013-08-15 12:25:58.400 test[38829:a0b] <NSIBPrototypingLayoutConstraint:0x8c80770
'IB auto generated at build time for view with ambiguity' H:|-(136@251)-
[UISwitch:0x8c7cc90](LTR) priority:251   (Names: '|':UIView:0x8c7cab0 )>
2013-08-15 12:25:58.400 test[38829:a0b] <NSIBPrototypingLayoutConstraint:0x8c80a50
'IB auto generated at build time for view with ambiguity' V:|-(268@251)-
[UISwitch:0x8c7cc90] priority:251    (Names: '|':UIView:0x8c7cab0 )>
```

You created the first of these three constraints by following Figure 3-6. IB adds the other two constraints on your behalf, to remove ambiguity. The duplicated constraint, the first of the two IB-created items, seems a bit like a bug. I have submitted a bug report (this is also called "filing a radar") with Apple to that effect. Therefore, by the time you try this example, you might get different output.

Size Constraints

As you read in Chapter 1, "Introducing Auto Layout," every view requires at least two constraints along each axis to set position and size. So where are the other constraints beyond inferred and direct placement constraints?

Every switch control provides a fixed intrinsic content size. This content size establishes the width and height of its view. To uncover the switch's "missing" constraints, you can create a new IBOutlet named mySwitch connected to your switch and add the following code to your custom viewDidAppear: method:

```
// Check the intrinsic content size
NSLog(@"Intrinsic content size: %@",
    NSStringFromCGSize(mySwitch.intrinsicContentSize));

// Look for constraints stored in the switch
for (NSLayoutConstraint *constraint in mySwitch.constraints)
    NSLog(@"%@", constraint);
```

When you run this updated method, you'll discover both the intrinsic content size and the two missing constraints IB built for you:

```
2013-07-05 13:50:12.040 IBTest[16646:a0b] Intrinsic content size: {49, 31}
2013-07-05 13:50:12.040 IBTest[16646:a0b] <NSContentSizeLayoutConstraint:0x8b231d0
H:[UISwitch:0x8b1e240(49)] Hug:750 CompressionResistance:750>
2013-07-05 13:50:12.040 IBTest[16646:a0b] <NSContentSizeLayoutConstraint:0x8b23320
V:[UISwitch:0x8b1e240(31)] Hug:750 CompressionResistance:750>
```

The default iOS switch is automatically sized at 49×31 points. Switches use a high hugging priority to ensure that they're not resized larger than their art. The default high compression resistance priority keeps the switch from clipping in tight layout situations.

Between size layout constraints, the one constraint you built in Figure 3-6, and IB-supplied constraints, the switch does indeed contain *at least* two constraints per axis—setting position and extent.

A Guided Tour of IB Elements

Table 3-1 offers a guided tour of IB elements that you'll find in the visual editor. Take a few minutes to read through this table and identify the components you use to create constraint-based layouts. Don't worry about messing up your current project by testing these options. You can easily revert your project to its one-switch, one-constraint state or create a new project when you continue on with this chapter.

Table 3-1   **What's What in the IB Editor**

Element	Description
	This entry arrow to the left of a view indicates that this is the app's initial view controller. It appears only on iOS storyboards. Set the initial view controller in the Attributes Inspector by checking Is Initial View Controller.
	This toolbar underneath the view offers connection targets that refer to the owning view controller, the active first responder, and the unwind segue. This toolbar is an iOS-only, storyboard-only editor feature. Drag the bar background to move scenes around the storyboard editor.
	This document outline toggle button at the bottom left shows and hides the document detail outline, which, among other things, contains hierarchical lists of views and layout constraints for each storyboard scene. When working with constraint-based layout, the document outline plays an important role. Keep your outline open, visible, and easily accessible.
	This form factor toggle button appears as the first of the three grouped tools at the bottom right. It enables you to switch from a 3.5-inch-based phone scene to a 4.0-inch-based one and back. This button is specific to phone projects and does not appear for tablet projects or in OS X interfaces. This is purely a design-time convenience and a helpful tool for testing your layout in both configurations. You can also switch your editor layout from portrait to landscape and back by selecting the view controller in the document outline. Open the Attributes Inspector and update Simulated Metrics > Orientation.
	This second set of tools offers constraint-building options. From left to right, these are the tools: • Alignment • Pinning (sizing, spacing, and size matching) • Constraint issue resolution • Resizing behaviors These tools largely mirror options offered in Xcode's Editor menu.

Element	Description
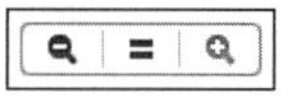	This rightmost set of tools at the bottom right of the editor window control zooming, which is an iOS editor feature. You can also double-click the editor's background for similar behavior.
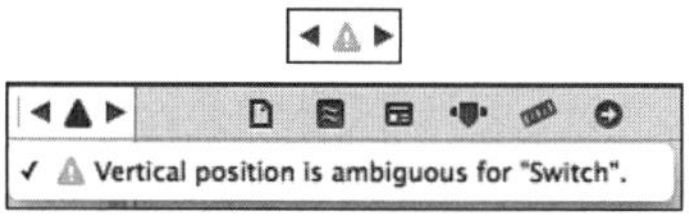	At the very top-right of the editor window, you find the Issue Stepper. Click the arrows to walk through any issues associated with your storyboard. The example you just built should have a single problem: its ambiguous vertical placement. The single constraint you created addressed only horizontal layout.
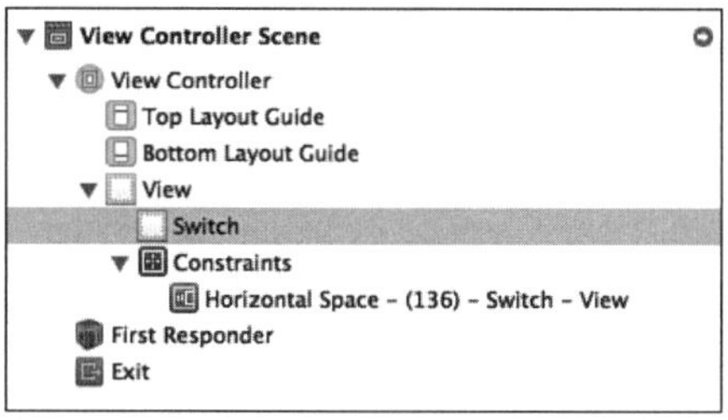	When toggled open, this outline view appears at the left of the editor window. It consists of a hierarchy of items contained in each scene.
	The Top and Bottom Layout Guide proxies enable you to constrain items to the visible portions of your interface so they won't disappear behind navigation bars or status bars. Drag from views to these elements to use them as natural components of your layout.
	A circled arrow appears to the right of any scene root that has layout issues. Click this circle to expose an issues list for each scene.
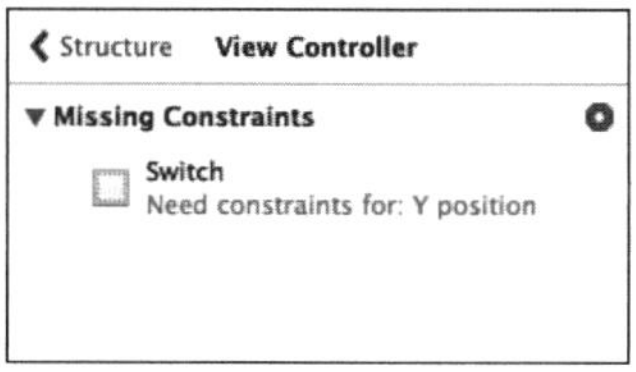	This issues list displays problems on a scene-by-scene basis. Typical issues include missing constraints, conflicting constraints, and misplaced views.
	Click Structure to return to the normal outline.
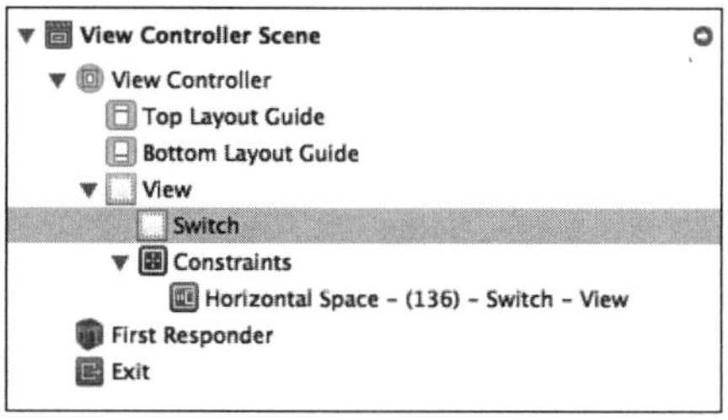	Constraints appear in this outline under the view they're installed to. (See Chapter 2, "Constraints," to learn how IB chooses which view goes with which constraints.)
	The constraint you added to set the switch's left inset appears in the constraint collection owned by its superview.
	As a rule, the only constraints installed at the same level as a given view are user-built size constraints. IB does not reveal internal `NSContentSizeLayoutConstraint` instances.

Element	Description
	The single constraint you've built appears with an orange color in the editor. Orange constraint lines warn you that views are insufficiently constrained.
	When you see blue constraint lines, they reassure you that view layout is unambiguous. A well-constrained view participates in at least two location constraints: one vertical and one horizontal. A view that expresses intrinsic content size does not require additional height and width constraints. To update your layout to blue constraints, choose Editor > Resolve Auto Layout Issues > Add Missing Constraints *or* Reset to Suggested Constraints. The Container variation of each command (found at the bottom of the resolution menu) generates constraints for the entire scene, not just the selected view.
	A dashed outline appears when a view's current position does not match the location specified by its constraints. This happens when you drag a view away from an already-constrained position. The outline indicates the position the view would occupy when Auto Layout applies its constraints. ■ To move the view back into position, choose Editor > Resolve Auto Layout Issues > Update Frames. The view frame refreshes to match the underlying constraints. ■ To update the constraints to match the dragged frame, choose Editor > Resolve Auto Layout Issues > Update Constraints. IB issues new constraints to match the changed layout.

Element	Description
	Red lines alert you to conflicting constraints from inconsistent layout. Fix these issues by editing the constraints directly (select and then delete extraneous items) or choose Editor > Resolve Auto Layout Issues > Reset to Suggested Constraints. A blue bubble indicates an inequality constraint, such as greater-than-or-equal-to. A number bubble indicates a constant value. Here, the constraint sets a 66-point width.
	As you've already seen, you add view-to-superview constraints by Ctrl+dragging from a view into the superview. Ctrl+drag from any view to another view to set constraints that relate two items. When you release the mouse, IB presents a list of possible constraints for you to select from: • The menu varies depending on whether you drag from view to superview (top), view to view (bottom), or view to same view (not shown here). • The direction you drag (horizontal, vertical, or diagonal) determines the choices in the pop-up menu. For example, when you drag horizontally between two views, the menu offers Horizontal Spacing; when you drag diagonally, the menu offers both horizontal and vertical options. • To select multiple items from the pop-up menu, hold Shift while selecting the items.

Element	Description
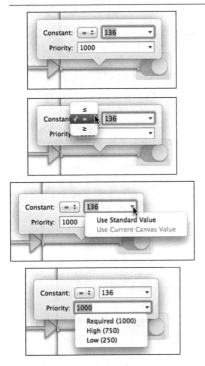	Double-click any constraint to reveal an adjustment pop-up dialog within the editor window. Edit the relation by selecting less than, equal to, or greater than. You may enter any constant—positive or negative, integer or float. Standard values are 20 points from the edge of a superview to a child view and 8 points between children. Predefined priorities are 1,000 (required), 750 (high), and 250 (low). You may enter any number from 1 to 1,000, although it's most common to adjust your numbers with respect to the predefined priorities. For example, 751 is slightly more important that 750, and 749 is slightly less important.
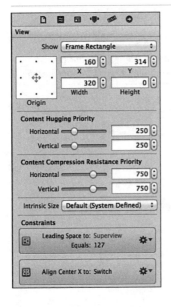	The Size Inspector (View > Utilities > Show Size Inspector) lists all constraints that mention the selected view. These constraints appear at the bottom of the inspector, in the Constraints section. Here, you can also see sliders that set content hugging and compression resistance priorities, as well as an Intrinsic Size adjustment tool. The priority sliders are context sensitive and do not always appear. If you're wondering where they've gone, try adding a width or height constraint to the view in question.

Element	Description
	The Intrinsic Size pop-up offers two options: a system-defined default size (best for system-supplied items like buttons and switches) and a placeholder option for custom views. Use the placeholder width and height in IB to provide a fixed stand-in for your real view for your design work. The values in this inspector default to the frame you lay out in the storyboard editor. The settings you add in the Size Inspector don't affect your compiled application. Instead, they help you better test your interface as you develop it in IB. Checking the None box applies values of `UIViewNoIntrinsicMetric`, such as -1, as discussed in Chapter 2. At runtime, your custom class reports its own size.
 	The Related Files menu appears in the top-left corner of the editor, above the outline view. Use this menu to open preview panes in the Assistant Editor. It looks like a series of eight small rectangles. Press and hold Option+Shift when picking a storyboard file to select a preview destination. A gray-backed placement dialog appears to help you place each preview. Click a star to place a preview into an already existing pane. Click a plus to add a new pane to the editor. The plus in the tab bar adds the preview to a new tab. The Cover Flow-style slanted plus to the left and behind the main "window" adds a new window. Press Return to apply your selection.

Element	Description
	A toolbar appears at the bottom of all preview panes. From left to right, here's what you find there:
	- **A firmware toggle**—Select either iOS 7 and Later or 6.1 and Earlier. The presentation updates to reflect the selected system style.
	- **An orientation toggle**—Switch between portrait and landscape.
	- **A form size toggle**—Choose either 4-inch or 3.5-inch layout.
	If you're not seeing this toolbar, you may be looking at an editor window instead of a preview window.
	Ctrl+Shift+click anywhere within the IB editor to reveal a list of all items placed at that point. Click any item to select it.
	This trick enables you to select items in an otherwise crowded or layered section of your editor.

Constraint Listings

A Constraints section appears in the document outline for all views that store constraints. This section corresponds to each view's `constraints` property, which is where layout constraints are normally stored. The way a constraint is listed tells you a lot about it.

In the one-switch example you worked on earlier in this chapter, the single constraint is attached to the view controller's main view (see Figure 3-7). This view represents the nearest common ancestor between the switch and its parent.

Constraint icons hint at the role each constraint plays. Table 3-2 provides a basic cheat sheet for these items. It shows the icon for each constraint type, a description of what the constraint does, and the destination where each constraint installs.

If you're reading this book in electronic format on a color screen, you'll note the color of the constraint icons in this table is blue. That's because they are taken from the pop-ups at the bottom of the editor. They appear in purple in constraint listings. These colors no longer have any meaning in Xcode 5, although they once did in Xcode 4.x.

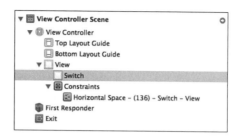

Figure 3-7   The constraints listed in the IB outline correspond to the `constraints` property for each view.

The table's vocabulary corresponds to the layout constraint attributes you have already read about in this book. These constraint rules may seem somewhat more limited to you than those you can express through code. They are. IB offers a common, but not exhaustive, set of constraints. For example, in IB, you can say "Match the width of this view to that view." In code, you can say "Set the width of this view to half the width of that view." IB doesn't offer the fine-detail constraint edits that allow you to tweak that relationship the way you can in code.

Table 3-2   **IB Constraints**

Constraints	Type	Description
Single View		
▣ Width ▣ Height	Size	Width and height constraints explicitly set a view's size. *Installed directly to view.*
▣ Horizontal Center in Container ▣ Vertical Center in Container	Centering	Center a view in its superview. *Installed to superview.*
▣ Leading Space to Superview ▣ Trailing Space to Superview ▣ Top Space to Superview ▣ Bottom Space to Superview	Offsets	Space a view away from its superview. *Installed to superview.*

Constraints	Type	Description
Multiple Views		
Horizontal Centers Vertical Centers Baselines	Align centers	Align all selected views to a common center: horizontal, vertical, or baseline. *Installed to nearest common ancestor of the selected views.*
Left Edges Right Edges Top Edges Bottom Edges	Align edges	Align all selected views to a common edge. *Installed to nearest common ancestor of the selected views.*
Equal Widths Equal Heights	Match dimensions	Constrain all selected views to match either width or height. *Installed to nearest common ancestor of the selected views.*
Horizontal Spacing Vertical Spacing	Pin space	Constrain the spacing between the views to the current offset in the layout editor. *Installed to nearest common ancestor of the selected views.*

Xcode Labels

IB assigns each new constraint a default name that explains its role. In the switch example, the constraint name (`Horizontal Space-(136)`) defines what the constraint does in a basic way. If you resize the outline to its full extent, as I did in Figure 3-7, you also see that each constraint description is appended by a list (for example, `Switch - View`). The items in this list refer to the default IB names for the constraint's first and second items. In this example, the two items are `Switch` and `View`.

If you added a button, its name would be `Button - Button`. The button's name derives from its class (`Button`) and its label (`Button`), and for an extra bit of fun, IB sticks a hyphen between these items, adding a certain *je ne sais quoi* of obfuscation. Override default naming by adding an Xcode-specific identity to each view. To do this, select any Xcode object and open the Identity Inspector (View > Utilities > Show Identity Inspector). Enter a name in the Document > Label field, as shown in Figure 3-8. Xcode uses the text you enter to label items.

Alternatively, you can select any item in the document outline and press Return to enter edit mode. A text field opens, and you can edit the same document label directly from the outline. This is usually handier than opening the Identity Inspector.

Figure 3-8   You assign Xcode-specific labels to views in the Identity Inspector.

Adding custom view labels improves the readability of the constraint listings. Figure 3-9 shows the document outline after the switch gets a custom name. You can now more easily see that the horizontal spacing constraint applies to a specific switch.

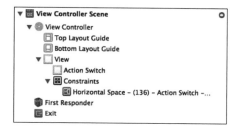

Figure 3-9   Using Xcode labels improves constraint listing readability.

Adding Xcode Identities

Xcode labels play no role in coding and execution, but Xcode identities *do*, at least to the limited extent that they can make your debugging logs slightly more readable. Unfortunately, at this time, this feature is for OS X only. Figure 3-10 shows the Identity Inspector. This screenshot is taken from an OS X project that's the equivalent of the one-switch iOS app you've already built. It substitutes a check box (an NSButton) for the switch.

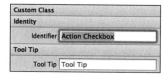

Figure 3-10   Assigning view identities enhances debugging output logs.

The constraints generated by OS X don't always match the ones produced by iOS. In this example, you end up with five auto-generated constraints instead of three. What's important is how those constraints are listed in the debugging console. Here's the default output you see before you add the view identifier:

```
2013-07-05 13:52:42.437 IBTest OS X[16736:303] <NSLayoutConstraint:0x10050d740 'IB
auto generated at build time for view with ambiguity' H:|-(191@251)-
[NSButton:0x101a0af90'Check'](LTR) priority:251    (Names: '|':NSView:0x101a0a300 )>
```

And here's the same constraint, in another run of the application, after you view the name:

```
2013-07-05 13:47:13.717 IBTest OS X[16510:303] <NSLayoutConstraint:0x10056d810 'IB
auto generated at build time for view with ambiguity' H:|-(191@251)-[Action
Checkbox](LTR) priority:251    (Names: Action Checkbox:0x101b13110,
'|':NSView:0x101b124a0 )>
```

Custom names enhance the clarity of console output and assist you in debugging. Because this feature is not cross-platform, I ended up writing my own view- and constraint-naming and logging routines. I discuss the technology I used to implement naming in Chapter 5, "Debugging Constraints."

If you are interested in exploring the identification technology in more depth, I refer you to Apple's NSUserInterfaceItemIdentification documentation:

> The NSUserInterfaceItemIdentification protocol is used to associate a unique identifier with objects in your user interface.

You can set an OS X view's identifier property in code as well as in IB.

Adding Constraints

In IB, you add constraints in several ways:

- Ctrl+drag from a view to another view or from a view to its superview. IB presents a context-specific pop-up menu based on the direction of the drag and the number of items involved.

- Select one or more items and use the Editor menu or the Pin and Align items in the toolbar at the bottom right of the editor pane to add constraints.

- Use the Editor menu or the toolbar to have IB automatically add constraints on your behalf regardless of the current selection.

Table 3-3 details the kind of requests you can create by using these approaches.

Table 3-3 **Adding Layout Requests in IB**

Pin Request	Result
Width or Height	Adds a constraint to fix the width or height of the selected view or views to the current value.
Horizontal or Vertical Spacing	When more than one view is selected, adds constraints that fix the relative spacing between those views.
Leading, Trailing, Top, and Bottom Space to Superview	Adds constraints to fix the offset of the selected view or views to the current distance from the superview.
Widths or Heights Equally	When more than one view is selected, constrains the view sizes (width or height) to match each other.
Alignment Request	Result
Left, Right, Top, or Bottom Edges	Aligns the selected views along the specified edge.
Horizontal and Vertical Centers	Aligns the selected views' centers along the requested axis.
Baselines	Aligns views along their baselines.
Horizontal or Vertical Center in Container	Center-aligns the selected views to their superview.

Dragging

When you add constraints by dragging, the direction you move your mouse affects the choices IB presents to you. Horizontal drags offer horizontal-axis constraints, such as width, horizontal spacing, or offsets from the leading and trailing edges of the superview. Vertical drags focus on top-to-bottom layout. Diagonal drags offer both choices. This rule applies whether you're dragging from a view to its superview or between two child views.

To continue the walk-through, follow these steps, starting with a single switch with one constraint and offsetting the switch from the parent's leading edge:

1. Drag a label into the editor and place it to the left of the existing switch.

2. Ctrl+drag from the label to the switch.

3. Press Shift. Select Horizontal Spacing and Center Y (see Figure 3-11).

4. Press Return. IB adds the two new constraints. The first constraint sets a fixed space between the label and the switch. The second constraint aligns both views along their vertical centers. Since the label is shorter than the switch, it centers vertically with a little extra space above and below it.

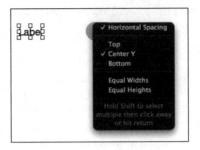

Figure 3-11   Use Shift to add multiple constraints at once. Selecting both Horizontal Spacing and Center Y alignment builds two constraints.

All three constraints you've added so far appear attached to the main view controller's view (see Figure 3-12). In the outline, you can see one Center Y constraint and two Horizontal Space constraints. To determine which constraint is which, click each one to highlight it in the main editor.

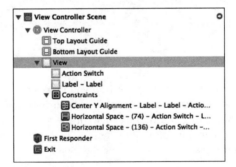

Figure 3-12   You review added constraints in the scene outline. Selecting a constraint in the outline highlights the corresponding constraint in the visual editor.

You also find the constraints in the Size Inspector (View > Utilities > Show Size Inspector). The constraints vary by view. The switch lists all three constraints it participates in (see Figure 3-13), the label lists two constraints, and the controller's view lists just one constraint.

To select a constraint, either click the constraint listing in the document outline or select a view and then click directly on any of its visualized constraints. Selecting a constraint highlights the constraint. Optionally, you can highlight the associated views as well by enabling Editor > Canvas > Show Involved Views for Selected Constraint (see Figure 3-14).

Figure 3-13   The switch participates in three constraints so far.

Figure 3-14   Involved views appear with a yellow overlay when you enable Editor > Canvas > Show Involved Views for Selected Constraints.

Continue the walkthrough as follows:

1. Double-click the constraint that sets a horizontal space between the label and the switch. A pop-up editor appears (see Figure 3-15).

2. Adjust the constraint to use a standard constant. Click the downward arrow in the Constant field to reveal the Use Standard Value option. The label pops to the right, almost (but not quite) meeting up with the switch. Save your changes.

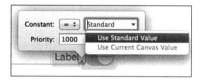

Figure 3-15   Use the constraint pop-up in the visual editor to tweak a constraint's constant, relation, and priority.

Pinning and Aligning

Both the editor and the bottom-right toolbars offer Pin and Align menus, but the ways they're presented are quite different. *Pinning* means fixing a size or offset. *Aligning* means placing items in a coordinated position with some shared aspect. You might align views along their left sides or bottoms. As you see in Figure 3-16, available options vary by the method you use to apply them.

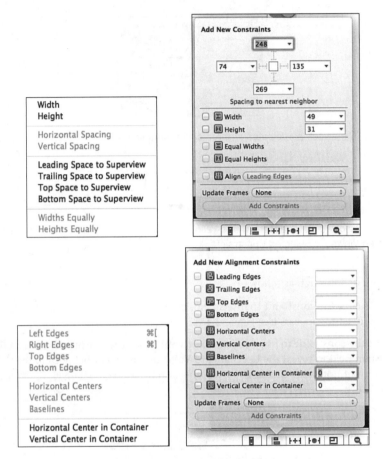

Figure 3-16   Top items: pinning views. Bottom items: aligning views. Left items: Editor menu. Right items: toolbar pop-ups.

For example, to set an item's width, you can select it and choose Editor > Pin > Width. IB adds a constraint that fixes the view's width to the current size. If you go the toolbar route, you click the Pin button, which looks like a TIE fighter with a plus in the middle. Check the Width option and, if desired, adjust the target width in the text field. Click Add Constraints to finish.

Or you might want to pin a view to the trailing edge. To do this, you choose Editor > Pin > Trailing Space to Superview, and the new constraint picks up the current offset. Alternatively, you can open the toolbar Pin menu and click the right-hand T-beam strut at the top of the pop-up.

Say that you want to align two views' bottoms. To do this, select them and either choose Editor > Align > Bottom Edges or use the Align pop-up and check the Bottom Edges choice.

As a rule, the pop-ups offer more powerful ways to add constraints:

- You can build multiple constraints at once by checking several items.

- You adjust constants as you're defining the constraints instead of taking extra editing steps.

- The T-beam struts provide a simple interface for adding connections to the superview.

- The pop-ups enable you to decide between automatically updating your frames to match the current constraint set (by enabling Update Frames) and just adding the constraints.

Continue the walkthrough with these steps, which use the tools you just read about:

1. Drag the label out of the way for the moment and then select the switch.

2. Open the pop-up Align menu by clicking the bar graph icon in the bottom toolbar of the editor window. Check Vertical Center in Container, select Update Frames > Items of New Constraints, and click Add Constraints. All constraints associated with the switch should now turn blue, as you have now established both a horizontal position and a vertical position.

3. When you dragged away the label, you disengaged its frame from its otherwise fully constrained position. Confirm this by noting the circled yellow arrow at the top-right of the outline. To fix this problem, select the label. Choose Update Frames from either the Editor > Resolve Auto Layout Issues menu or the pop-up resolution menu. When you do this, the layout resolves, and all constraints turn blue as you see in Figure 3-17.

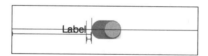

Figure 3-17   After you add a vertical placement constraint to the switch and updating frames, the layout constraints display in blue.

At this point, you have established rules that fix both the switch and the label in place:

- The switch is offset 136 points from the leading edge of its superview and is centered vertically in that superview.

- The label is vertically aligned with and offset from the switch by a standard spacer.

Previewing Layouts

To fully test an interface, there are certain regular checks every developer performs. For example, do all interaction spots cover at least 44×44 points on the screen? Does the app supply appropriate art for both Retina and non-Retina targets? Is that art sized for most audiences on full-sized iPads, iPad minis, 3.5-inch phones, and 4-inch phones?

In addition to these common checks, you should be thinking of Auto Layout–specific tests. Answer the following questions:

- Does the interface adjust appropriately between iPad geometry, 3.5-inch geometry, and 4-inch geometry?

- Does the interface re-orient seamlessly when the device rotates?

- Does the interface adjust correctly when the user changes font selections in Settings and the app receives a dynamic font update?

- Does the interface adapt properly when the text is localized?

At this time, IB offers simple ways to preview layout across device geometry and orientation, which you'll see in these next few steps. Chapter 5 discusses testing for dynamic fonts and localized text, which are not features you find in IB. The following are IB-specific steps:

1. Close any inspectors and/or the debugging console to make the most possible room in your workspace. Previewing layout takes up a *lot* of room.

2. Locate the related file's menu at the very top left of the IB outline. It's to the left on the Xcode jump bar. Its icon looks like a grid of eight small rectangles.

3. While holding Shift+Option, select Preview and then your iPhone storyboard. A gray destination dialog appears. Click the plus on the right (see the top image in Figure 3-18) to open the preview in a new assistant editor pane and press Return. Repeat to open a second editor pane below the first one.

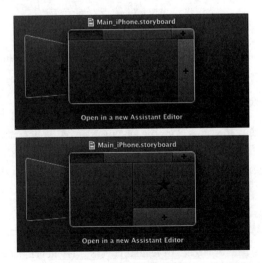

Figure 3-18   If screen space permits, you can add multiple panes to preview your application in both orientations.

4. At this point, your interface should look as shown in Figure 3-19. Locate the rotation toggle in the bottom preview. It's the middle button in the toolbar and looks like a downward-pointing arrow. Click it to rotate the lower preview to landscape.

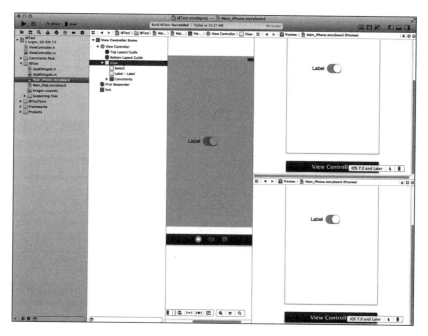

Figure 3-19   The IB interface after you add two preview panes to the assistant editor. What you see in this screenshot from left to right is the gray-backed project navigator, followed by the IB editor, followed by a pair of previews stacked top and bottom. This is an overview screenshot, which is not meant to be read in detail. Rather it shows the basic layout you create after opening both previews.

5. Adjust the panels so you can see your editing space and both previews at once (see Figure 3-20).

At this point, IB previews how your interface looks in both portrait and landscape orientations. Any changes you make in your editor are reflected in the previews. From here, you can do the following:

- Switch between iOS 7 preview and iOS 6.1 and earlier styles. The newer layout is whiter, starker, and lacking in features such as the black status bar. These are preview-only features and do not affect the editor.

- Toggle between 3.5-inch and 4-inch layout (for iPhone previews only). This enables you to see how your layout adjusts from one geometry to the other.

In the sample app, the switch stays at a fixed distance from the left edge, regardless of orientation. Because you see both orientations at once, this detail jumps out in your design, alerting you to the problem.

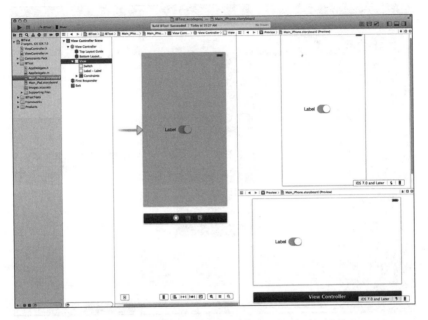

Figure 3-20   Rotating the bottom preview and adjusting the panel sizes helps you see your application in both orientations. You see the change at the bottom-right of the screen, which now takes up much less vertical space than in Figure 3-21. Again, this screenshot is not meant to show fine details.

This switch was placed using a leading-edge constraint rather than a centering constraint. To get a sense of how IB's preview helps you correct your layout, follow these steps:

1. Locate the Horizontal Space – (136) constraint in the organizer. Select it and delete it.

2. Select the switch and choose Editor > Align > Horizontal Center in Container.

The landscape preview updates immediately. The switch moves to the center, providing a more pleasing layout in both orientations.

Inspecting Constraints

Xcode allows you to inspect any selected constraint by using the Attributes Inspector (View > Utilities > Show Attributes Inspector) or by double-clicking any constraint from the editor. Figure 3-21 shows the Center X constraint you just added to the switch.

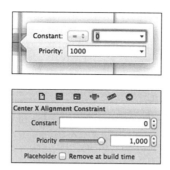

Figure 3-21   This vertical constraint aligns the switch to the center of its container.

The inspectors you see in Figure 3-21 reinforce the *y R mx + b* relation that underlies all constraints. In this instance, the relation (*R*) is equal, the constant (*b*) is 0, and the multiplier (*m*, which you do not see and cannot adjust here) is 1.

These inspectors enable you to make the following tweaks to constraints:

- For constraints that allow it, you can select a different relation. Consider the constraint that offsets the label from the switch. If you edit that constraint to be greater than or equal to 50 points, the visualized constraint adds a ≥ badge, as shown in Figure 3-22. This indicates at a glance that the constraint now refers to an inequality.

  Second, at least in this example, the IB constraint system would find itself expressing ambiguity. Under this new relation, the label no longer has a certain place to live, so the constraint turns orange.

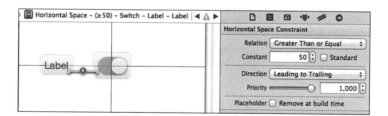

Figure 3-22   This horizontal constraint specifies that the label should be at least 50 points away from the switch. The Placeholder check box enables you to remove a constraint at build time. This is handy when you want to create a fully satisfied layout for design time but need to replace an item with a code-based constraint at runtime.

- You change offsets and size extents by editing a constraint's Constant value. In the example in Figure 3-22, adjustments would move the label closer to or farther away from the switch.

Checking the Standard box updates the constraint to use Aqua spacing—basically, 20-point offsets from edges and 8-point offsets between views. Apple's Aqua user interface standards are the primary visual theme used in OS X design. Many Aqua patterns also appear in iOS.

When Standard is checked, standard spacing overrides any Constant value you've already entered or set through layout.

- You adjust constraint priority from its default setting of required (1,000) to another value either by moving the slider or entering a new value into the text box.

View Size Inspector

A view's Size Inspector (View > Utilities > Show Size Inspector) plays a different role in the constraints story from the constraint editor in the Attributes Inspector. When you select a view, the Size Inspector lists all constraints that mention the view and provides support for editing the view's content size priorities.

Figure 3-23 shows the Size Inspector for this project's label. This is where you edit properties that affect a view's size and where you can see all the constraints that the view participates in.

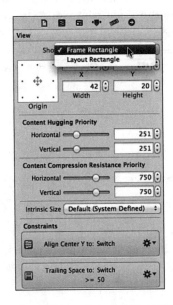

Figure 3-23   A view's Size Inspector enables you to set its content size priorities and lists its constraints.

Frame and Layout Rectangles

In the top section of the inspector shown in Figure 3-23, you can view and edit either the frame rectangle or the layout rectangle for the view. *Layout rectangle* is IB-speak for an alignment rectangle, which you read about in earlier chapters. Alignment rectangles define a view's Auto Layout geometry attributes, like left edge, trailing edge, baseline, top, bottom, and center. For control instances, the rectangles may vary slightly between the frame and the alignment rectangle. You can spot the difference by switching between the two options in the Show pop-up.

To better visualize frames and alignment rectangles, select Editor > Canvas > Show Layout Rectangles or Editor > Canvas > Show Bounds Rectangles. These options add overlays to the visual editor, as shown in Figure 3-24. Bounds rectangles appear in blue, and layout rectangles appear in red.

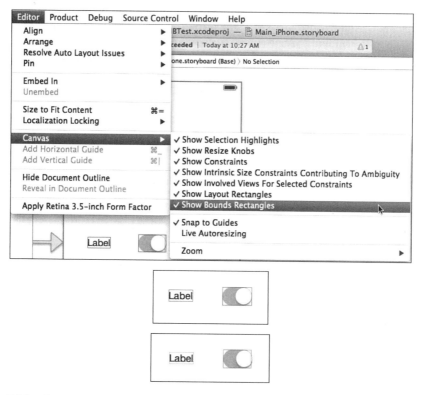

Figure 3-24 The Editor > Canvas menu (top) enables you to visualize bounding rectangles (frames—shown in blue) and layout rectangles (alignment rectangles—shown in red). As you can see, the switch's layout rectangle slightly clips its right-hand side, forcing centering slightly to the left. Its bounding rectangle completely encloses all art.

Other Size Inspector Items

Next in the inspector, below the rectangle editors, lie two sections in which you can set content hugging and content compression priorities for the view. Auto Layout uses these to generate content size constraints. As you read in earlier chapters, these values allow you to adjust view padding and clipping. Below this you find the Intrinsic Size pop-up, which enables you to set proxy view sizes.

Constraints that mention the view are listed at the bottom of the inspector pane. These constraints are not necessarily owned by the view in question. Always check the document outline—and not the Size Inspector—for ownership.

The Resolution Menu

Xcode 5's new resolution menu (Editor > Resolve Auto Layout Issues; see Figure 3-25) allows you to manage common constraint issues. The menu consists of two halves. The top half of the menu applies to the currently selected view. The bottom half affects all views within the active scene. The options in the two halves mirror each other.

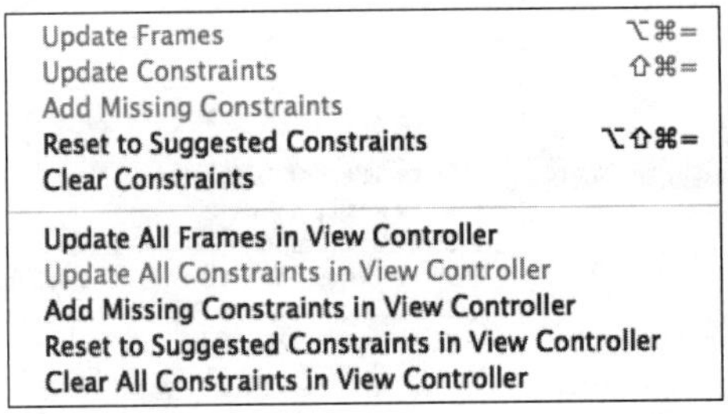

```
Update Frames                              ⌥⌘=
Update Constraints                         ⇧⌘=
Add Missing Constraints
Reset to Suggested Constraints            ⌥⇧⌘=
Clear Constraints
─────────────────────────────────────────────
Update All Frames in View Controller
Update All Constraints in View Controller
Add Missing Constraints in View Controller
Reset to Suggested Constraints in View Controller
Clear All Constraints in View Controller
```

Figure 3-25   Use the resolution menu to address common constraint issues.

Updating Frames and Constraints

When you move an already-constrained view within the IB editor, you encounter the dashed rectangles you read about earlier in this chapter. Orange dashes outline the position that the view would live in if Auto Layout applied its current set of constraints.

Two update options appear at the start of the resolution menu. Update Frames allows you to adjust view frames to match the current set of constraints, and Update Constraints lets you change your constraints to match the current set of view frames.

If your movement was deliberate—as opposed to temporarily nudging a view out of the way—you can go ahead and update your constraints. IB replaces any constraints that set the view's original position. If the movement was administrative, you can reset the frames. This moves views back into place with respect to the current constraint set.

Adding and Resetting Constraints

The next two options are Add Missing Constraints and Reset to Suggested Constraints. The Add option creates just enough new constraints to remove any ambiguity. It adds these constraints to any constraints you've already established. The Reset option replaces the constraints with a full, sufficient set. In both cases, IB must guess at what constraints you want. Sometimes it gets this right. Often it does not.

IB is not a mind-reader. If you centered a view, IB *may* correctly surmise that you meant that view to be centered when adding its constraints. Or it may center the view along one axis and add a fixed offset along the other.

The constraints you add with the Add and Reset options are not the same as the inferred frame constraints discussed at the start of this chapter. IB's auto-generated constraints for fixed frame views set position and size exactly as you laid out the view, without guessing intent.

Clearing Constraints

The final menu option is Clear Constraints, and it does exactly what it says on the wrapper: It removes all constraints associated with a view or within the entire scene, depending on which version you select from the menu. This action is the equivalent of opening a view's Size Inspector and individually deleting each constraint listed there.

Constraints/Resizing Pop-Up Menu

So far, you've seen the functionality of the first three of the four items that live in the tools group at the bottom of the editor screen. The first two of these are alignment and pinning options, which you use to add constraints to your layout. The third item provides constraint resolution. The last offers a pair of preferences, as shown in Figure 3-26.

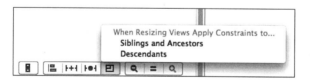

Figure 3-26   IB can apply constraints during resizing.

These global options enable and disable automatic constraint application for siblings/ancestors and children during resizing. When this is enabled, IB maintains constraints as you resize views in the editor. This is best explained through an example. Figure 3-27 shows three views (two siblings and one child) and the constraints that relate them. One constraint separates the top view from the bottom view, using a fixed distance. Additional constraints embed a child view within the parent at the bottom, adding fixed offsets from each edge to the superview.

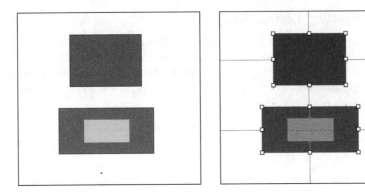

Figure 3-27   Three views consist of two siblings, one with a child view.

You're about to see how IB enforces these constraints during resizing, using the pop-up menu options. When you allow IB to enforce constraints, it coordinates your resize request with any existing layout rules. First, you'll see the Descendants option and then the Siblings and Ancestors option.

Descendants

Figure 3-28 shows the bottom view during resizing. The Descendants option is enabled on the left and disabled on the right. In the left example, IB applies its constraints to the child during resizing. The child view updates to match the changes in the bottom view, maintaining the fixed offsets established during layout.

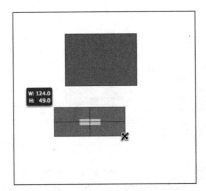

Figure 3-28   Enabling the Descendants option (left) maintains the relationship constraints that offset the child view from its superview. When this option is disabled (right), the constraints have no effect during resizing.

After you revert and disable the Descendants option, the results change. The child view no longer responds to its parent view as it resizes. The constraints are ignored, and the child view remains in place, the same size as it began.

Siblings and Ancestors

The Siblings and Ancestors option works the same way as the Descendants option, but with sibling and ancestor views. Figure 3-29 demonstrates this as the bottom view resizes in an upward direction.

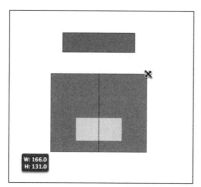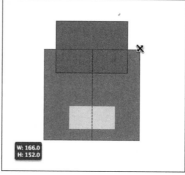

Figure 3-29   Resizing with Siblings and Ancestors enabled on the left and disabled on the right.

With the Siblings and Ancestors option enabled, the top view maintains the offset constraint between the two views, shrinking to accommodate. When the option is disabled, the bottom view resizes without consideration to that constraint, and the top view remains at its original size.

The Missing Views Problem

As in code, conflicting priorities may cause views to "go missing." Although IB can guarantee a consistent and unambiguous interface, it does not guarantee an interface where every view is visible. Next, you'll see why this can happen.

For the next example, you need a blank canvas to work with, so create a new single-view application and open the iPhone storyboard. Display it in portrait orientation.

In this example, imagine that you are building a corporate information application as you follow these steps:

1. Drag a label into the view and center-align it just below the top, using constraints. Next, drag in a second label and left-align it with the standard inset, again just below the top of the screen (see Figure 3-30). Use the resolution menu to add missing constraints. IB adds several for you.

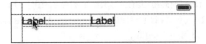

Figure 3-30   Here you add two labels to the portrait view.

2. Double-click the left label to enter edit mode. Update the name of the left label to Department Name. The label should automatically resize to accommodate the new text. The two labels will now overlap when they use the default fonts assigned to labels.

3. Select both labels in the document outline. Choose Editor > Pin > Horizontal Spacing.

4. Select the new Horizontal Spacing constraint. It probably has a negative constant value because the two views overlap, with the start of the second label to the left of the end of the first. Open the Attributes Inspector and check the Standard box. This requests a standard 8-point spacer between the two views. The left label should now clip, as in Figure 3-31.

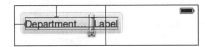

Figure 3-31   Forcing a row with standard spacing squeezes the Department Name label.

5. Select the Department Name label and open the Size Inspector. Adjust the Horizontal Content Compression Resistance Priority setting up, from 750 to 751. Then select Update All Frames in View Controller from the constraint resolution menu. The Department Name label resizes (somewhat), and the Label label (the item on the right) disappears entirely.

6. Select Label – Label from the document outline. (You cannot select it from the IB editor.) Examine its size in the size editor (see Figure 3-32). It will have a 0 width, which is why it disappears from the IB layout.

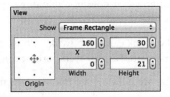

Figure 3-32   Due to conflicting constraints, a view's size may slip to 0 and disappear from the layout, even in IB.

In this example, the Auto Layout constraint system could be satisfied but only by squeezing the right label to 0. That's because several constraints came into conflict. The rightmost label's compression-resistance rule loses. Its width falls to 0, and the view disappears entirely from the screen.

If you now select the view controller again and switch the orientation to Landscape in Attributes Inspector > Simulated Metrics > Orientation, the missing view springs back. The extra layout space ensures that the view can be presented with these rules. If you flip it to portrait, the view goes away again.

When designing in Auto Layout, you should ensure that your views are laid out properly in every orientation and every legal window size. This example demonstrates how things can go wrong and why you should always consider edge conditions.

Balancing Requests

Whenever you design with Auto Layout, be sure to think about extremes. For example, how should items respond to minimum and maximum sizing? Which objects should take precedence during that resizing? The key to succeeding at Auto Layout is having a gestalt understanding of your desired layout *before* attempting to express that layout. Next, you'll explore common layout scenarios.

To get started, create another new one-view iPhone storyboard project with a custom view controller class. In this example, I use a `ViewController` class, but your class may vary. The key is to use a custom subclass of `UIViewController` with editable code.

Follow these steps to set up a basic test bed, which you'll use to explore these Auto Layout issues:

1. Add a navigation controller to your storyboard. Select the default table view controller supplied as the navigation controller's root view controller and delete it. Select the navigation controller, open the Attributes Inspector, and check Is Initial View Controller.

2. Drag a new view controller into the storyboard editor to replace the now-deleted table view controller. Ctrl+drag from the navigation controller to the view controller. Choose Root View Controller from the IB pop-up.

3. Select the new view controller and open the Identity Inspector. Adjust the class in the Custom Class > Class tool to match your primary view controller class. You now have a navigation controller setup that loads your custom class.

4. Add two labels. In this case, align the labels left and right instead of left and center. Edit the first label to say Department Name. Edit the second label to say Value. Pin the left label a standard distance from the leading edge of its parent and the right label a standard distance from the trailing edge of its parent.

5. Select both labels and choose Editor > Pin > Horizontal Spacing. Select the new constraint and edit the relation to Greater Than or Equal. Then check Standard. Figure 3-33 shows the updated interface with its two labels and its fixed minimum spacing.

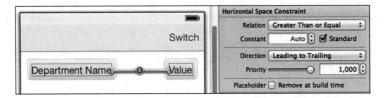

Figure 3-33   Set up the interface so that the two labels cannot grow any closer than standard spacing (8 points).

6. Drag a bar button item to the right side of your root controller navigation bar. Edit the title from Item to Switch. This button adjusts the text displayed in the right label so that you can test a variety of layout conflicts.

7. Open the Assistant Editor (View > Assistant Editor > Show Assistant Editor) so that it shows your primary view controller interface. Ctrl+drag from the Value label into your interface declaration. Create a new Outlet connection named valueLabel.

8. Ctrl+drag from the Switch bar button item into your interface declaration. Create a new Action connection named switch:, as shown in Figure 3-34. (A method name like switchLabelText: would also be a good choice, since switch is a keyword in C.)

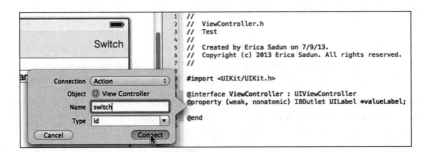

Figure 3-34   You connect an outlet to the right label and add an action to the Switch bar button item.

9. Edit your view controller source code to match the following snippet:

```
@implementation ViewController
- (IBAction) switch: (id) sender
{
    static int numberOfTimes = 1;
    NSMutableString *string = [NSMutableString string];
```

```
        for (int i = 0; i <= numberOfTimes; i++)
            [string appendString:@"Value"];
        _valueLabel.text = string;
        numberOfTimes = (numberOfTimes + 1) % 5;
    }
    @end
```

In this code, you add a local instance variable and update the `switch` method you just created. This method adjusts repetitions of the word *Value*, growing the right-side label to test constraint behavior.

Compile and run the app, testing it both in portrait orientation and landscape orientation. In portrait orientation, when the Value label contains several repetitions, one of the two labels must get clipped. At this point, it cannot be determined *which* label will be clipped because both items have identical content compression resistance, and you haven't added constraints about the two view widths. Your output might look like either sample in Figure 3-35.

Figure 3-35   Auto Layout helps you balance clipping rules, choosing which item gets clipped first.

In real-world deployment, information often competes for space onscreen, as you see in Figure 3-35. Value labels (that is, data derived from the application model) often compete against field name labels (that is, identifying labels). The identifying labels should usually win out (as shown on the left in Figure 3-35), creating a consistent interface regardless of what data is being presented. This is a good reason to keep your labels short and to the point.

With Auto Layout, you usually specify precedence through rules rather than by declaring explicit widths. In this example, lowering the Value label's horizontal content compression with respect to the Department Name label allows Auto Layout to unambiguously prefer the first of the two layouts shown in Figure 3-35. Select the Value label, open the Size Inspector, and lower the Content Compression Resistance Priority setting to 749. When you run the app again, the behavior should consistently match the image on the left in Figure 3-35.

Raising and lowering priorities by one are common practices when you're balancing layout requests. They're more or less equivalent solutions. You're either saying "make this layout more important" or "reduce the importance of this other layout." Both approaches work.

Hybrid Layout

Many developers have invested substantial time in creating Autosizing-based views they want to keep using in Auto Layout projects. In hybrid development, you load Autosizing views from code and arrange them using Auto Layout.

Building a Nib File for Testing

Follow these steps to create a nib file that you'll use to try using the hybrid layout approach:

1. Create a new iOS single-view project and add a new interface file (File > New > User Interface > View). Choose iPhone and click Next. Name it View and save the file, adding it to your project.

2. In the view's File Inspector > Interface Builder Document, uncheck Use Auto Layout. IB builds its document using Autosizing.

3. In the view's Attributes Inspector > Simulated Metrics, change its size to Freeform and remove the status bar.

4. In the Attributes Inspector > View, set the background to some easily viewed color, such as bright yellow.

5. In the view's Size Inspector, set the size to 200 by 200.

6. Populate the view. For example, you can drag in a new subview and set a contrasting view color, such as blue. Set up the children however you like, using Autosizing struts and springs (see Figure 3-36). It doesn't really matter how you perform your layout, but be aware that the parent will be resizing, and its child should behave in a known and set manner, using consistent Autosizing rules.

7. Save the file.

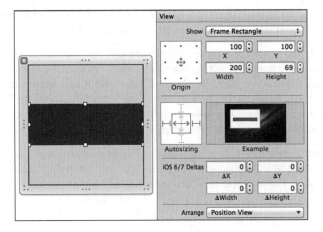

Figure 3-36   Add Autosizing rules in the Size Inspector.

Adding the Nib File in Code

You have now built an Autosizing-based nib file that you can use in Auto Layout. Listing 3-1 demonstrates how you do this: You load the view from its nib file, prepare it for Auto Layout, and then add constraints as you would have if you had built the view in code. The result is an IB-designed view that is leveraged in a code-based Auto Layout implementation.

This example adds several constraints to the custom view. The first five constraints center the view in its parent, ensure that it maintains a 1:1 aspect ratio, and then limit the size to its parent, with a 20-point inset. This produces a view that hugs the parent in either landscape or portrait orientation, without touching its edges.

Strictly speaking, this layout is underconstrained because size inequalities can be ambiguous. Two final constraints address this. Added at low priorities, they request an exact match to the inset-from-parent sizing. This ensures that the view displays at the biggest possible size in both orientations, while respecting insets.

Figure 3-37 shows the resulting interface in both orientations.

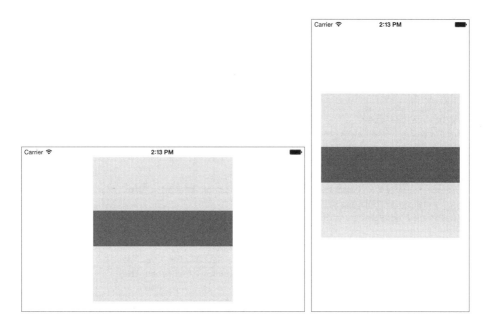

Figure 3-37   The resulting hybrid interface in portrait and landscape orientations.

Advantages of Hybrid Layout

Using both IB and code offers tangible benefits, such as the following:

- **Orthogonal design**—This design pattern compartmentalizes subview details. You can freely return to IB and update the nib you created without affecting code, or you can update the layout code without affecting the subview. All design work within IB is essentially self-contained. The Autosizing and Auto Layout rules don't cross boundaries.

- **IB-based layout**—This approach fully leverages IB view design. The visual details of the subview remain in IB, which is the preferred design environment for many developers.

- **Mix-and-match development**—You can easily hybridize autoresizing and Auto Layout development. Although this view was created with autoresizing rules, it happily lives in an Auto Layout interface.

- **Reduced complexity**—Even if you were to design in IB using Auto Layout, the constraints you have to manage inside a modular nib file are limited to those directly involved in laying out that view, so the complexity goes way down. Reduced complexity improves readability and inspection. So modular development is as valuable for those working with Auto Layout as for those working with Autosizing.

Listing 3-1   Loading an Autosizing View into Auto Layout

```
- (void) loadView
{
    // Create the view
    self.view = [[UIView alloc] init];
    self.view.backgroundColor = [UIColor whiteColor];

    // Load the subview from the nib file
    UIView *subview = [[[NSBundle mainBundle] loadNibNamed:@"View"
        owner:self options:nil] lastObject];
    [self.view addSubview:subview];

    // Prepare it for Auto Layout
    // Even though the view was laid out using Autosizing, you're
    // adding it *to* Auto Layout. This property only affects the
    // subview's relation to its parent, and not its subviews.
    subview.translatesAutoresizingMaskIntoConstraints = NO;

    // Add constraints
    NSLayoutConstraint *constraint;

    // Center it along its parent X and Y axes
    constraint = [NSLayoutConstraint
        constraintWithItem:subview
        attribute:NSLayoutAttributeCenterX
        relatedBy:NSLayoutRelationEqual
        toItem:self.view
```

```
        attribute:NSLayoutAttributeCenterX
         multiplier:1
          constant:0];
[self.view addConstraint:constraint];

constraint = [NSLayoutConstraint
    constraintWithItem:subview
    attribute:NSLayoutAttributeCenterY
    relatedBy:NSLayoutRelationEqual
    toItem:self.view
    attribute:NSLayoutAttributeCenterY
    multiplier:1
    constant:0];
[self.view addConstraint:constraint];

// Set its aspect ratio to 1:1
constraint = [NSLayoutConstraint
    constraintWithItem:subview
    attribute:NSLayoutAttributeWidth
    relatedBy:NSLayoutRelationEqual
    toItem:subview
    attribute:NSLayoutAttributeHeight
    multiplier:1
    constant:0];
[subview addConstraint:constraint];

// Constrain it with respect to the superview's size
constraint = [NSLayoutConstraint
    constraintWithItem:subview
    attribute:NSLayoutAttributeWidth
    relatedBy:NSLayoutRelationLessThanOrEqual
    toItem:self.view
    attribute:NSLayoutAttributeWidth
    multiplier:1
    constant:-40];
[self.view addConstraint:constraint];
constraint = [NSLayoutConstraint
    constraintWithItem:subview
    attribute:NSLayoutAttributeHeight
    relatedBy:NSLayoutRelationLessThanOrEqual
    toItem:self.view
    attribute:NSLayoutAttributeHeight
    multiplier:1
    constant:-40];
[self.view addConstraint:constraint];

// Add a weak "match size" constraint
constraint = [NSLayoutConstraint
    constraintWithItem:subview
```

```
        attribute:NSLayoutAttributeWidth
        relatedBy:NSLayoutRelationEqual
        toItem:self.view
        attribute:NSLayoutAttributeWidth
        multiplier:1
        constant:-40];
    constraint.priority = 1;
    [self.view addConstraint:constraint];
    constraint = [NSLayoutConstraint
        constraintWithItem:subview
        attribute:NSLayoutAttributeHeight
        relatedBy:NSLayoutRelationEqual
        toItem:self.view
        attribute:NSLayoutAttributeHeight
        multiplier:1
        constant:-40];
    constraint.priority = 1;
    [self.view addConstraint:constraint];
}
```

Removing IB-Generated Constraints

At times you may build a storyboard or xib file that's purposely underconstrained so that you can add custom layout from code. Inferred constraints, created on your behalf, don't work well with this scenario. Of the possible approaches you may take, only one—using placeholders—is suitable for production work.

The "best practices" solution starts with a fully constrained layout in IB. Unambiguous layout prevents IB from adding inferred constraints on your behalf. The constraints in your storyboard or xib file will match the ones loaded by iOS in your app.

Next, select each constraint you want to remove from your layout and open the Attributes Inspector. Check the Placeholder box, as shown in Figure 3-38. This option enables IB to use the constraint to validate design-time layout but removes that constraint at runtime.

Figure 3-38   The Placeholder check box enables you to choose which constraints will not be added at runtime.

> **Note**
> Constraints are first-class objects in IB. You can use the same techniques to build outlets that point to them as you would with views. Ctrl+drag from any constraint to a header file interface to create that outlet. This enables you to refer to specific constraints when you need to. This approach is particularly useful for animating constraints by adjusting their constants.

Exercises

After reading this chapter, test your knowledge with these exercises:

1. Add three buttons to your view. Add constraints so the three buttons remain centered within the view, regardless of orientation and platform, with fixed offsets (see Figure 3-39). Extra credit: Extend this to 5 buttons instead of 3.

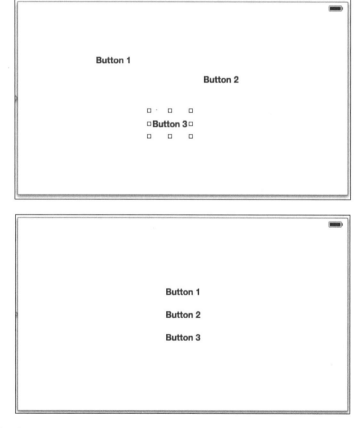

Figure 3-39   Center three buttons.

2. Add a view with a colorful background color to a view controller. Constrain it so it's inset on each side by 40 points, regardless of orientation (see Figure 3-40).

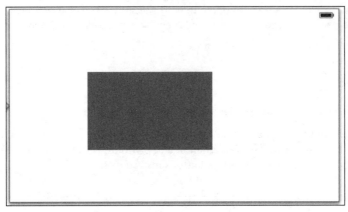

Figure 3-40   Stretch a view with an inset.

3. Add three views to a new view controller (see the top image in Figure 3-41). Using IB alone, create a constraint system, as in the middle image in Figure 3-41, that when applied by updating frames produces the equally sized results you see in the bottom image in Figure 3-41.

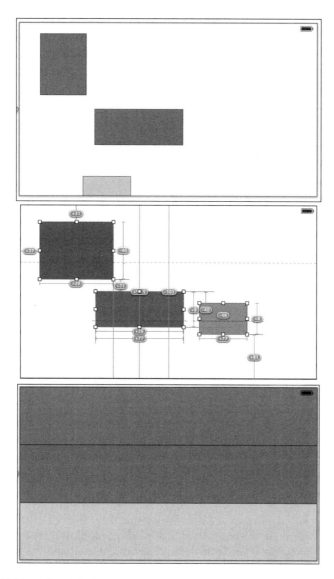

Figure 3-41   Divide and match view areas.

4. Create a table that consists of left-aligned labels and two buttons in a row on the right (see Figure 3-42). Add constraints so the label and buttons remain properly aligned in every orientation, with all three items centered vertically.

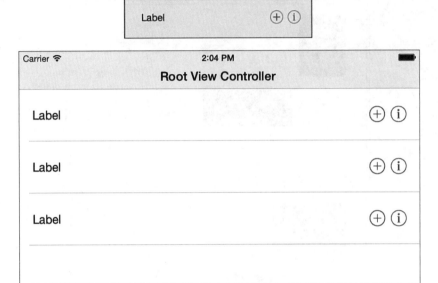

Figure 3-42   Lay out items in cells.

Conclusions

This chapter provides a tour through the world of IB-based Auto Layout. You have seen how to add, delete, and modify constraints in IB, and you have explored the edges of the design space. Before you continue on to other chapters, here are a few final thoughts:

- In the last edition of this book, I wrote, "If I could rewrite IB from the ground up, I'd remove its ambiguity oversight system entirely. I'd rather add constraints iteratively and then test for ambiguity at the end of my layout." In Xcode 5, IB now does this.

  If I had sway with the IB team, I'd now request that they remove constraints from the overview pane entirely and instead add them to their own floating inspector. Here, developers could group related constraints together and freely annotate their design choices. IB should support the visual design process rather than mirror underlying implementation details.

- When testing IB Auto Layout interfaces, you may need to apply deductive reasoning to figure out which constraints are producing the behavior you don't expect. This problem is especially pronounced when you allow IB to add constraints on your behalf, so proceed cautiously.

Visual Formats

Auto Layout builds constraints in three ways. So far, you've read about two of them. First, you can lay out your constraints in Interface Builder (IB) and customize them to your needs. Second, you can build single constraints in code. The NSLayoutConstraint *class offers the* constraintWithItem: attribute:relatedBy:toItem:attribute:multiplier:constant: *method, which enables you to create constraints one at a time, relating one item's attribute to another. In this chapter, you'll read about the third way: using a visual formatting language to express how items are laid out along vertical and horizontal axes.*

This chapter explores what these visual constraints look like, how you build them, and how you use them in your projects. You'll read about how metrics dictionaries and constraint options extend visual formats for more flexibility. And you'll see numerous examples that demonstrate these formats and explore the results they create.

There's one thing to keep in mind throughout: All constraints are members of the NSLayoutConstraint *class, regardless of how you build them. Every constraint stores a "y relation mx + b" rule within an Objective-C object and expresses that rule through the Auto Layout engine. Visual formats are another tool that takes you to that same place.*

Introducing Visual Format Constraints

As with individual constraints, you build visual format constraints by calling an NSLayoutConstraint class method. Although visual formats can relate any number of views, they translate down to instances that relate just one or two views at a time. You supply a text-based specification and any options, and the class creates a group of constraints from that description.

The visual format consists of a text string that describes the view layout. You list items in sequence as they appear in the interface. Text sequences specify spacing, inequalities, and priorities. The result is a short visual picture of the layout in text. In a way, it's a bit like ASCII art for Objective-C nerds.

The following code snippet demonstrates constraint creation using visual formats. I boldfaced the two key items in this request. They are the visual format itself and an option that says how to align the layout:

```
[self.view addConstraints: [NSLayoutConstraint
    constraintsWithVisualFormat:@"V:[view1]-8-[view2]"
    options:NSLayoutFormatAlignAllLeading
    metrics:nil
    views:NSDictionaryOfVariableBindings(view1, view2)]];
```

This call creates a pair of constraints that say "Create a left-aligned vertical column of view1 followed by view2, leaving an 8-point spacer between the two views." The boldfaced items are the visual format and options parameters. Here are a few things to note about how this constraints formatting example is created:

- The axis (or orientation, if you're using OS X) is specified first as a prefix, either H: or V:. When you omit the axis, the constraint defaults to horizontal layout. I encourage you to always use a prefix. Mandatory prefixes provide a consistent indication of design intent, ensuring that any missing prefix is guaranteed to be a mistake.

- Variable names for each view appear in square brackets (for example, [view1]).

- The order of the view names in the string matches the requested order of the views in the layout. The order is normally from top to bottom or left to right. In Arabic and Hebrew locales, the order is right to left. You can also override the order with layout format options.

- The fixed spacing appears between the two views as a number constant, -8-. Hyphens surround the number.

- The options parameter specifies alignment. In this example, it sets a *leading* alignment, which is left-aligned for English-like languages and right-aligned for languages like Arabic and Hebrew. Leading refers to the first horizontal edge encountered for the standard writing direction of the prevailing locale. Trailing refers to the final horizontal edge.

- A metrics dictionary parameter is not included in this example. When used, this parameter supplies constant numbers for value substitutions in constraints. For example, if you want to vary the spacing between these two views, you could replace 8 with a metric name like myOffset and assign that metric's value via a dictionary.

- The views: parameter does not, despite its name, pass an array of views. It passes a dictionary of variable bindings. This dictionary associates variable name strings (for example, "view1") with the objects they represent (the view instance whose variable name is view1). This indirection allows you to use developer-meaningful symbols like "nameLabel" and "requestButton" in your format strings.

This example creates two constraints. Visual format strings always produce an array of results. Some format strings are quite complex, and others are simple. It's not always easy to guess how many constraints will be generated from each string. You install the entire collection of constraints to satisfy the format string that you processed. Here are the two constraints for this example:

```
[NSLayoutConstraint
    constraintWithItem:view2
    attribute:NSLayoutAttributeTop
    relatedBy:NSLayoutRelationEqual
    toItem:view1
    attribute:NSLayoutAttributeBottom
    multiplier:1.0
    constant:8.0];
[NSLayoutConstraint
    constraintWithItem:view1
    attribute:NSLayoutAttributeLeading
    relatedBy:NSLayoutRelationEqual
    toItem:view2
    attribute:NSLayoutAttributeLeading
    multiplier:1.0
    constant:0.0];
```

The first constraint aligns view2's top to view1's bottom and adds 8 points of spacing. This constraint derives from the visual format string. The second constraint is produced from the options argument. It aligns both views' leading edges, which is the left edge in English's left-to-right layout system.

So, why build with visual formats if the results are identical to manually built constraints?

- First, they are more concise. A single visual format can express layout conditions that would take several constraints to describe.

- Second, they are more easily inspected. The visual format tells a little layout story, allowing you to focus your attention on more concentrated ideas.

- Third, they can be easily tweaked. If you want to update the alignment or adjust the spacing, you have to modify just one call.

Apple recommends using visual format constraints over standard layout constraints and prefers IB solutions to code-based ones. I recommend that you use the layout solutions that best match your individual development comfort.

Options

Table 4-1 lists the options you can supply to the visual format method. These options include alignment masks (left column) and formatting directions (right column). You can supply only one format direction. Prior to iOS 7, Apple also required that you choose only one alignment mask at a time. That requirement is now gone. To combine options, you use a bitwise OR.

For most layout work, you need only the values from the left column of Table 4-1. These choices set the alignment used to augment the visual format you specify. In a rare case in which you need to flip formatting directions, you use the options in the right column of Table 4-1. The leading-to-trailing direction is the default. You do not have to set it explicitly.

Table 4-1 **Layout Options**

Alignment Masks	Format Direction Masks
NSLayoutFormatAlignAllLeft	NSLayoutFormatDirectionLeadingToTrailing
NSLayoutFormatAlignAllRight	NSLayoutFormatDirectionLeftToRight
NSLayoutFormatAlignAllTop	NSLayoutFormatDirectionRightToLeft
NSLayoutFormatAlignAllBottom	
NSLayoutFormatAlignAllLeading	
NSLayoutFormatAlignAllTrailing	
NSLayoutFormatAlignAllCenterX	
NSLayoutFormatAlignAllCenterY	
NSLayoutFormatAlignAllBaseline	

Alignment

You should always apply alignment masks *perpendicular* to your format. When you create a horizontal row, you specify a vertical alignment (and vice versa). For example, imagine laying out a row of objects from left to right—for example, H:[view1]-[view2]-[view3]-[view4]. You can align their tops, their middles, or their bottoms simply by tweaking them up or down a bit.

However, you can't align their lefts or rights because doing so would force them out of the layout order you specified. All the views would have to scoot left or scoot right, essentially contradicting the visual format.

Breaking this rule raises an exception, as you see in the following log text. In this case, I attempted to apply a horizontal alignment (leading edges) to a horizontal constraint (H:[view1]-8-[view2]):

```
2013-01-22 12:35:23.885 HelloWorld[25429:c07] *** Terminating app due to uncaught
exception 'NSInvalidArgumentException', reason: 'Unable to parse constraint format:
Options mask required views to be aligned on a horizontal edge, which is not allowed
for layout that is also horizontal.
```

Skipping Options

You skip options by supplying `0` to the options parameter. `NSLayoutConstraint` builds constraints from the visual format you supply but doesn't add any alignment constraints:

```
[self.view addConstraints: [NSLayoutConstraint
    constraintsWithVisualFormat:@"H:[view1]-8-[view2]"
    options:0
    metrics:nil
    views:NSDictionaryOfVariableBindings(view1, view2)]];
```

Variable Bindings

When you're working with visual constraints, the layout system associates name strings like "`view1`" and "`view2`" with the objects they represent. Variable bindings build these associations. You create them by calling `NSDictionaryOfVariableBindings()`, a macro defined in `NSLayoutConstraint.h`. You pass the macro an arbitrary number of local view variables, as in this example:

```
NSDictionaryOfVariableBindings(view1, view2, view3, view4)
```

As you see, this macro doesn't require a `nil` semaphore to terminate your list. It builds a dictionary from the passed variables, using the variable names as keys and the objects they point to as values. For example, this call:

```
NSDictionaryOfVariableBindings(leftLabel, rightLabel)
```

builds this dictionary:

```
@{@"leftLabel":leftLabel, @"rightLabel":rightLabel}.
```

If you'd rather not use the variable bindings macro, you can easily create a dictionary by hand and pass it to the visual format constraints builder. Visual constraints don't work well with view arrays, which is one reason you should create a custom bindings dictionary.

The Problem with Indirection

Consider the following code, which attempts to create a visual format around a view array:

```
NSDictionary *bindings =
    NSDictionaryOfVariableBindings(views[0], views[1]);
constraints = [NSLayoutConstraint constraintsWithVisualFormat:
    @"H:|[views[0]]-[views[1]]|" options:0 metrics:nil views:bindings];
```

Here is the bindings dictionary built by this call:

```
2013-01-24 09:40:17.403 HelloWorld[46260:c07]
{
    "views[0]" = "<TestView: 0x8a6af50; frame = (0 0; 0 0);
```

```
        layer = <CALayer: 0x8a6b010>>";
    "views[1]" = "<TestView: 0x8a6e850; frame = (0 0; 0 0);
        layer = <CALayer: 0x8a6e8c0>>";
}
```

Although this compiles without error, it raises a runtime exception. The format string parser cannot handle the indexed view references. You are, essentially, embedding Objective-C calls into the format, which is a step too far for the NSLayoutConstraint class:

```
2013-01-24 09:12:02.374 HelloWorld[45646:c07] *** Terminating app due to uncaught
exception 'NSInvalidArgumentException', reason: 'Unable to parse constraint format:
views is not a key in the views dictionary.
H:|[views[0]]-[views[1]]|
```

Indirection Workaround

As the example you just saw demonstrates, visual formats work poorly with any items that are not explicitly declared in the local context. Visual formats depend on simple name-to-instance translations. The way you refer to non-local instances in code (for example, [self.view viewWithTag:99] or views[0]) doesn't parse correctly within the format string.

To work around this, you can build both the dictionary and your format string from code. The following code snippet demonstrates one approach:

```
// Initialize the format string and bindings dictionary
NSMutableString *formatString = [NSMutableString string];
NSMutableDictionary *bindings = [NSMutableDictionary dictionary];

// View counter
int i = 1;

// Build a format string that lays out the views in a row
// e.g. @"H:|-[view1]-[view2]-[view3]..."
[formatString appendString:@"H:|-"];
for (UIView *view in views)
{
    // Create a view name
    NSString *viewName =
        [NSString stringWithFormat:@"view%0d", i++];

    // Add the new view to the layout string
    [formatString appendFormat:@"[%@]%@",
        viewName, (i <= views.count) ? @"-" : @""];

    // Store the view and its name in the bindings dictionary
    bindings[viewName] = view;
}
```

Assigning each item a name and an entry in the bindings dictionary allows you to work around the impossibility of indexing items from within the format string. Once populated, this dictionary can be passed as the variable `bindings` parameter for the `formatString` built by this method:

```
// Build constraints with centerY alignment
constraints = [NSLayoutConstraint
    constraintsWithVisualFormat:formatString
    options:NSLayoutFormatAlignAllCenterY
    metrics:nil views:bindings];

// Install the constraints
[self.view addConstraints:constraints];
```

Metrics

When you don't know a constant's value a priori, a metrics dictionary supplies that value to your visual format string. For example, consider this:

```
@"V:[view1]-spacing-[view2]"
```

Here, the word `spacing` represents some spacing value, which has not yet been determined. You pass that value by building a dictionary that equates the word string with its value. For example, this dictionary associates `spacing` with the number `10`:

```
NSDictionary *metrics = @{@"spacing":@10};
```

You supply this dictionary to the `metrics` parameter of the visual format creation method:

```
[NSLayoutConstraint
    constraintsWithVisualFormat:@"V:[view1]-spacing-[view2]"
    options:NSLayoutFormatAlignAllCenterX
    metrics:metrics
    views:bindings];
```

`NSLayoutConstraint` uses the metrics dictionary to substitute the value `10` for the `spacing` string. Unlike the bindings dictionary, which equates views to names, the metrics dictionary supplies numbers.

Real-World Metrics

Metrics are most useful when you build constraints programmatically. For example, consider the following method. It constrains a view's width to a size you supply. When writing this method, you cannot know what view will be supplied or what width it needs to be constrained to:

```
- (void) constrainView: (VIEW_CLASS *) view toWidth: (CGFloat) width
{
    NSString *formatString = @"H:[view(==width)]";
    NSDictionary *bindings = NSDictionaryOfVariableBindings(view);
    NSDictionary *metrics = @{@"width":@(width)};

    NSArray *constraints = [NSLayoutConstraint
        constraintsWithVisualFormat:formatString
        options:0 metrics:metrics views:bindings];
    [view addConstraints:constraints];
}
```

The metrics dictionary used here associates the "width" string in the visual format with the width parameter passed to the method. This allows you to construct readable, maintainable format strings using parameter indirection.

> **Note**
>
> VIEW_CLASS is used throughout this book to refer to UIView on iOS and NSView in OS X.

Format String Structure

The format strings used to create constraints follow a grammar, which is specified as follows:

(<orientation>:)? (<superview><connection>)? <view>(<connection><view>)*
(<connection><superview>)?

The question marks refer to an optional item, and the asterisk refers to an item that may appear zero or more times.

Although this definition is daunting to look at, these strings are actually quite easy to construct. The sections that follow offer an introduction to these format string elements and provide examples of their use.

Orientation

Visual formats start with an optional orientation, either H: for horizontal or V: for vertical alignment. This alignment specifies whether the constraint applies from the leading edge toward the trailing edge or from the top downward.

Consider this constraint format: "[view1][view2]". When prefixed with V:, it says to place View 2 just below View 1. With H:, it says to place View 2 to the right of View 1. Figure 4-1 shows these two constraint requests displayed in a simple iOS test bed application.

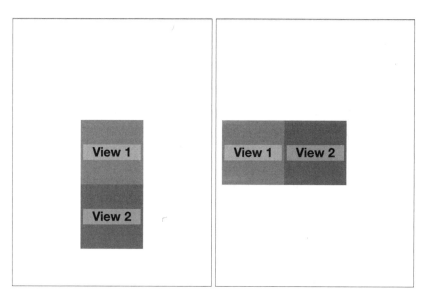

Figure 4-1   These two images were built with "V:[view1][view2]" (left) and "H:[view1]
[view2]" (right) visual format strings.

You can produce a horizontal layout by skipping the orientation prefix, although I don't
recommend you do so. Mandatory prefixes enhance your code checks, helping you find
mistakes at a glance. The horizontal axis for both iOS and OS X is the default.

Retrieving Constraints by Axis

Because Auto Layout design is axis specific, you might want to separate a view's constraints
into horizontal and vertical members. During debugging, you may use the constraints
AffectingLayoutForAxis: view method (this is constraintsAffectingLayoutFor
Orientation: on OS X) to retrieve all constraints that affect either the horizontal or vertical
layout. This code isn't intended for deployment use, and Apple states in its documentation that
it is not App Store-safe. The horizontal axis is enumerated with a value of 0. The vertical axis is
enumerated with 1.

View Names

As the two examples you just saw demonstrate, view names are encased in square brackets. For
example, you might work with "[thisview]" and "[thatview]". When working with a variable bindings dictionary, the view name refers to the local variable name of your view. So if
you've declared this:

```
UIButton *myButton;
```

your format string can refer to "[myButton]".

As you saw earlier in this chapter, you associate view *names* with view *instances* through a dictionary of variable bindings. You pass the dictionary to the constraint creation method to map names to objects.

Superviews

A special character, the vertical pipe (|) always refers to the superview. You see it only at the beginning or end of format strings. At the beginning, it appears just after the horizontal or vertical specifier ("V: | ..." or "H: | ..."). At the end, it appears just before the terminating quote character (" ... | ").

You do not need to name the superview in your bindings dictionary. Auto Layout understands that | refers to the view's superview.

Typical cases for using the superview character include the following:

- Stretching a view to fit its superview—for example, "H: | [view] | "

- Offsetting a view from its superview's edge—for example, "V: [view] -8-| "

- Creating a superview-aligned row or column of views—for example, "V: | - [view1] - [view2] - [view3] - [view4] "

Connections

Connections specify inter-view spacing. Listed between each view (including superview references), they mark out the distance to add. The following discussion surveys the connection types to use in your apps.

Empty Connections

An empty connection looks like this: H: [view1] [view2] or V: | [view3]. Nothing is specified between the square brackets of View 1 and View 2, or between the vertical pipe and the square bracket of View 3. These examples respectively lay out View 2 directly to the right of View 1 (see the top image in Figure 4-2) and View 3 at the very top of its superview (see the bottom image in Figure 4-2).

You use the empty connection to place views that should naturally abut each other. For example, you may need segmented view art to work together to form a single natural presentation onscreen and operate as a single entity. The empty connection allows the views to lay one directly after the other. The empty connection specified in the visual format relating view1 and view2 creates an NSLayoutConstraint instance that relates view1's NSLayoutAttributeTrailing edge to view2's NSLayoutAttributeLeading edge using an equality relation.

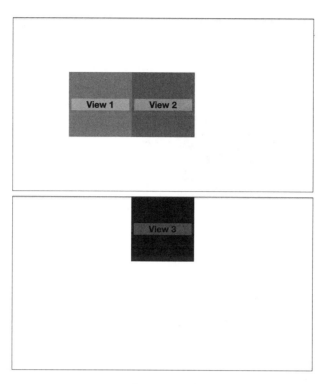

Figure 4-2   Top: `"H:[view1][view2]"`. Bottom: `"V:|[view3]"`. Omitting connections forces views to abut along the constraint axis.

Standard Spacers

A hyphen (-) represents a standard fixed space. The constraint `"H:|-[view1]-[view2]"` leaves a small gap between View 1 and View 2 and between View 1 and its superview (see Figure 4-3). Although officially undocumented, this standard is generally 8 points for view-to-view layout and 20 points for view-to-superview layout.

Apple engineers have stated that visual formats use "Aqua spacing" for layout. These 8- and 20-point values derive from Apple's Aqua user interface standards, the primary visual theme used in OS X design.

Standard gaps ensure that related but distinct views are shown with sufficient visual space. For example, you might use spacers to offset labels from the controls (switches, buttons, text fields, and so on) they describe.

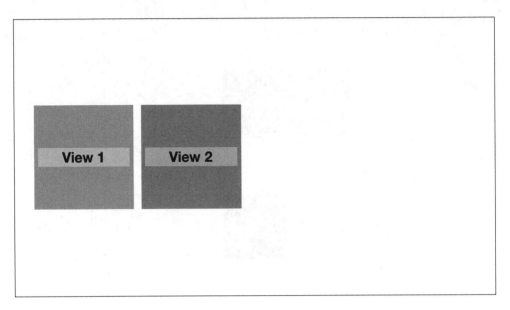

Figure 4-3   `"H:|-[view1]-[view2]"` adds standard spacer connections between the views.

Numeric Spacers

A numeric constant placed between hyphens sets an exact gap size. The constraint
`"H:[view1]-30-[view2]"` adds a 30-point gap between the two views, as shown in Figure 4-4.
This is visibly wider than the small default gap produced by the single hyphen, shown in
Figure 4-3.

Referencing the Superview

The format `"H:|[view1]-[view2]|"` specifies a horizontal layout that starts with the super-
view. Notice the vertical pipe to the right of the axis specifier. The superview is immediately
followed by the first view, then a spacer, the second view, and then, with another vertical pipe,
the superview.

The constraint left-aligns View 1 and right-aligns View 2 flush with the superview. To accomplish this, something has to give. Either the left view or the right view must resize. When I ran
the test app, it happened to be View 1 that adjusted, as you can see in Figure 4-5. It could just
as easily have been View 2.

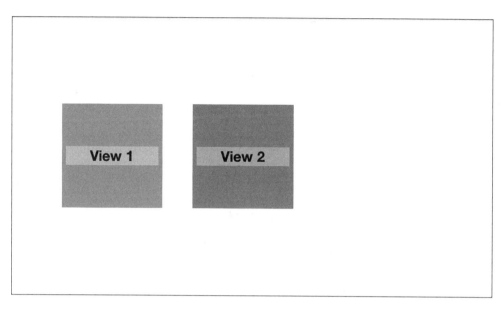

Figure 4-4   `"H:[view1]-30-[view2]"` uses a fixed-size gap of 30 points, producing a notice-ably larger distance between the two views than the standard spacer.

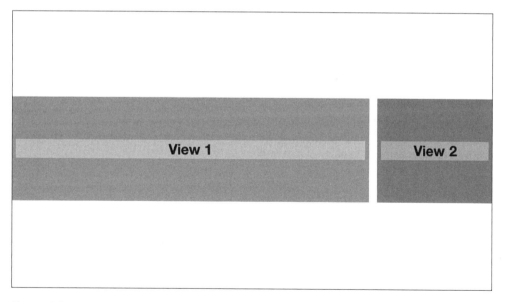

Figure 4-5   `"H:|[view1]-[view2]|"` tells both views to hug the edges of their superview. With a fixed-size gap between them, at least one of the views must resize to satisfy the constraint.

Spacing from the Superview

Often, you don't want to bang right up against the superview edges. The `"H:|-[view1]-` `[view2]-|"` format adds an inset between the edges of the superview and the start of View 1 and end of View 2 (see Figure 4-6). The standard superview inset (20 points) is wider than the view-to-view gap (8 points).

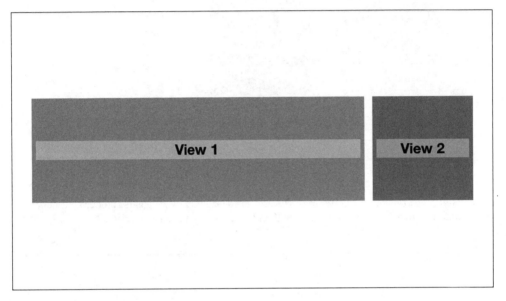

Figure 4-6   `"H:|-[view1]-[view2]-|"` introduces edge insets between the views and their superviews.

Insets give your views visual breathing room, allowing them to move away from the edges of the screen or a parent window. If you need to inset with a nonstandard distance, you can specify a number between hyphens (for example, `"H:[view2]-50-|"`).

Flexible Spaces

If your goal is to add a flexible space between views, there's a way to do that, too. You add a relation rule between the two views (for example, `"H:|-[view1]-(>=0)-[view2]-|"`) to allow the two views to retain their sizes and separate while maintaining gaps at their edges with the superview, as shown in Figure 4-7.

This rule, which you can read as "at least 0 points distance," provides a more flexible way to let the views spread out. By using a small number here, you don't inadvertently interfere with a view's other geometry rules.

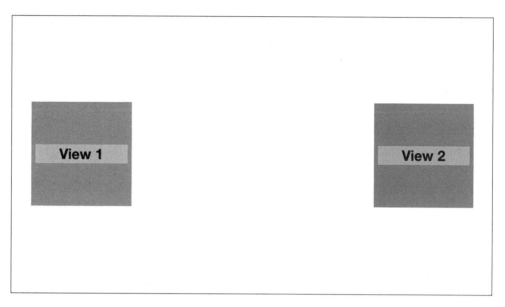

Figure 4-7 `"H:|-[view1]-(>=0)-[view2]-|"` uses a flexible space between the two views, allowing them to separate while maintaining their sizes.

While you can say "at least 50 points" (`>=50`) or "no more than 30 points" (`<=30`), you cannot relate distance to the standard (Aqua) space. For example, saying `>=-` or `<=-` is illegal. You just use equivalent numeric values. Remember that standard view-to-view spacing is 8 points, and view-to-superview spacing is 20 points.

Parentheses

There's an important syntactic difference between the format used in Figure 4-7 (`"H:|-[view1]-(>=0)-[view2]-|"`) and a fixed spacing format (for example, `"H:|-[view1]-30-[view2]-|"`)—namely that the relation (`>=0`) has been placed within parentheses for clarity. Parentheses distinguish spacing that's not a simple positive number or metric name.

You have a lot of flexibility with visual constraints in how you express rules. The following rules all have two views that abut one another:

- `[view1][view2]`
- `[view1]-0-[view2]`
- `[view1]-(0)-[view2]`
- `[view1]-(==0)-[view2]`
- `[view1]-(>=0,<=0)-[view2]`

- `[view1]-(==0@1000)-[view2]`

- `[view1]-(>=0,<=0,==0,<=30)-[view2]`

When you add multiple relations within parentheses, you separate items with commas. The `@` sign specifies a priority, as you'll see in the "Priorities" section.

Negative Numbers

You *must* use parentheses for any spacer that involves a negative number. These constraints are both illegal:

- `V:[view1]--5-[view2]`

- `V:[view1]- -5-[view2]`

The errors raised by these constraints are as follows. The first item complains about the repeated - sign:

```
2013-01-31 18:52:27.735 HelloWorld[88684:c07] *** Terminating app due to uncaught
exception 'NSInvalidArgumentException', reason: 'Unable to parse constraint format:
Cannot tell if this - is a minus sign or an accidental extra bar in the connection.
Use parentheses around negative numbers.
V:[v1]--5-[v2]
```

The second catches on the space before the minus:

```
2013-01-31 18:53:18.756 HelloWorld[88713:c07] *** Terminating app due to uncaught
exception 'NSInvalidArgumentException', reason: 'Unable to parse constraint format:
Expected a number or key from the metrics dictionary, but encountered something else
V:[v1]- -5-[v2]
```

There is a legal solution. The following constraint says, "Set the top edge of view 2 to 5 points above the bottom edge of View 1":

```
V:[view1]-(-5)-[view2]
```

Negative constants *are* allowed in visual constraints.

Priorities

You prioritize layout requests by adding an optional value to the format string. Append any connection or sizing rule with an `@` sign followed by the numeric priority you want to assign.

For example, in this visual format:

```
"H:|-5@20-[view1]-[view2]-|"
```

the first spacing request between the superview and View 1 is prioritized at 20, a very low value. Normally, spacing rules are required unless you specify otherwise.

For clarity, you can surround the spacing request with parentheses, although they are not strictly necessary in this case:

```
"H:|-(5@20)-[view1]-[view2]-|"
```

Because you've lowered the priority to 20, the way the two views are sized may affect layout. For example, if the views are small due to a high priority, they may not end up reaching the left side of the screen at all. Sized large, they might shoot off too far to the left. The rule that links them to the superview's left side may no longer be important enough to pin down the leftmost edge.

Multiple Views

Format constraints are not limited to just one or two views. You can easily stick in a third, fourth, or more. Consider this constraint string:

```
"H:|-[view1]-[view2]-(>=8)-[view3]-|"
```

It adds a third view, separated from the other two views by a flexible space that is at least a standard distance wide. Figure 4-8 shows what this might look like. This approach enables you to specify entire rows or columns at a time, using a single constraint request.

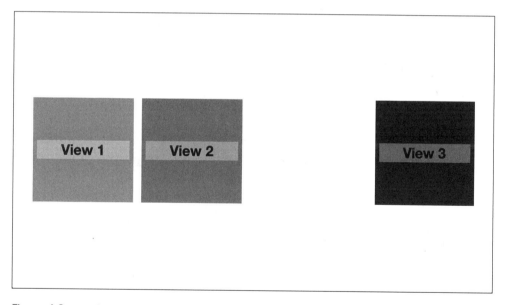

Figure 4-8 `"H:|-[view1]-[view2]-(>=8)-[view3]-|"` demonstrates a rule that references three views.

View Sizes

The visual constraint formatting language optionally specifies view sizing within the square brackets that otherwise delimit the view name. You add the sizing specifications in parentheses after the name, like this:

- You might specify a view with a fixed 120-point width: `@"H:[view1(120)]"`. If you prefer to state the relation explicitly, you can add that as well: `@"H:[view1(==120)]"`.

- You might specify that the width of a view is at least 50 points, using the following format: `@"H:[view1(>=50)]"`. A similar approach lets a view's size range between 50 and 70 points. As with spacing, separate your rules with commas for compound items: `"H:[view1(>=50,<=70)]"`.

- You can refer to other views in sizing requests. For example, this format matches View 1's width to View 2's width: `"H:[view1(view2)]"`. If you add size matching to the `"H:|-[view1]-[view2]-|"` format originally shown in Figure 4-6, you ensure that both subviews are the same size, fixing the lopsided random layout (that is, `"H:|-[view1(view2)]-[view2]-|"`). Figure 4-9 shows the updated result.

Incidentally, because constraints are nondirectional and can be self-referential, you produce an equivalent layout with this format: `"H:|-[view1(view2)]-[view2(view1)]-|"`, where View 1 matches View 2 and View 2 matches View 1. Circular definitions don't produce performance hits.

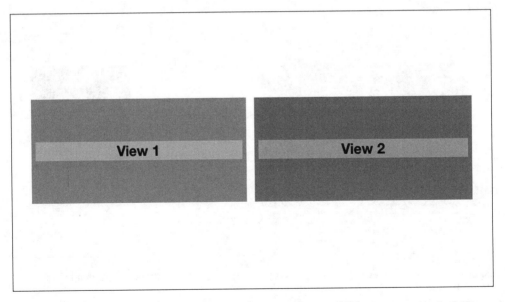

Figure 4-9　`"H:|-[view1(view2)]-[view2]-|"`. Adding size matching ensures that both views have equal widths.

- Not all views need to participate in size matching. The next request creates matching flanking views around a primary view while stretching all three views across the superview: `@"H:|-[view1(<=80)]-[view2]-[view3(view1)]-|"`. The format limits View 1's size to 80 points and matches it to View 3, ensuring that View 2 stretches to occupy the remaining space. Figure 4-10 shows the resulting layout.

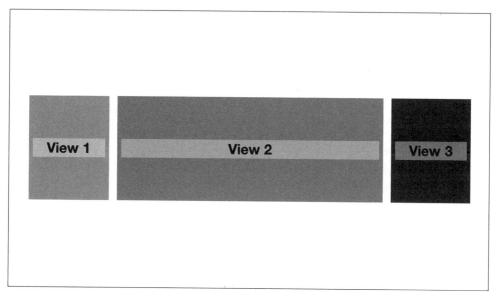

Figure 4-10   With `"H:|-[view1(<=80)]-[view2]-[view3(view1)]-|"`, the two outer views are matched in size and limited to a maximum width, allowing View 2, which has no real intrinsic size, to expand to occupy the remaining room.

- View sizes can also express priorities. In the format string `"H:|-[view1(==250@700)]-[view2(==250@701)]-|"`, both View 1 and View 2 request to be 250 points wide. View 2 wins (see Figure 4-11) because its request has a higher priority.

- Although you can easily produce constraints in code that express relative size using multipliers, you cannot do so in visual constraints. This is an illegal constraint: `"H:|-[view1(==2*view2)]-[view2]-|"`. If you want to say "View 1 is twice the width of View 2," you need to do so in code.

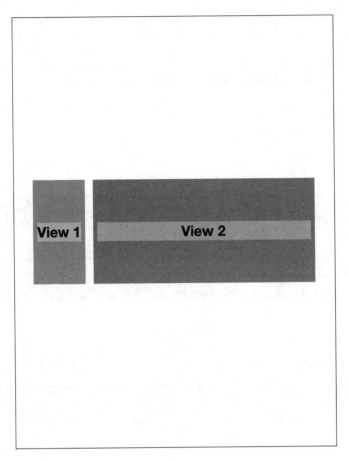

Figure 4-11   With `"H:|-[view1(==250@700)]-[view2(==250@701)]-|"`, View 2's request to be 250 points wide wins as it has a higher priority.

Format String Components

Table 4-2 summarizes the components used to create layout constraints through visual formats. You can combine multiple conditions with commas within parentheses—for example, `(>=0, <=250)`.

Table 4-2   **Visual Format Strings**

Type	Format	Example
Horizontal or vertical arrangement	`H:` `V:`	`V:[view1]-15-[view2]` Puts View 2's top 15 points below View 1's bottom.
Views	`[item]`	`[view1]` The view bindings dictionary matches the bracketed name to a view instance.
Superview	`|`	`H:|[view1]|` Makes View 1's width size to that of the superview.

Relations	`==`
	`<=`
	`>=`
		`H:[view1]-(>=20)-[view2]`
		Sets View 2's leading edge at least 20 points from View 1's trailing edge.

Metrics	`metric`	`H:[view1(<=someWidth)]V:[view1]-mySpacing-[view2]` Metrics are keys. `someWidth` and `mySpacing` must map to `NSNumber` values in the passed metric dictionary.
Flush alignment	`[item][item]`	`H:[view1][view2]` Sets View 1's trailing edge flush with View 2's leading edge.
Flexible space	`[item]-(>=0)-[item]`	`[view1]-(>=0)-[view2]` Views can stretch apart as needed, "at least zero points apart."
Fixed space	`[item]-gap-[item]`	`V:[view1]-20-[view2]` Sets View 1's bottom 20 points from View 2's top.
Fixed distance (view to view)	`[item]-[item]`	`[view1]-[view2]` Leaves a small fixed space (8 points) between the two views.
Fixed width or height	`[item(size)]` `[item(==size)]`	`[view1(50)]` Sets View 1's extent to exactly 50 points along this axis.
Minimum and maximum width/height	`[item(>=size)]` `[item(<=size)]`	`[view1(>=50)][view1(<=50)]` Limits View 1's minimum or maximum size for this axis.

Type	Format	Example

Match width/height with another view	`[item(==item)]`
	`[item(<=item)]`
	`[item(>=item)]`
		`[view1(==view2)]`
		Matches View 1 to View 2's size along this axis.

Flush with superview	`|[item]` `[item]|`	`V:|[view1]` Sets View 1's top flush with the superview's top.
Inset from superview	`|-[item]` `[item]-|`	`|-[view1]` Places a fixed space (20 points) between the superview and View 1 along this axis.
Custom inset from superview	`|-gap-[item]` `[item]-gap-|`	`H:|-15-[view1]` Insets the view from the superview by 15 points on the leading edge.
Priority (from 0 to 1,000)	`@value`	`[view1(<=50@20)]` Gives View 1 a maximum size of 50 along this axis, with a very low priority (20).

> **Note**
>
> iOS 7 and Xcode 5 introduce two properties for laying out your formats with respect to a container's bars. The `topLayoutGuide` and `bottomLayoutGuide` conform to the `UILayoutSupport` protocol, establishing offsets for view controllers whose views may extend behind parent bars. At the time of writing this book, you must assign those properties to local variables to refer to them in your format strings.

Getting It Wrong

Xcode provides no compiler check that ensures the validity of your format strings. A poorly formatted string throws an exception at runtime. For example, you may have skipped a colon, as shown here:

```
2013-01-23 11:40:17.169 HelloWorld[35717:c07] *** Terminating app due to uncaught
exception 'NSInvalidArgumentException', reason: 'Unable to parse constraint format:
Expected ':' after 'H' to specify horizontal arrangement
H|[view1]-[view2]
```

Or you may have forgotten to close the square bracket ending a view declaration. Where possible, the log messages attempt to instruct you on how to fix your mistake, as shown here:

```
2013-01-23 11:41:35.897 HelloWorld[35750:c07] *** Terminating app due to uncaught
exception 'NSInvalidArgumentException', reason: 'Unable to parse constraint format:
Expected a ']' here. That is how you give the end of a view.
H:|[view1-[view2]
```

Common errors include stray or missing characters, views that don't exist in the bindings dictionary, missing metrics values, and invalid priorities. The exceptions raised by these errors demonstrate why it's absolutely critical to fully inspect and test all format strings.

NSLog and Visual Formats

Xcode adds visual format representations wherever it can into NSLayoutConstraint logs. Even if you build your constraints entirely in IB or through single constraint instances, you'll be well served by learning this layout language. Here's an example of a visual format–based log. I've bolded both the format and the binding between the superview pipe (|) character and the view it represents (stored at memory address 0x71c7f50):

```
2013-01-23 11:21:39.378 HelloWorld[35535:c07] <NSLayoutConstraint:0x71cf290 H:|-
(55@20)-[TestView:0x71c8390] priority:20    (Names: '|':UIView:0x71c7f50)>
```

Not all constraints can be expressed with visual formats, and even those that can be may not produce the output you expect. Consider the following code, which builds and logs what are basically two identical constraints:

```
// This provides no visual format
NSLayoutConstraint *c = [NSLayoutConstraint
    constraintWithItem:view1
    attribute:NSLayoutAttributeBottom
    relatedBy:NSLayoutRelationEqual
    toItem:self.view
    attribute:NSLayoutAttributeBottom
    multiplier:1.0f constant:0.0f];
NSLog(@"%@", c);

// This basically identical constraint does.
c = [NSLayoutConstraint
    constraintWithItem:self.view
    attribute:NSLayoutAttributeBottom
    relatedBy:NSLayoutRelationEqual
    toItem:view1
    attribute:NSLayoutAttributeBottom
    multiplier:1.0f constant:0.0f];
NSLog(@"%@", c);
```

The logs for these two constraints showcase the difference. The first log shows a y R $mx + b$ relation, and the second shows a visual format:

```
2013-01-23 11:55:08.961 HelloWorld[36083:c07] <NSLayoutConstraint:0x958c650
TestView:0x9566b30.bottom == UIView:0x9568790.bottom>
2013-01-23 11:55:08.962 HelloWorld[36083:c07] <NSLayoutConstraint:0x7565790
V:[TestView:0x9566b30]-(0)-|    (Names: '|':UIView:0x9568790 )>
```

Expect to see both of these logs in your development work. So, why does swapping the order of the two views make a difference? It's an Apple implementation detail, and one that seems as inconsistent to me as it probably does to you.

Constraining to a Superview

Visual formats offer a great match for view fallback conditions, as you can express and implement those edge conditions using a series of format strings instead of code. You see this in Listing 4-1, where the format strings power these requirements.

This function succinctly constrains a view to its superview, using a priority you specify. The `for` loop iterates through four format strings, each of which describes a view boundary: The first two keep the view inside the parent's leading and trailing edges, and the second two do the same for the top and bottom edges. Inequality relations ensure that the view's edges are at least within those bounds, without specifying any further position.

The function adds its minimum sizing requests, using the same priority. You pass that minimum size as an argument to the function. For example, a 40×40 or 100×100 view can easily be seen in most interfaces.

You generally call this function with a very low priority, such as 1, establishing a fallback set of rules for the view. The function mandates that the view must appear onscreen and that it must have an easy-to-view size so that your views don't go missing. You should add these rules early (for example, in your `loadView` or `viewDidLoad` methods).

A simple `viewDidAppear:` method can inventory your views:

```
- (void) viewDidAppear:(BOOL)animated
{
    for (UIView *view in self.view.subviews)
        NSLog(@"View: %@", NSStringFromCGRect(view.frame));
}
```

You're ready to start building Auto Layout–powered interfaces where you don't experience the "missing views" issue that plagues so many new Auto Layout developers.

Listing 4-1   Constraining Views to Their Superview

```
void constrainToSuperview(VIEW_CLASS *view,
    float minimumSize, NSUInteger priority)
{
    if (!view || !view.superview)
        return;

    for (NSString *format in @[
        @"H:|->=0@priority-[view(==minimumSize@priority)]",
        @"H:[view]->=0@priority-|",
```

```
     @"V:|->=0@priority-[view(==minimumSize@priority)]",
     @"V:[view]->=0@priority-|"])
{
    NSArray *constraints = [NSLayoutConstraint
        constraintsWithVisualFormat:format options:0
        metrics: @{@"priority":@(priority),
            @"minimumSize":@(minimumSize)}
        views:@{@"view": view}];
    [view.superview addConstraints:constraints];
}
}
```

View Stretching

Stretching views is another common view task you can easily address with visual formats. Listing 4-2 creates a function that stretches the view you supply to its superview, leaving an indentation that you specify. Figure 4-12 shows the interface built by ramping up the indentation for a series of four views.

Like the previous example, this method builds constraints from an array of format strings, using a metrics dictionary to specify the indentation requested. Although this method builds both vertical and horizontal stretching rules, you could easily adapt this code for separate requests per axis.

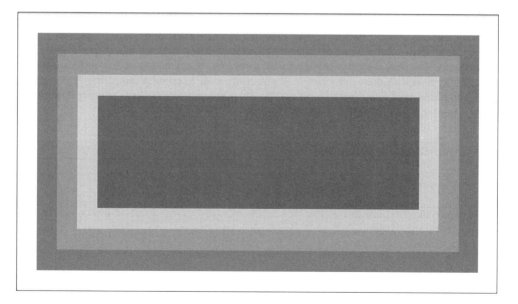

Figure 4-12   These stepped views were built from visual formats. The stepped indentations represent a 20-point value multiplied by the view number.

Listing 4-2   Stretching Views to Their Superview

```
void stretchToSuperview(VIEW_CLASS *view,
    CGFloat indent, NSUInteger priority)
{
    for (NSString *format in @[
        @"H:|-indent-[view]-indent-|",
        @"V:|-indent-[view]-indent-|"
        ])
    {
        NSArray *constraints = [NSLayoutConstraint
            constraintsWithVisualFormat:format options:0
            metrics:@{@"indent":@(indent)} views:@{@"view": view}];
        for (NSLayoutConstraint *constraint in constraints)
        {
            constraint.priority = priority;
            [view.superview addConstraint:constraint];
        }
    }
}
```

Constraining Size

Listing 4-3 uses visual formats to constrain a view to the size that you specify. You choose the priority, which can range from a mild suggestion all the way up to required. The method adds two visual constraints and sets their exact sizes. You can easily adapt this function to support minimum and maximum sizes by simply replacing the equalities in the two strings with inequalities. If you do this, consider creating a private helper function to do the work without redundancy. The code is similar enough for all three tasks that you'd want to build just one place for it, even with three entry points. If you really want to create a complete API experience, often you must constrain a view's width or height without affecting the other dimension. This expansion is left for you to do as an exercise.

Listing 4-3   Constraining View Size

```
void constrainViewSize(VIEW_CLASS *view,
    CGSize size, NSUInteger priority)
{
    NSDictionary *bindings =
        NSDictionaryOfVariableBindings(view);
    NSDictionary *metrics = @{
        @"width":@(size.width),
        @"height":@(size.height),
        @"priority":@(priority)};
```

```
    for (NSString *formatString in @[
        @"H:[view(==width@priority)]",
        @"V:[view(==height@priority)]",
        ])
    {
        NSArray *constraints = [NSLayoutConstraint
            constraintsWithVisualFormat:formatString
            options:0 metrics:metrics views:bindings];
        [view addConstraints:constraints];
    }
}
```

Building Rows or Columns

Listing 4-4 demonstrates how to create a row or column from an array of views. You specify an alignment option, a spacer, and a priority. The code determines which axis to use from the alignment you supply. The alignment must be orthogonal to the axis, so if the alignment is horizontal, the layout is vertical or vice versa.

The function in Listing 4-4 builds pairs of constraints, iterating through the views array you pass it. It creates a layout based on both the calculated axis and the spacing constant you provided. For standard spacing, you use @"-", and for no spacing, you use @"". Otherwise, you can pass any string that describes how the spacers should act (for example, @">=15-").

This function uses the custom `install` method that was first introduced in Chapter 2, "Constraints." It installs each constraint safely to its natural destination.

Listing 4-4   **Placing Views into a Line**

```
#define IS_HORIZONTAL_ALIGNMENT(ALIGNMENT) \
    [@[@(NSLayoutFormatAlignAllLeft), @(NSLayoutFormatAlignAllRight),\
    @(NSLayoutFormatAlignAllLeading), @(NSLayoutFormatAlignAllTrailing),\
    @(NSLayoutFormatAlignAllCenterX)] containsObject:@(ALIGNMENT)]

void buildLineWithSpacing(NSArray *views, NSLayoutFormatOptions alignment,
    NSString *spacing, NSUInteger priority)
{
    if (views.count == 0)
        return;

    VIEW_CLASS *view1, *view2;

    // Calculate the axis and its string representation.
    // The axis is orthogonal to the requested alignment
    // eg, centerX alignment creates a column, and
    // trailing builds a row.
```

```
BOOL axisIsH = IS_HORIZONTAL_ALIGNMENT(alignment);
NSString *axisString = (axisIsH) ? @"H:" : @"V:";

// Build the format
NSString *format = [NSString
    stringWithFormat:@"%@[view1]%@[view2]",
    axisString, spacing];

// Apply the format to view pairs
for (int i = 1; i < views.count; i++)
{
    view1 = views[i-1];
    view2 = views[i];
    NSDictionary *bindings =
        NSDictionaryOfVariableBindings(view1, view2);
    NSArray *constraints = [NSLayoutConstraint
        constraintsWithVisualFormat:format options:alignment
        metrics:nil views:bindings];
    for (NSLayoutConstraint *constraint in constraints)
        [constraint install:priority];
}
}
```

Matching Sizes

Listing 4-5 shows how to use visual formats to match the sizes for all members of a view array. It ensures that you've passed at least one view and then matches each of the remaining views to that first one. You specify the axis, and the function applies the visual constraints.

As with Listing 4-4, this function uses the install method from Chapter 2, which is a safe way to install constraints.

Listing 4-5   Matching View Sizes to Each Other

```
void matchSizes(NSArray *views,
    NSInteger axis, NSUInteger priority)
{
    if (views.count == 0)
        return;

    // Create the axis-appropriate format
    NSString *format = axis ?
        @"V:[view2(==view1@priority)]" :
        @"H:[view2(==view1@priority)]";
```

```
// Iterate through the views
VIEW_CLASS *view1 = views[0];
for (int i = 1; i < views.count; i++)
{
    VIEW_CLASS *view2 = views[i];
    NSArray *constraints = [NSLayoutConstraint
      ` constraintsWithVisualFormat:format options:0
        metrics:@{@"priority":@(priority)}
        views:NSDictionaryOfVariableBindings(view1, view2)];
    for (NSLayoutConstraint *constraint in constraints)
        [constraint install];
}
}
```

Why You Cannot Distribute Views

You can't distribute views along an axis under the current constraint system for equal spacing. Adding a " [A] - (>=0) - [B] - (>=0) - [C] " constraint doesn't distribute the views along an axis with equal spacing, as you might expect. The basic reason is that each constraint can reference only two views at a time.

An equal spacing or distribution rule must refer to a minimum of three. You can't say, "The space between View 1 and View 2 equals the space between View 2 and View 3," nor can you talk about the distances of their leading edges, tops, centers, or other geometries. There aren't enough references in any NSLayoutConstraint instance to encapsulate (let alone implement) rules like this:

> *Some distance* such that *A.center + distance = B.center* and *B.center + distance = C.center*

You also can't declare simultaneous equations that equate two constraint constant properties, like this:

```
A. center == B. center + spacer1;
B. center == C. center + spacer2;
spacer1 == spacer2
```

There is simply no way to express these relations in the *y R mx + b* format used by the iOS constraint system, where the *b* offset must be known and relations are only between view attributes. The best you can do is to calculate how far apart you want the items to be and then use a multiplier and offset to manually fix each view's position.

I do, however, offer two workarounds for your consideration.

How to Pseudo-Distribute Views (Part 1: Equal Centers)

The first of my two solutions works by dividing the superview into N equal sections, where N is the number of views. It co-aligns each view's center X to the middle of its section.

That's where a little multiplier hack comes into play. As shown in Listing 4-6, use a function that calculates the percent extent along the superview that reaches to the section's middle and multiplies it by the "right" attribute, which amounts to the full distance along the view.

Listing 4-6   **Distributing Views by Equal Center Placement**

```
void pseudoDistributeCenters(
    NSArray *views, NSLayoutFormatOptions alignment,
    NSUInteger priority)
{
    if (!views.count)
        return;

    if (alignment == 0)
        return;

    // Check the alignment for vertical or horizontal placement
    BOOL horizontal = IS_HORIZONTAL_ALIGNMENT(alignment);

    // The placement is orthogonal to that alignment
    NSLayoutAttribute placementAttribute = horizontal ?
        NSLayoutAttributeCenterY : NSLayoutAttributeCenterX;
    NSLayoutAttribute endAttribute = horizontal ?
        NSLayoutAttributeBottom : NSLayoutAttributeRight;

    // Cast from NSLayoutFormatOptions to NSLayoutAttribute
    NSLayoutAttribute alignmentAttribute =
        attributeForAlignment(alignment);

    // Iterate through the views
    NSLayoutConstraint *constraint;
    for (int i = 0; i < views.count; i++)
    {
        VIEW_CLASS *view = views[i];

        // midway across each section
        CGFloat multiplier =
            ((CGFloat) i + 0.5) / ((CGFloat) views.count);
```

```
        // Install the item position
        constraint = [NSLayoutConstraint
                    constraintWithItem:view
                    attribute:placementAttribute
                    relatedBy:NSLayoutRelationEqual
                    toItem:view.superview
                    attribute:endAttribute
                    multiplier:multiplier
                    constant: 0];
        [constraint install:priority];

        // Install alignment
        constraint = [NSLayoutConstraint
                    constraintWithItem:views[0]
                    attribute:alignmentAttribute
                    relatedBy:NSLayoutRelationEqual
                    toItem: view
                    attribute:alignmentAttribute
                    multiplier:1
                    constant:0];
        [constraint install:priority];
    }
}
```

This function produces a set of views whose centers are equally distributed. The gaps between the views, however, vary by the size of each view. This works best when all views are matched in size, to produce equally spaced results, as shown at the top of Figure 4-13. As the bottom image in Figure 4-13 shows, the results can look a little odd with unmatched sizing. The view-to-view spaces are not even.

This code stretches completely across the parent. If you want to adjust this, you must carefully manipulate the multiplier (to set a different endpoint) and/or constant (to set the starting point). The math is left as an exercise for you.

So, why can't you use `NSLayoutAttributeWidth` directly? Unfortunately, you can only relate location attributes to location attributes. You cannot relate them to size attributes. Doing so crashes your application, as shown here:

```
2013-01-26 23:45:59.739 HelloWorld[16073:c07] *** Terminating app due to uncaught
exception 'NSInvalidArgumentException', reason: '*** +[NSLayoutConstraint
constraintWithItem:attribute:relatedBy:toItem:attribute:multiplier:constant:]: Invalid
pairing of layout attributes'
```

Figure 4-13   Distributing centers works best with equal-sized views placed entirely across a shared superview (top). When you distribute centers for unequal-sized views, the spacing becomes visually haphazard (bottom).

Pseudo-Distributing Views (Part 2: Spacer Views)

A far better but less elegant solution than the one just shown is to add a series of views *between* each source view. As you can see in Figure 4-14, it works equally well for same-sized views, views with variable sizes, and even groups whose first and last members have been pinned to odd locations. By adding spacer views, you bypass the "no rules about spaces" problem described earlier. Because your spacers are views themselves, you can add constraint rules that establish the similarity of these views to each other.

Listing 4-7 shows the code that powers this distribution. It builds an array of disposable transparent view spacers. It then adds constraints built like this:

```
"[view1][spacer(==firstspacer)][view2]"
```

These constraints add spacers between pairs of views, matching the size of each spacer view. This forces each pair of views to space apart an equal amount.

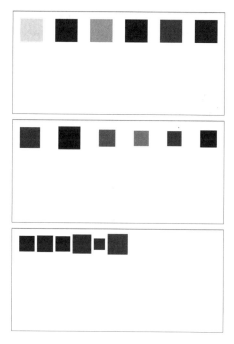

Figure 4-14   By creating inter-item spacing views, you can add constraint rules that relate spaces to each other.

This distribution strategy involves a few things you need to think about in deployment:

- First, the layout is underconstrained. This function adds no rules about the placement of the first and last views. So you need to pin those views elsewhere in your code.

- Second, you must pin *both* the first and last views. Unlike in Listing 4-4, these spacers are underspecified until after the last view is pinned into position.

- Third, it uses a *lot* of extra views that you need to keep track of. This becomes especially troublesome when your design changes between portrait and horizontal orientations and you need to re-layout your views. Each spacer view plays a particular role, and you can't just reuse spacers arbitrarily. You must track each role, track the spacer that fulfills it, and associate that layout geometry with that particular instance.

- Fourth, it's inherently more fragile. You must provide enough space to lay out all your views, especially if you size them with a required priority. If the extent of all your views and spacers is larger than the available width (between the starting edge of the first view and the ending edge of the last view), Auto Layout starts breaking constraints on your behalf.

Work around this fragility by adjusting constraint priorities. For example, if your views can resize to take up the slack, let them do so. If you know your views are equally sized, you can diminish the impact of view resizing by adding a view-size matching rule to the layout format:

`"[view1][spacer(==firstspacer)][view2(==view1)]"`

Unfortunately, if you work with mixed view sizes, you cannot specify rules that state "resize each view proportionally." You must accept that some views may shrink significantly and randomly when faced with insufficient space.

Listing 4-7   Adding Spacer Views to Provide Even Distributions

```
void pseudoDistributeWithSpacers(
    VIEW_CLASS *superview, NSArray *views,
    NSLayoutFormatOptions alignment, NSUInteger priority)
{
    // Must pass views, superview, non-zero alignment
    if (!views.count) return;
    if (!superview) return;
    if (alignment == 0) return;

    // Build disposable spacers
    NSMutableArray *spacers = [NSMutableArray array];
    for (int i = 0; i < views.count; i++)
    {
        // Create a view, install it, and prepare for autolayout
        [spacers addObject:[[VIEW_CLASS alloc] init]];
        [spacers[i] setTranslatesAutoresizingMaskIntoConstraints:NO];
        [superview addSubview:spacers[i]];
    }

    BOOL horizontal = IS_HORIZONTAL_ALIGNMENT(alignment);
    VIEW_CLASS *firstspacer = spacers[0];

    // Structure format
    NSString *format = [NSString stringWithFormat:
        @"%@:[view1][spacer(==firstspacer)][view2]",
        horizontal ? @"V" : @"H"];

    // Lay out the row or column
    for (int i = 1; i < views.count; i++)
    {
        VIEW_CLASS *view1 = views[i-1];
        VIEW_CLASS *view2 = views[i];
        VIEW_CLASS *spacer = spacers[i-1];
```

```
    // Create bindings
    NSDictionary *bindings = NSDictionaryOfVariableBindings(
        view1, view2, spacer, firstspacer);

    // Build and install constraints
    NSArray *constraints = [NSLayoutConstraint
        constraintsWithVisualFormat:format
        options:alignment metrics:nil views:bindings];
    for (NSLayoutConstraint *constraint in constraints)
        [constraint install:priority];
    }
}
```

Exercises

After reading this chapter, test your knowledge with these exercises:

1. How many constraints does the format @"H:[view1]-[view2]" produce?
   How many constraints does it produce if the options parameter is
   NSLayoutFormatAlignAllBaseline?

2. How many constraints does the format @"H:[view1]" produce? How many constraints
   does it produce if the options parameter is NSLayoutFormatAlignAllTop?

3. Your format string is @"H:[view1]-[view2]". (a) You pass NSDictionaryOfVariable
   Bindings(view1, view2, view3, view4, view5) to the views parameter. What
   happens? (b) You pass NSDictionaryOfVariableBindings(view1, view3) to the
   views parameter. What happens?

4. How do you request a set of views to align both on the top and on the bottom?

5. How do you request a bottom alignment for a vertical format string, such as
   @"V:[view1][view2]"?

6. What result does the visual format @"H:|-(50@100)-[view1(==320@200)]-
   (50@300)-|" produce on a screen that is 320 points wide? On a screen 480 points wide?

7. How wide will this view be: @"H:[view(>=20, <=10)]"?

8. Describe the results the constraint @"H:|-(-20)-[view1(==50)]" produces.

Conclusions

This chapter introduces Auto Layout's text-based visual formatting language. You discovered
how these formats are built and saw many examples that demonstrate their flexibility. Here are
a few final thoughts about this technology:

- Although visual formats are not as nuanced as building straight `NSLayoutConstraint` instances, they offer the benefit of concise expression, along with self-documenting format strings. Visual formats cover enough ground to match many developers' light layout needs.

- While alignment is not a necessary part of constraint creation, it helps condense your code as much as possible. When you set an option with visual formats, you eliminate any need to build separate alignment constraints.

- All constraints you generate with visual formats have a default 1,000 (required) priority unless you specify otherwise within your text. If you find readability suffering as a result of carefully prioritized layout, consider switching to individual layout constraints for more direct control.

- Visual constraints are more intuitive to use for layout. Specifying `@"H:[nameLabel]-[nameTextField]"` is far easier than working out that the text field's leading edge lies 8 points to the right of the label's trailing edge, transferring that knowledge to a seven-parameter call, and then testing whether you got the order of the arguments and the sign of the constant right on the first go.

- Visual formats have an intrinsic flexibility, and there are usually several ways to accomplish your goal. As you read in this chapter, slightly different formats (for example, `-0-`, `-(0)-`, `-(==0)-`) can produce identical constraints, allowing you to customize rules to your personal style.

Debugging Constraints

So, you have taken the plunge and added constraints to your project. Now, things either don't work the way you expect or you are seeing dreaded errors about conflicting constraints. Constraints can be maddeningly opaque. The code and interface files you create them with don't lend themselves to easy perusal. It takes only a few "helpful" Xcode log messages to make some developers start pulling out their hair. This chapter is dedicated to shining light upon the lowly constraint.

You're about to dive into varied and exhaustive ways to read logs and explore constraints more manageably. Helper functions make your code more debugger friendly and minimize time spent diagnosing layout issues. You'll find ideas that will help reduce the pain of reviewing, understanding, and debugging your layout. Read on to learn how to simplify Auto Layout debugging.

Xcode Feedback

Xcode 5 provides constraint feedback throughout the creation of your interfaces. You receive important status updates during *development*, at *compilation*, and at *runtime*. Use them to diagnose and fix layout issues.

Development Feedback

During development, Interface Builder (IB) provides immediate updates on the state of your storyboard and xib layout. As you see in Figure 5-1, constraint colors in the canvas and view outlines express how your layout is functioning. When you see orange (ambiguous) and red (conflicting) items, you know you need to fix problematic layout. The overall color you're aiming for is blue. An interface drawn entirely with blue constraint lines is fully satisfied.

At the top right of the jump bar, the Issue Stepper pop-up details immediate Auto Layout issues. In Figure 5-1, the list warns about problems with frames and conflicting constraints for this storyboard.

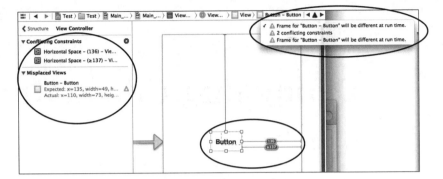

Figure 5-1   Xcode 5 provides cues about the state of your views and constraints under Auto Layout.

An issues pane for each storyboard scene appears in the outline view. You can reach it by clicking the circled arrow associated with problematic scenes. Here, IB lists problems such as conflicting constraints and misplaced views on an issue-by-issue basis.

Compiler Feedback

The Issue Navigator (see Figure 5-2) lists errors and warnings created at compile time. Here, you find items that raise warnings about your layout. These mirror the design-time warnings you see in the Issue Stepper at the top-right of Figure 5-1.

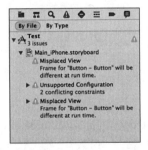

Figure 5-2   Xcode's Issue Navigator lists compile-time interface defects.

Select a warning to open the associated file—in this case the storyboard—and for most warnings, Xcode highlights the problematic item within the file.

Runtime

At runtime, the debugging console at the bottom of the Xcode workspace (see Figure 5-3) offers real-time feedback about the state of Auto Layout issues. Here you find updates that highlight problems sourced from storyboard, xib, and code-based constraint management. You use these messages to diagnose and resolve layout problems in your app.

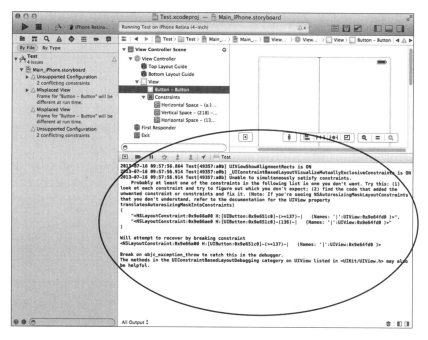

Figure 5-3   The debugging console shows Auto Layout feedback at runtime.

Reading Console Logs

The most common problems you encounter when adding constraints programmatically are ambiguous and unsatisfiable layouts. Expect to spend time at the Xcode debugging console, and don't be surprised when you see a large dump of information that starts with the phrase "Unable to simultaneously satisfy constraints."

Auto Layout does its best during runtime to let you know which constraints could not be satisfied and which constraints it has to break in order to proceed. Often, it suggests a list of constraints that you should evaluate to see which item is causing the problem.

This section introduces two common conflict scenarios and explains the console information provided to you.

Autosizing Issues Example

The console output in Example 5-1 is typical of what you should expect to see in the debugger console. It shows a common Auto Layout message. I have bolded the pertinent parts.

Example 5-1   **Autosizing Console Output**

```
2013-01-31 08:57:42.184 HelloWorld[81805:c07] Unable to simultaneously satisfy
constraints.
        Probably at least one of the constraints in the following list is one you
don't want. Try this: (1) look at each constraint and try to figure out which you
don't expect; (2) find the code that added the unwanted constraint or constraints
and fix it. (Note: If you're seeing NSAutoresizingMaskLayoutConstraints that you
don't understand, refer to the documentation for the UIView property
translatesAutoresizingMaskIntoConstraints)
(
    "<NSAutoresizingMaskLayoutConstraint:0x750f280 h=--& v=--&
H:[UIView:0x7507860(320)]>",
    "<NSAutoresizingMaskLayoutConstraint:0x750d860 h=--& v=--& UILabel:0x7507c70.midX
== + 50>",
    "<NSLayoutConstraint:0x7509c20 UILabel:0x7507c70.centerX == UIView:0x7507860.
centerX>"
)

Will attempt to recover by breaking constraint
<NSLayoutConstraint:0x7509c20 UILabel:0x7507c70.centerX == UIView:0x7507860.centerX>
Break on objc_exception_throw to catch this in the debugger.

The methods in the UIConstraintBasedLayoutDebugging category on UIView listed in
<UIKit/UIView.h> may also be helpful.
```

Here's a breakdown of the message this output displays:

- Logs start with a complaint. In this example, the problem is unsatisfiability. Auto Layout cannot simultaneously satisfy all the constraints currently added to the system.

- An informative message explains what you should do to resolve this issue. Here, you're told to examine a list of constraints and determine which one may be causing your issue.

- Next, you see the list of problem candidates. Each constraint's full description explains the item's role in the interface.

- Sometimes, the Auto Layout system takes action. The next section explains what that action is. In this example, Auto Layout attempts to recover by breaking one of the constraints. It tells you which constraint was affected. Here, it's a centering constraint.

- Finally, you're referred to any further documentation or APIs that may assist you.

Solution: Switch Off Autosizing Translation

Always look carefully at the list of problematic constraints. In Example 5-1, there are three. I highlighted the start of each item, which specifies the item's class. Two of these constraints belong to the NSAutoresizingMaskLayoutConstraint class, and one belongs to NSLayoutConstraint. This is where Auto Layout Debugging Rule 1 may apply.

Auto Layout Debugging Rule 1

When you see autoresizing constraints listed in your console output, check your `translatesAutoresizingMaskIntoConstraints` properties. You may have forgotten to switch this setting off for one or more of your views.

In Example 5-1, in fact, I had added a `UILabel` instance to my view and centered it using Auto Layout constraints, like this:

```
UILabel *label = [self createLabel]; // Create label
[self.view addSubview:label]; // Add to view
centerView(label, 1000); // Add Auto Layout centering
```

I did not, however, prepare it for Auto Layout by switching off the translation property. The translation property defaulted to YES. Auto Layout saw that and created Autosizing constraints on my label's behalf. This was expressed as a pair of layout constraints (`0x750f280` and `0x750d860`).

These constraints conflicted with the Auto Layout constraint (`0x7509c20`) that I created and added. The view was attempting to live in both the Autosizing world and the Auto Layout world at the same time. That's where the problem was born. To fix this situation, I just switched the translate property off:

```
label.translatesAutoresizingMaskIntoConstraints = NO
```

Once I did this, my app recovered and worked as I intended.

You may find it helpful to use an Auto Layout preparation macro so that you don't have to remember the long property name each time you build a new view:

```
#define PREPCONSTRAINTS(VIEW) \
    [VIEW setTranslatesAutoresizingMaskIntoConstraints:NO]
```

Auto Layout Conflicts Example

Rule conflicts represent another common Auto Layout scenario. Your required constraints may contradict each other, as shown in Example 5-2. This console output shows a mismatch between two layout constraints, with Auto Layout breaking one of the two in order to continue.

Example 5-2   **Conflicting Constraint Rules**

```
2013-01-31 09:35:26.157 HelloWorld[82130:c07] Unable to simultaneously satisfy
constraints.
        Probably at least one of the constraints in the following list is one you
don't want. Try this: (1) look at each constraint and try to figure out which you
don't expect; (2) find the code that added the unwanted constraint or constraints
and fix it. (Note: If you're seeing NSAutoresizingMaskLayoutConstraints that you
```

don't understand, refer to the documentation for the UIView property
translatesAutoresizingMaskIntoConstraints)
(
    "<NSLayoutConstraint:0x714e500 **H:|-(80)-[UILabel:0x714bf30]**   (Names:
'|':UIView:0x714bb20)>",
    "<NSLayoutConstraint:0x714e200 **H:|-(50)-[UILabel:0x714bf30]**   (Names:
'|':UIView:0x714bb20)>"
)

Will attempt to recover by breaking constraint
<NSLayoutConstraint:0x714e500 H:|-(80)-[UILabel:0x714bf30]   (Names:
'|':UIView:0x714bb20)>

Break on objc_exception_throw to catch this in the debugger.
The methods in the UIConstraintBasedLayoutDebugging category on UIView listed in
<UIKit/UIView.h> may also be helpful.

Solution: Adjusting Priorities

Auto Layout often makes choices. When two constraints come into conflict, it may recover by
breaking one of the constraints. Here is where Auto Layout Debugging Rule 2 comes
into play.

Auto Layout Debugging Rule 2

Constraints must not contradict each other. Two required constraints cannot ask Auto
Layout to do inconsistent things at the same time. Try removing constraints or adjusting
priorities to resolve the conflict.

The bolded items in Example 5-2 hint at the underlying problem. In this scenario, I added a
label and then told the label to move both 50 and 80 points away from its parent's leading
edge:

```
UILabel *label = [self createLabel]; // create label
[self.view addSubview:label]; // add it
pin(label, @"H:|-50-[view]"); // Place it 50 points in
pin(label, @"H:|-80-[view]"); // Place it 80 points in
```

My pin function added each constraint at a required (1,000) priority. This created an unsatisfiable system. Both rules are required, but they contradict each other. You can satisfy this kind of
conflict by using either of two approaches: going nuclear or balancing the rules.

The Nuclear Approach

The nuclear approach is the simpler of the two. When two constraints conflict, you can kill one
of them. (I mentally imagine a rather juicy "splat" sound.) Deleting either constraint immediately resolves the inconsistency.

This is the best solution for any interface where you didn't *intend* the two constraints to contradict. For example, you may experience this scenario when your code goes up against a layout introduced by IB. Or you may have forgotten to remove older layout requests when tweaking your code. In both cases, extraneous constraints are throwing off your layout.

Constraints should always express your immediate design intent. You should review the constraints being applied and remove any stray items you find. There's nothing sacred about IB-generated items. You can assertively and confidently trim away any rules that stand between you and a great interface.

The Balance Approach

The second approach, the balance approach, involves more nuance. When two rules run counter to each other and both are required, remove the requirement instead of the rule. Adjust the priority of one or both rules until Auto Layout can be satisfied (or, as the great Mick Jagger might say, you "can get satisfaction").

In this example, I actually intended the 50-point offset to act as a fallback priority. Its job was to ensure that my label would have a set position to move to if the 80-point offset went away. Lowering the priority of the 50-point offset allows both rules to coexist and resolves the conflict.

If I have both constraints in place simultaneously, I can animate my button by removing the rule that pins it at the 80-point offset. When the required constraint goes away, Auto Layout expresses the other rule, and the button can move to a well-defined secondary layout position.

Tracing Ambiguity

Auto Layout offers an undocumented tracing feature for iOS that scans an entire view hierarchy for ambiguous layout issues. The _autolayoutTrace method descends the view tree and marks any items of concern. You call it on the key window (although it works just as well on nearly any view in the hierarchy), and it reports a complete ambiguity trace.

You can execute the trace in code, although for obvious reasons, *you shouldn't ship code that references this method*:

```
NSLog(@"%@", [[[UIApplication sharedApplication] keyWindow]
    performSelector:@selector(_autolayoutTrace)]);
```

Or at the debug console, you can use this:

```
(lldb) po [[UIWindow keyWindow] _autolayoutTrace];
$0 = 0x075795f0
*<UIWindow:0x7684a60>
|   *<UILayoutContainerView:0x8ab6300>
|   |   *<UINavigationTransitionView:0x8ab8bb0>
|   |   |   *<UIViewControllerWrapperView:0x719cd90>
|   |   |   |   *<UIView:0x7197c50>
```

```
|    |    |    |    |    *<UILabel:0x71980b0> - AMBIGUOUS LAYOUT
|    |    <UINavigationBar:0x8ab6590>
|    |    |    <_UINavigationBarBackground:0x8ab6250>
|    |    |    |    <UIImageView:0x8ab7110>
|    |    |    <UINavigationItemView:0x8ab96e0>
|    |    |    <UINavigationButton:0x719b0b0>
|    |    |    |    <UIImageView:0xea82380>
|    |    |    |    <UIButtonLabel:0x719bae0>
```

This trace easily finds the troublesome label underlying Example 5-2.

Examining Constraint Logs

Auto Layout console output is self-documenting when you know what to look for. This is the basis of another debugging rule.

Auto Layout Debugging Rule 3

Every logged constraint tells you what it does. The better you understand your logs, the more easily you can identify constraints and connect them to your coding.

The following sections provide examples of constraint logs and explain the items you typically encounter.

Alignment Constraint Example

Example 5-3 shows a basic alignment constraint. It is typical of the kind you may encounter in your logs.

Example 5-3   **A Constraint Log**

```
<NSLayoutConstraint:0x8a64de0 V:|-(0)-[UIView:0x8a64300]
       (Names: '|':UIView:0x8a422f0 )>
```

Here are a few points to consider as you look at this console output:

- Every constraint listing starts with its class. All constraints you create directly belong to the NSLayoutConstraint class, although you may see other classes mentioned in the console output. When that happens, try to figure out why those constraints were created and why your constraints conflict with them.

- The memory addresses matter. Memory addresses help distinguish instances, acting as built-in names for otherwise similar objects. The address for the constraint in Example 5-3 is 0x8a64de0.

- Every constraint offers a self-description. This particular example uses a visual format to explain its role, which I boldfaced. This format reveals that the constraint flush-aligns the top of a view instance (0x8a64300) with its superview (0x8a422f0). Some self-descriptions are based on constraint equations instead.

- The Names section of the log appears in parentheses just after the visual format. You'll see this for superview-to-view visual descriptions. This example expresses a binding between the superview (0x8a422f0) and its mention in the visual format ('|').

- This Names dictionary may be confusing for developers new to Auto Layout. It's there because the single pipe character in the visual format can't associate the superview with a specific instance and its memory reference. Adding the dictionary after the format expresses that binding.

Standard Spacers Example

NSSpace entries (as in Example 5-4) refer to "standard" spaces, specifically 20-point insets from superviews and 8-point boundaries between views. You create this by using hyphen spacers in your formats or when checking the standard constants in IB. You may see this for yourself by generating layouts from hyphen-powered formats, such as "H:|-[view]" and "V:[view1]-[view2]" and then logging the returned constraints.

Example 5-4   **An IB-Sourced Constraint**

```
<NSLayoutConstraint:0x10c3fbf0 H:[UIRoundedRectButton:0x10c3d530]-
    (NSSpace(20))-|(Names: '|':UIView:0x10c3bc20 )>
```

Equation-Based Constraint Example

Not all constraints provide a visual format when logged. Consider Example 5-5. This constraint vertically aligns a button's and a label's centers. This relationship cannot be expressed as a visual format, and the log output uses a mathematical presentation instead. Equation-based constraint listings don't use a Names binding dictionary.

Example 5-5   **A Constraint Equation**

```
<NSLayoutConstraint:0x10c3fc30
    UIRoundedRectButton:0x10c3d530.centerY ==
    UILabel:0x10c3e830.centerY>
```

Complex Equation Example

Example 5-6 shows the console output for a constraint that limits a view's width to half the width of its superview. As you can see, its description includes a little extra math, using a multiplier in the equation.

Example 5-6   **A Constraint with a Multiplier**

```
<NSLayoutConstraint:0x7534dc0 UIView:0x7533780.width ==
    0.5*UIView:0x75334e0.width>
```

You can create this constraint in code but you cannot build the equivalent in IB. IB does not offer multipliers. This is an example of the kind of expressiveness that code-sourced layout offers.

You encounter multipliers whenever you work with aspect ratios and proportional sizes. Example 5-5's constraint derives from a function I built to add grid backsplashes to a view, as shown in Figure 5-4. These consist of two views, each colored light gray. One view covers the vertical left half of the parent, and the other covers the horizontal bottom half. The darker gray portion shows where the two views overlap.

Figure 5-4   The constraint math shown in Example 5-5 allows two overlapping backdrop views to form a grid. The subviews reach halfway across and halfway up their parent. One view appears on the left half of the screen and the other on the bottom half. The section where they overlap appears as the darkest gray.

Each backdrop view is set to hug its parent's edge (respectively, left and bottom), stretch fully in one direction (respectively, vertically and horizontally), and stretch just halfway in the other direction. Multipliers, also called coefficients in some documentation, limit the aspect in relation to other views.

Multiplier and Constant Example

I didn't want to finish up this section without showing you an example of a constant as part of a logged equation. I tweaked Example 5-6's constraint to create Example 5-7's console output. I added a 20-point spacer to the rule that created the proportional sizes. There's no real difference to see between these results and those in Figure 5-4, except the width on the left backdrop extends *ever so slightly* more to the right.

Example 5-7   **A Constraint with a Multiplier and a Constant**

```
<NSLayoutConstraint:0x754d2c0 UIView:0x754cd10.width ==
    0.5*UIView:0x754b390.width + 20>
```

To be fair, I should mention that the times you need to include both a multiplier *and* a constant to your constraints are exceedingly rare. You will have to think long and hard to come up with physical layout examples best described in this way. This is particularly true because the constant cannot be described in respect to the parent's attributes. So, although you may want to place a half-size view one-quarter of the way across its parent, you need to do so with two constraints: one that sets its size and the other that positions its edge.

If you think of a rational use (the best I could come up with is multiple subviews with a fixed leading padding between them and the superview), drop me a note and let me know.

A Note About Layout Math

There's a reason Apple recommends using visual formats whenever possible. Here's an example that demonstrates why. Consider this visual constraint: `@"V:[view1]-50-[view2]"`. Now, quick, which of the following four rules correctly describes the equivalent constraint?

Candidate 1:

```
[NSLayoutConstraint
    constraintWithItem:view1
    attribute:NSLayoutAttributeBottom
    relatedBy:NSLayoutRelationEqual
    toItem:view2
    attribute:NSLayoutAttributeTop
    multiplier:1 constant:50]
```

Candidate 2:

```
[NSLayoutConstraint
    constraintWithItem:view1
    attribute:NSLayoutAttributeBottom
    relatedBy:NSLayoutRelationEqual
    toItem:view2
    attribute:NSLayoutAttributeTop
    multiplier:1 constant:-50]
```

Candidate 3:

```
[NSLayoutConstraint
    constraintWithItem:view2
    attribute:NSLayoutAttributeTop
    relatedBy:NSLayoutRelationEqual
    toItem:view1
    attribute:NSLayoutAttributeBottom
    multiplier:1 constant:50]
```

Candidate 4:

```
[NSLayoutConstraint
    constraintWithItem:view2
    attribute:NSLayoutAttributeTop
    relatedBy:NSLayoutRelationEqual
    toItem:view1
    attribute:NSLayoutAttributeBottom
    multiplier:1 constant:-50]
```

Answers 2 and 3 are correct. Both describe View 2's top as starting 50 points after View 1's bottom ends. As discussed in Chapter 2, "Constraints," if you want to keep the constant positive, you need to make the leading, left, or top attribute item the `firstItem` and the trailing, right, or bottom attribute item the `secondItem`.

Sign errors are a common issue when you're working directly with items because of this unintuitive flow. Whenever possible, use visual formats for view layout. If you must use items, develop and debug a reusable function, method, or macro to implement that layout. This leads to another debugging rule.

Auto Layout Debugging Rule 4

When creating layouts using items instead of formats, *rigorously check your math*. It's way too easy to flip the sign of your constant. And, if you can, *just use formats*.

Constraint Equation Strings

To improve the clarity of my personal logs, I like to be able to produce a string representation of any constraint on demand. I prefer a description that is not tied to each constraint's `description` or `debugDescription`, and one that I can repurpose as needed.

Listing 5-1 transforms constraint instances into simple and clean mathematical representations. Its `stringValue` method describes the algebra stored in each constraint instance to produce a descriptive string. Here are a few examples:

```
<UIView:0x987a640>.leading == <UIButton:0x987a530>.trailing + 8.0
<UIButton:0x987a530>.centerY <= <UIView:0x987a640>.centerY
<UIView:0x714a040>.height == 20.0
<UIView:0x8b50f80>.width == <UIView:0x8b50ce0>.width * 0.5
```

These descriptions are built mechanically. Class methods transform attribute and relation properties into string equivalents. The stringValue method uses these, appending any multiplier and constant. In the end, you retrieve an easy-to-read on-demand description for each constraint.

Listing 5-1   **Describing Constraint Relations as Strings**

```
// Transform the attribute to a string
+ (NSString *) nameForLayoutAttribute: (NSLayoutAttribute) anAttribute
{
    switch (anAttribute)
    {
        case NSLayoutAttributeLeft: return @"left";
        case NSLayoutAttributeRight: return @"right";
        case NSLayoutAttributeTop: return @"top";
        case NSLayoutAttributeBottom: return @"bottom";
        case NSLayoutAttributeLeading: return @"leading";
        case NSLayoutAttributeTrailing: return @"trailing";
        case NSLayoutAttributeWidth: return @"width";
        case NSLayoutAttributeHeight: return @"height";
        case NSLayoutAttributeCenterX: return @"centerX";
        case NSLayoutAttributeCenterY: return @"centerY";
        case NSLayoutAttributeBaseline: return @"baseline";
        case NSLayoutAttributeNotAnAttribute:
        default: return @"not-an-attribute";
    }
}

// Transform the relation to a string
+ (NSString *) nameForLayoutRelation: (NSLayoutRelation) aRelation
{
    switch (aRelation)
    {
        case NSLayoutRelationLessThanOrEqual: return @"<=";
        case NSLayoutRelationEqual: return @"==";
        case NSLayoutRelationGreaterThanOrEqual: return @">=";
        default: return @"not-a-relation";
    }
}
```

```objc
// Represent the constraint as a string
- (NSString *) stringValue
{
    if (!self.firstItem)
        return nil;

    // Establish firstView.firstAttribute
    NSString *firstView = self.firstView.objectName;
    NSString *firstAttribute = [NSLayoutConstraint
        nameForLayoutAttribute:self.firstAttribute];
    NSString *firstString = [NSString stringWithFormat:@"<%@>.%@",
        firstView, firstAttribute];

    // Relation
    NSString *relationString =
        [NSLayoutConstraint nameForLayoutRelation:self.relation];

    // Handle Unary Constraints
    if (self.isUnary)
        return [NSString stringWithFormat: @"%@ %@ %0.01f",
                firstString, relationString, self.constant];

    // Establish secondView.secondAttribute
    NSString *secondView = self.secondView.objectName;
    NSString *secondAttribute = [NSLayoutConstraint
        nameForLayoutAttribute:self.secondAttribute];
    NSString *secondString = [NSString stringWithFormat:
        @"<%@>.%@", secondView, secondAttribute];

    // Initialize right-hand side string
    NSString *rhsRepresentation = secondString;

    // Add multiplier
    if (self.multiplier != 1.0f)
        rhsRepresentation = [NSString stringWithFormat:
            @"%@ * %0.1f", rhsRepresentation, self.multiplier];

    // Initialize constant
    NSString *constantString = @"";

    // Positive constant
    if (self.constant > 0.0f)
        constantString =
            [NSString stringWithFormat:@"+ %0.1f", self.constant];

    // Negative constant
    if (self.constant < 0.0f)
```

```
    constantString =
        [NSString stringWithFormat:@"- %0.1f", fabs(self.constant)];

// Append constant
if (self.constant != 0.0f)
    rhsRepresentation = [NSString stringWithFormat:@"%@ %@",
        rhsRepresentation, constantString];

return [NSString stringWithFormat:@"%@ %@ %@",
    firstString, relationString, rhsRepresentation];
}
```

Adding Names

Working with memory addresses grows very old very fast, especially when they're the only way to identify what object you're working with. Sadly, iOS does not support the NSUserInterfaceItemIdentification protocol. This is an OS X–only feature that adds a custom identity property to any object. It enables you to tag your objects from code or IB and, as discussed in Chapter 3, "Interface Builder Layout," enhances Auto Layout console feedback.

Custom-built object nametags provide another way to annotate objects for easier tracking and viewing, and they do so cross-platform. Listing 5-2 shows an NSObject category that adds simple string-based developer-provided names. It's built around associative references, a feature first introduced in OS X 10.6/iOS 5. Associated objects add key–value storage to an existing class without modifying that class's original declaration. They work by building an association between an Objective-C object and a unique void pointer key. You specify a storage policy such as retain, copy, or assign, and establish whether the assignments are atomic (that is, thread-safe but with a slight performance hit) or not.

Adding these methods to a custom category (Nametags) allows Listing 5-2 to essentially extend all NSObject behavior.

Listing 5-2   **Adding Object Nametags**

```
@implementation NSObject (Nametags)
// Nametag getter
- (id) nametag
{
    return objc_getAssociatedObject(self, @selector(nametag));
}

// Nametag setter
- (void)setNametag:(NSString *) theNametag
{
    objc_setAssociatedObject(self, @selector(nametag),
        theNametag, OBJC_ASSOCIATION_RETAIN_NONATOMIC);
}
```

```
// Return 'Class description : hex memory address'
- (NSString *) objectIdentifier
{
    return [NSString stringWithFormat:@"%@:0x%0x",
        self.class.description, (int) self];
}
```

Using Nametags

I use nametags in ways that push well beyond OS X's identifier properties when I label constraints. Instead of providing individual identities, I create categories that use nametags to group related items by task, such as establishing a view's size or setting its position.

For many tasks, multiple rules express a single design goal. A fully specified view size defines both width and height. Constraining a view to its superview involves no fewer than four rules that limit a view's position and reach. When grouping constraints, nametags treat them as coherent units for the purpose of reference, retrieval, removal, and updating.

Here is an example of this philosophy in action. This method retrieves all position constraints that match a view parameter. It then updates each constant value to the specified point offsets. Nametags allow this code to fetch and update with a minimum of fuss and bother:

```
- (void) repositionView: (UIView *) view atPoint: (CGPoint) point
{
    NSArray *constraints = [self.view
        constraintsNamed:@"Position Constraint" matchingView:view];
    for (NSLayoutConstraint *constraint in constraints)
    {
        if (constraintIsHorizontal(constraint))
            constraint.constant = point.x;
        else
            constraint.constant = point.y;
    }
}
```

Retrieval by name typically follows three patterns:

- You modify constant values on the retrieved collection, as is done here. This constraint update approach is especially friendly for animation and direct manipulation tasks, where you want to tweak views in place so views move or resize as needed. You'll see more of this in Chapter 6, "Building with Auto Layout," and Chapter 7, "Layout Solutions."

- You remove an entire constraint group that's no longer needed. This allows an interface to return to a fallback layout, so you can "close" a drawer view or collapse a spring-loaded folder's icons.

- You remove a constraint group and replace it with a fresh set of new constraints. This is important for any modification that involves properties other than `constant`. When working with installed constraints (that is, constraints that have been added to the Auto Layout system and expressed on live views), you cannot update other properties. I hope the irony of the modifiable property being called `constant` isn't lost on you.

Naming Views

Nametags are not limited to constraints. They also enable you to label views meaningfully— certainly more meaningfully than the default descriptions produced by constraint logs (for example, `UIButton:0x987a530` or `UIView:0x714a040`). These identifiers are produced from the view class and the view memory location.

To use nametags with views, you simply assign a string to a property. Here's a simple example:

```
self.view.nametag = @"RootView"
```

This assignment gives your primary view controller an easy-to-recognize identity for you to use in custom descriptions. The following constraint output better identifies the views involved—in this case the root view and a "contrast view," which was loaded to provide a visual backsplash:

```
<RootView:0x7534660>.bottom >= <ContrastView:0x7534a50>.bottom
```

You can add custom nametags in IB as easily as you would in code. The Identity Inspector (View > Utilities > Show Identity Inspector) provides a User Defined Runtime Attributes tool (see Figure 5-5). Add a `nametag` key path, set its type to String, and set any value you'd like to use.

Figure 5-5   Runtime attributes provide an easy solution for adding custom nametags to IB-designed views.

Describing Views

Your interface's layout isn't limited to `NSLayoutConstraint` instances. Each view may generate its own constraints via its hugging priority, compression resistance priority, and intrinsic content size. Therefore, describing views is just as important as describing constraints. Listing 5-3 details a report-generation method that creates a view description and that lists that view's constraints.

I use this approach to describe views I've built in code. It's even better at helping me understand the layouts I've established in IB than in code. Just load a storyboard or xib and ask for a view report:

```
UIViewController *c = [[UIStoryboard storyboardWithName:@"Storyboard"
    bundle:[NSBundle mainBundle]] instantiateInitialViewController];
NSLog(@"%@", [c.view viewLayoutDescription];
```

Listing 5-3 shows the main report method. It skips several helper items, such as the `readableFrame` method and the platform-sensitive `SIZESTRING`, hug, and resistance macros. (You can find these in the examples in this chapter.) You'll also discover a few more view descriptions that I omitted for space reasons (for example, readable alignment rectangles and view ancestry). Even after these cuts, Listing 5-3 is a big, ugly method.

Here are a couple final notes on this subject:

- Content modes only affect `UIView` instances; they are not part of OS X. Content modes flag how a view lays out content with respect to the view bounds. For example, views can use content mode to stretch their content either proportionally or not, or center it, pin it to the top, left, and so forth. Compiler directives guard the call that displays a view's content model, limiting it to iOS deployment.

- Intrinsic content size defaults to `(-1, -1)`. When you see a pair of `-1`s, you know the view does not express a natural size.

Listing 5-3   View Reports

```
// Create view layout description
- (NSString *) viewLayoutDescription
{
    NSMutableString *description = [NSMutableString string];

    // Specify view address, class, and superclass
    [description appendFormat:@"<%@> %@ : %@",
        self.objectName, self.class.description,
        self.superclass.description];

    // Test for Autosizing and Ambiguous Layout
    if (self.translatesAutoresizingMaskIntoConstraints)
        [description appendFormat:@" [Autosizes]"];
    if (self.hasAmbiguousLayout)
        [description appendFormat:@" [Caution: Ambiguous Layout!]"];
    [description appendString:@"\n"];

    // Show description for autoresizing views
    if (self.translatesAutoresizingMaskIntoConstraints &&
        (self.autoresizingMask != 0))
```

```objc
    [description appendFormat:@"Mask...........%@\n",
        [self maskDescription]];

// Frame and content size
[description appendFormat:@"Frame:.........%@\n",
    self.readableFrame];
[description appendFormat:@"Content size...%@",
    SIZESTRING(self.intrinsicContentSize)];

// Add content mode, but only for iOS
#if TARGET_OS_IPHONE
if ((self.intrinsicContentSize.width > 0) ||
    (self.intrinsicContentSize.height > 0))
    [description appendFormat:@" [Content Mode: %@]",
        [UIView nameForContentMode:self.contentMode]];
#endif
[description appendFormat:@"\n"];

// Content Hugging
[description appendFormat:@"Hugging........[H %d] [V %d]\n",
    (int) HUG_VALUE_H(self), (int) HUG_VALUE_V(self)];

// Compression Resistance
[description appendFormat:@"Resistance.....[H %d] [V %d]\n",
    (int) RESIST_VALUE_H(self), (int) RESIST_VALUE_V(self)];

// Constraint count
[description appendFormat:@"Constraints....%d\n",
    (int) self.constraints.count];

// Constraint listings
int i = 1;
for (NSLayoutConstraint *constraint in self.constraints)
{
    BOOL isLayoutConstraint = [constraint.class isEqual:
        [NSLayoutConstraint class]];

    // List each constraint
    [description appendFormat:@"%2d. ", i++];

    // Display priority only for layout constraints
    if (isLayoutConstraint)
        [description appendFormat:@"@%4d ", (int) constraint.priority];

    // Show constraint
    [description appendFormat:@"%@", constraint.stringValue];
```

```
    // Add non-standard classes
    if (!isLayoutConstraint)
        [description appendFormat:@" (%@)",
            constraint.class.description];

    [description appendFormat:@"\n"];
    }

    return description;
}
```

Unexpected Padding Example

Consider the view report shown in Example 5-8. Generated by the report code in Listing 5-3, it provides much of the information you usually need to know about a view and its constraints. This particular report describes the view shown in Figure 5-6. It tells a story about the view and why it presents the way it does.

Example 5-8   **An Image View Report**

```
<UIImageView:0x8c33c20> UIImageView : UIView
Frame:.........(110 202; 100 100)
Content size...{64, 64} [Content Mode: Center]
Hugging........[H 50] [V 50]
Resistance.....[H 750] [V 750]
Constraints....4
1. @ 250 <UIImageView:0x8c33c20>.width == 100.0
2. @ 250 <UIImageView:0x8c33c20>.height == 100.0
3. <UIImageView:0x8c33c20>.width == 64.0 (NSContentSizeLayoutConstraint)
4. <UIImageView:0x8c33c20>.height == 64.0 (NSContentSizeLayoutConstraint)
```

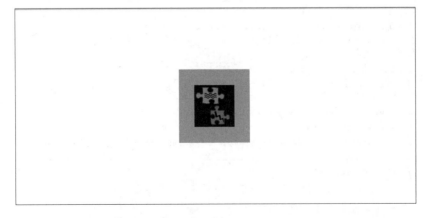

Figure 5-6   An image view with unexpected padding.

The view's class and superclass are listed in the first line of the report. This particular view is a member of the UIImageView class. Its frame is (110 202; 100 100), and it has a 64×64-point content size. Now turn your attention to the image view's light background splash, which indicates the full extent of its frame. This splash reaches well beyond the image it presents. What's going on in this view to create that difference?

The frame is sized 100 points in both directions. This contrasts with the view's intrinsic content size, which is just 64 points on each side. Why doesn't this image occupy the entire frame? The view's content mode tells you why. It uses a center mode, specifically UIViewContentModeCenter. This mode centers content in the view bounds, restricting proportions to match the native data. The 64×64 source cannot reach the view's edges.

Constraints tell the rest of the story. The content hugging priority is just 50 along both axes. Thus, the view's desire to limit padding is outweighed by constraints 1 and 2. Prioritized at a higher value (250), these two constraints expand the width and height of the view beyond the intrinsic content.

Even the two system-generated size constraints (3 and 4) cannot overrule the layout. These two constraints list no specific priorities because the class implementation is internal to Apple, and the exposed values are generally nonsense. The actual priorities are set by any hugging and resistance numbers you assign to each axis.

These priorities are expressed internally by NSContentSizeLayoutConstraint instances and factored into the linear algebra satisfaction system that powers Auto Layout.

The Hugged Image Example

This example considers the opposite problem just examined. Figure 5-7 shows an image view whose size was constrained to 100×100 points and whose content mode allows it to scale to fill available space. The problem? As both the screenshot and the report in Example 5-9 reveal, the view is still just 64×64 points in size. Why?

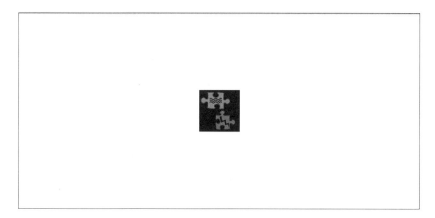

Figure 5-7   This image view is much smaller than its requested size.

Example 5-9   **A Small Image View Report**

```
<UIImageView:0x8d3bd80> UIImageView : UIView
Frame:.........(131 223; 64 64)
Content size...{64, 64} [Content Mode: Scale Aspect Fill]
Hugging........[H 750] [V 750]
Resistance.....[H 750] [V 750]
Constraints....4
 1. @ 500 <UIImageView:0x8d3bd80>.width == 100.0
 2. @ 500 <UIImageView:0x8d3bd80>.height == 100.0
 3. <UIImageView:0x8d3bd80>.width == 64.0 (NSContentSizeLayoutConstraint)
 4. <UIImageView:0x8d3bd80>.height == 64.0 (NSContentSizeLayoutConstraint)
```

The answer lies, again, with relative priorities. In this example, I ramped up the hugging priorities for both axes to 750. Constraints 1 and 2, with their 500 priorities, are overruled by constraints 3 and 4.

The frame wants to be exactly 100 points along each dimension, but it only wants this at a 500 priority. It also wants to hug the intrinsic content, which is just 64×64 points in size. And it wants this *more*. The 750 priorities of the hugging request win out over the 500 priority size requests. The resulting frame is expressed with just a 64×64 point size.

There's an important lesson to pay attention to here, and Auto Layout Debugging Rule 5 spells it out.

Auto Layout Debugging Rule 5

Content compression resistance and content hugging are first-class players in Auto Layout. Their priorities can and will overrule layout constraints. Don't forget to review these values when debugging your layouts.

View Centering Example

There is a big story missing from the previous two reports. Nowhere in those listings do the reports describe how their image view is centered in its superview. None of the constraints listed in this report mention the view's position, and yet the ambiguity warning in Listing 5-3 does not trigger. That's because position constraints are always installed higher up the view hierarchy. Looking at the parent view's report, which is shown in Example 5-10, immediately clears up this mystery. Its parent owns two constraints that reference this image view, assigning its center position.

Positioning constraints are *always* added to superviews. You cannot describe a view's location by using constraints installed directly to that view.

Example 5-10 **Looking at the Parent's Constraints**

```
<RootView:0x8c33970> UIView : UIResponder
Frame:.........(0 0; 320 504)
Hugging........[H 250] [V 250]
Resistance.....[H 750] [V 750]
Constraints....2
1. @1000 <UIImageView:0x8c33c20>.centerX == <RootView:0x8c33970>.centerX
2. @1000 <UIImageView:0x8c33c20>.centerY == <RootView:0x8c33970>.centerY
```

Retrieving Referencing Constraints

Constraints that reference a view can occur in nearly any view ancestor, from the view itself all the way up to the root of the hierarchy. This leads to Auto Layout Debugging Rule 6.

Auto Layout Debugging Rule 6

When debugging, you must consider all constraints your view participates in, not just the ones installed directly to the view itself. Constraint references may reside in any ancestor view and positioning references will *always* reside in ancestor views.

With this rule in mind, consider the methods in Listing 5-4. They retrieve an exhaustive array of constraints that reference any given view:

- The first method is `refersToView:`. It's a constraint method that returns a Boolean value. It indicates whether the passed view is mentioned as the constraint's first or second item.

- The second method is `referencingConstraintsInSuperviews`. A view method, it ascends the view tree to find all constraints in superviews that contain a reference to the given view, either as `firstItem` or `secondItem`. When applied to Example 5-9's image view, it would easily find the two constraints installed to its superview.

- The third method is `referencingConstraints`. Another view method, it combines any references from the superviews with any references it finds in its own constraints. Don't forget that you install sibling constraints to a parent. A view may contain constraints that don't reference itself at all. Testing each constraint allows you to select just those items that provide concrete references.

This combined array returned from `referencingConstraints` equates to the one you find in IB's Size Inspector for any selected view. It offers a full list of installed constraints that mention the view in question.

Both methods reject any constraints that don't directly belong to the `NSLayoutConstraint` class. This excludes Autosizing constraints and system-generated hugging and resistance size constraints.

Listing 5-4   **Exhaustively Finding Referencing Constraints**

```
// (NSLayoutConstraint) Test for view reference
- (BOOL) refersToView: (VIEW_CLASS *) theView
{
    if (!theView)
        return NO;
    if (!self.firstItem) // shouldn't happen. Illegal
        return NO;
    if (self.firstItem == theView)
        return YES;
    if (!self.secondItem)
        return NO;
    return (self.secondItem == theView);
}


// (View) Return referencing constraints from superviews
// The superviews property is a custom class extension and does not
// ship with UIView/NSView by default
- (NSArray *) referencingConstraintsInSuperviews
{
    NSMutableArray *array = [NSMutableArray array];
    for (VIEW_CLASS *view in self.superviews)
    {
        for (NSLayoutConstraint *constraint in view.constraints)
        {
            if (![constraint.class isEqual:
                [NSLayoutConstraint class]])
                continue;

            if ([constraint refersToView:self])
                [array addObject:constraint];
        }
    }
    return array;
}


// (View) Return all constraints that reference this view
- (NSArray *) referencingConstraints
{
    NSMutableArray *array =
        [self.referencingConstraintsInSuperviews mutableCopy];
    for (NSLayoutConstraint *constraint in self.constraints)
    {
        if (![constraint.class isEqual:
            [NSLayoutConstraint class]])
            continue;
```

```
        if ([constraint refersToView:self])
            [array addObject:constraint];
    }
    return array;
}
```

Descent Reports

Generally, you'll want to provide reports for every view that participates in a given hierarchy. This allows you to see a full overview of the interface and enables you to inspect your layout and search for any potential issues.

Listing 5-5 offers an example of how you might approach this problem. This method descends the view hierarchy, creating reports for each view in the tree.

Listing 5-5   **Iterating Through View Subviews**

```
- (void) showViewReport: (BOOL) descend
{
    // Print view layout description for this view
    printf("%s\n", self.viewLayoutDescription.UTF8String);
    if (!descend) return;

    // Continue down the hierarchy?
    // This is described for Listing 5-6, which follows
    for (Class class in [self skippableClasses])
        if ([self isKindOfClass:class])
            return;

    // Recurse on children
    for (VIEW_CLASS *view in self.subviews)
        [view showViewReport: descend];
}
```

There's a problem, however, in performing an exhaustive descent. You don't want to descend into the custom subviews Apple uses to create system-supplied view classes like buttons, switches, and navigation bars. These classes are complex and detailed. They're also, mostly, not your concern as a developer.

Listing 5-6 offers a workaround. It stops the descent wherever it finds a "do not continue" class. This provides a way for you to concentrate on your views and your implementation details, without having to keep track of any system-created interface classes.

The classes listed in the skippableClasses method are absolutely arbitrary. Feel free to edit, tweak, or just replace the entire list. You can throw in new items as needed when your logs descend too low. You can also remove items that you really don't want in there. There's nothing magical about the list. If you have any specific improvement suggestions, please contact me and let me know.

Sadly, checking for UI and NS prefixes doesn't work here. There are good reasons you add subviews to standard class instances. To take the most obvious example, you do want to descend into UIView instances rather than treat them as atomic endpoints.

Listing 5-6   **Avoiding Exhaustive Descent While Inspecting Views**

```
- (NSArray *) skippableClasses
{
#if TARGET_OS_IPHONE
    return @[
            [UIButton class], [UILabel class], [UISwitch class],
            [UIStepper class], [UITextField class],
            [UIScrollView class], // Includes tables & collections
            [UIActivityIndicatorView class], [UIAlertView class],
            [UIPickerView class], [UIProgressView class],
            [UIToolbar class], [UINavigationBar class],
            [UISearchBar class], [UITabBar class],
            ];
#elif TARGET_OS_MAC
    // Left as an exercise for the reader
    return @[];
#endif
}

- (void) displayViewReports
{
    printf("%s\n", self.viewLayoutDescription.UTF8String);

    for (Class class in [self skippableClasses])
        if ([self isKindOfClass:class])
            return;

    for (VIEW_CLASS *view in self.subviews)
        [view displayViewReports];
}
```

Ambiguity Example

Example 5-11 examines the issue of ambiguity. Figure 5-8 shows the interface in question. This screenshot consists of a parent view with a single square child view. The fact that the view appears to be partially offscreen offers a hint of the underlying problem.

Figure 5-8   The child view in this example is underconstrained. Its vertical position is unknown.

This is where Auto Layout Debugging Rule 7 comes into play.

Auto Layout Debugging Rule 7

Common visual indications of underconstrained layout include missing views, partially displayed views, and random positions.

In this example, the child's vertical position is, in fact, unspecified. Because of this, the child has ambiguous layout. Just one constraint describes the view's position in its superview. In this case, it's the left edge offset. To fix this problem, add a centering or edge-positioning constraint to fix the vertical position.

Note

Views with undefined intrinsic content size report {-1, -1} as their `intrinsicContentSize` property. UIKit provides the corresponding `UIViewNoIntrinsicMetric` constant.

Apple writes, "Note that not all views have an `intrinsicContentSize`. `UIView`'s default implementation is to return (`UIViewNoIntrinsicMetric`, `UIViewNoIntrinsicMetric`). The *intrinsic* content size is concerned only with data that is in the view itself, not in other views."

Example 5-11   **Looking at the Parent's Constraints**

```
<RootView:0x71331c0> UIView : UIResponder
Frame:.........(0 0; 320 504)
Content size...{-1, -1}
Hugging........[H 250] [V 250]
Resistance.....[H 750] [V 750]
Constraints....1
1. @1000 <V0:0x7133370>.left == <RootView:0x71331c0>.left + 211.0
```

```
<V0:0x7133370> UIView : UIResponder   [Caution: Ambiguous Layout!]
Frame:.........(211 -25; 50 50)
Content size...{-1, -1}
Hugging........[H 250] [V 250]
Resistance.....[H 750] [V 750]
Constraints....2
1. @1000 <V0:0x7133370>.width == 50.0
2. @1000 <V0:0x7133370>.height == 50.0
```

Expanding on Console Dumps Example

Imagine that you're in the middle of developing an application. You run a test, and Xcode complains about conflicting constraints, producing the following console output (where I bold-faced the parts that matter):

```
2013-01-29 12:14:23.336 HelloWorld[54631:c07] Unable to simultaneously satisfy
constraints.
        Probably at least one of the constraints in the following list is one you
don't want. Try this: (1) look at each constraint and try to figure out which you
don't expect; (2) find the code that added the unwanted constraint or constraints
and fix it. (Note: If you're seeing NSAutoresizingMaskLayoutConstraints that you
don't understand, refer to the documentation for the UIView property
translatesAutoresizingMaskIntoConstraints)
(
    "<NSLayoutConstraint:0x755f2a0 H:|-(100)-[UIView:0x755e510](LTR)    (Names:
'|':UIView:0x755e260 )>",
    "<NSLayoutConstraint:0x755ef70 H:|-(118)-[UIView:0x755e510](LTR)    (Names:
'|':UIView:0x755e260 )>"
)

Will attempt to recover by breaking constraint
<NSLayoutConstraint:0x755ef70 H:|-(118)-[UIView:0x755e510](LTR)    (Names:
'|':UIView:0x755e260 )>

Break on objc_exception_throw to catch this in the debugger.
The methods in the UIConstraintBasedLayoutDebugging category on UIView listed in
<UIKit/UIView.h> may also be helpful.
```

The dump contains a lot of information, but it's clear that a view (0x755e510) wants to be both 100 and 118 points away from its parent's left edge. (The LTR acronym refers to left-to-right layout.) Which view is it?

You can try to track back the view using the standard debugging tools, or you can quickly peruse the report in Example 5-12 to connect the address with the name you assigned. The report provides additional detail, showing where the conflicting constraints have been installed (specifically, the root view) and which view (v0) is causing the problem.

Note that the v0 view does not warn about ambiguity in Example 5-12. This report was generated after Auto Layout had automatically broken Constraint 1. The constraint remains attached to the parent, but it no longer has an effect over layout.

Example 5-12   **Expanding on Console Dumps**

```
<RootView:0x755e260> UIView : UIResponder
Frame:........(0 0; 320 504)
Content size...{-1, -1}
Hugging........[H 250] [V 250]
Resistance.....[H 750] [V 750]
Constraints....3
1. @1000 <V0:0x755e510>.left == <RootView:0x755e260>.left + 118.0
2. @1000 <V0:0x755e510>.top == <RootView:0x755e260>.top + 124.0
3. @1000 <V0:0x755e510>.left == <RootView:0x755e260>.left + 100.0

<V0:0x755e510> UIView : UIResponder
Frame:........(100 124; 50 50)
Content size...{-1, -1}
Hugging........[H 250] [V 250]
Resistance.....[H 750] [V 750]
Constraints....2
1. @1000 <V0:0x755e510>.width == 50.0
2. @1000 <V0:0x755e510>.height == 50.0
```

Visualizing Constraints

When developing for OS X, you can visualize constraints on demand. You pass a request to any window, adding a list of constraints you want to see. Figure 5-9 shows a display that might result from doing this.

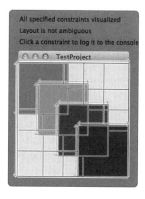

Figure 5-9   When visualized, clickable constraint lines appear over a window.

Click any constraint to log it to the console. When many constraints are shown in the same area, Xcode lists whatever constraints might apply to your click. As Example 5-13 shows, OS X constraint feedback differs slightly from iOS feedback. AppKit output can often be a little more detailed.

Example 5-13   **Output from Visualized Constraints**

```
2013-01-31 13:01:24.997 TestProject[85253:303] Clicked on overlapping
visualized constraints: (
    "<NSLayoutConstraint:0x100138980 H:[TestView:0x1001379d0(100)]>
        (Actual Distance - pixels):100",
    "<NSLayoutConstraint:0x100139570 V:|-(>=0)-[TestView:0x1001379d0]
        (Names: '|':NSView:0x100510800 )> (Actual Distance - pixels):80",
    "<NSLayoutConstraint:0x10013a6b0 V:|-(80@501)-[TestView:0x1001379d0]
        priority:501    (Names: '|':NSView:0x100510800 )>
        (Actual Distance - pixels):80"
)
```

Automating Visualization

In OS X, you can easily tie constraint visualization to a menu item during your development process. Listing 5-7 offers an example of an IB-friendly method that toggles constraints on and off. Hook it up to a menu item, and you're ready to switch constraint visualization at will.

Listing 5-7   **Toggling Constraints**

```
// Toggle constraint view on and off
- (IBAction)toggleConstraintView:(id)sender
{
    // allConstraints returns an exhaustive recursive collection
    // of constraints from self and subviews
    [_window visualizeConstraints:
        alreadyShowingConstraints ? nil : [self.view allConstraints]];
    alreadyShowingConstraints = !alreadyShowingConstraints;
}
```

In Figure 5-9, the layout is unambiguous, and all the constraints live happily with each other. You more generally want to view constraints when the layout can't be satisfied. An interesting alternative exists to showing the overlay on each run or using a menu item to toggle the presentation. Instead, you can tell your OS X application to automatically display whenever there is a conflict. A simple launch argument called NSConstraintBasedLayoutVisualizeMutuallyExclusiveConstraints brings up the constraint overlay for conflicted debug builds.

Launch Arguments

Xcode's scheme editor enables you to add launch arguments, which are passed to your app as default settings. These are undocumented and typically specific to debug builds. In addition, they are subject to change, and Apple can remove them at any time.

Launch arguments enable you to add runtime conditions or visualize onscreen items, which means they provide valuable ways to customize your testing environment. Here's the basic process you use to add them to a project:

1. Select Product > Scheme > Edit Scheme. (Alternatively, use the pop-up at the top left of the editor to the right of the stop button. Make sure to pull down on the project name and not on the selected platform.)

2. When the scheme editor opens, select your Run scheme and open the Arguments tab.

3. Add a new argument by clicking Arguments Passed on Launch > + or delete one by selecting it and clicking –. Note that an argument starts with a hyphen, followed by the argument name (for example, `AppleTextDirection`) followed by a value, typically `YES` or `NO`.

4. Make your changes and then click OK to close the scheme editor.

Figure 5-10 shows an example of the kinds of items you might add. Checked boxes are applied at launch, and unchecked items are skipped. When the app launches, especially on iOS, you may see console confirmation for arguments that have "taken." Here's an example:

```
2013-01-29 12:41:53.467 HelloWorld[55067:c07] UIViewShowAlignmentRects is ON
```

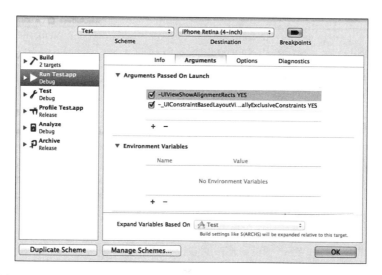

Figure 5-10   You add custom runtime arguments in Xcode's scheme editor.

When you add the "visualize automatically" launch option on OS X, you're assured that if any constraint conflicts arise, the purple overlay will automatically appear. Other helpful launch arguments enable you to visualize alignment rectangles for your views and to test internationalization. Table 5-1 offers a highly unscientific list of launch arguments and their effects.

Table 5-1   **Launch Arguments**

Argument	System	Value	Effect
NSShowAllViews	OS X	YES	Adds an outline around each view in the window.
NSViewShowAlignmentRects	OS X	YES	Displays alignment rectangles over views.
UIViewShowAlignmentRects	iOS	YES	Displays alignment rectangles over views.
NSDoubleLocalizedStrings	iOS, OS X	YES	Forces strings to be repeated, to more rigorously test internationalization.
AppleTextDirection and NSForceRightToLeftWritingDirections	OS X	YES YES	Forces RTL presentation, regardless of the system language.
NSConstraintBasedLayoutVisualize MutuallyExclusiveConstraints	OS X	YES	Automatically visualizes constraints upon encountering layout conflicts.

Other items that are mentioned in frameworks that do not seem to be implemented (at least not in any meaningful way for developers) include the following:

- UIConstraintBasedLayoutEngageNonLazily and
  NSConstraintBasedLayoutEngageNonLazily

  These are likely tied to the requiresConstraintBasedLayout calls that force a view to use constraint-based layout.

  In the header file for this method, Apple writes, "Constraint-based layout engages lazily when someone tries to use it (e.g., adds a constraint to a view). If you do all of your constraint set up in updateConstraints, you might never even receive updateConstraints if no one makes a constraint. To fix this chicken and egg problem, override this method to return YES if your view needs the window to use constraint-based layout."

- UIConstraintBasedLayoutPlaySoundWhenEngaged,
  UIConstraintBasedLayoutPlaySoundOnUnsatisfiable,
  NSConstraintBasedLayoutPlaySoundWhenEngaged, and
  NSConstraintBasedLayoutPlaySoundOnUnsatisfiable

- `UIConstraintBasedLayoutVisualizeMutuallyExclusiveConstraints`

  This may turn out to be the iOS counterpart of the working OS X argument.

- `UIConstraintBasedLayoutLogUnsatisfiable` and
  `NSConstraintBasedLayoutLogUnsatisfiable`

Note that some of these options seem to be "engagable" when prefixed with underscores, but nothing much otherwise happens. This console output shows that Xcode has responded to at least a couple of options:

```
2013-01-26 21:41:48.844 HelloWorld[13704:c07]
_UIConstraintBasedLayoutVisualizeMutuallyExclusiveConstraints is ON
2013-01-26 21:45:25.100 HelloWorld[13806:c07]
_UIConstraintBasedLayoutPlaySoundWhenEngaged is ON
```

Internationalization

You can use two sets of launch arguments to stress test your apps for worldwide deployment. These are string doubling and interface flipping. The first is available for both iOS and OS X. The second works only with OS X, but you'll learn a way around that in the sections that follow.

Doubled Strings (iOS/OS X)

Adding `NSDoubleLocalizedStrings` to your debug scheme doubles the text shown in any localized project. This is most useful in early development, when you have not yet translated your strings.

Doubling strings helps you plan for locales where phrases tend to run long. The English "Car Info" may become the German "Information zum Auto." Those strings may not arrive with enough advance time to calculate your largest extents. String doubling comes to the rescue in such a case, offering immediate ways to check size outliers.

You internationalize your text normally when using this feature using `NSLocalizedString()` to load localized text, as in this example:

```
[button setTitle:NSLocalizedString(@"changelabel", nil)
    forState:UIControlStateNormal];
```

The launch argument takes care of the rest, doubling each localized string in place. Figure 5-11 shows a simple interface without and with string doubling, respectively.

The "good enough" interface in the left image in Figure 5-11 quickly breaks down under doubled text, as shown in the right image. The buttons are enormous, the labels are badly clipped, and the value field has disappeared entirely. This graphical user interface (GUI) is ripe for reevaluation.

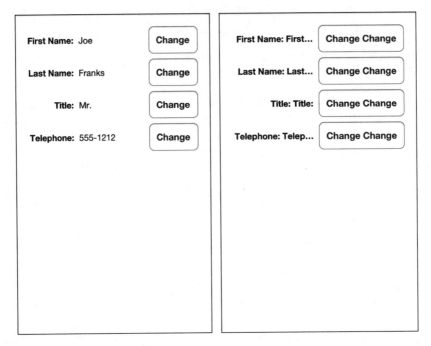

Figure 5-11   String doubling stress tests your interfaces, enabling you to test layout before receiving translation files.

Doubled text offers a valuable tool for finding weak points by stressing the entire interface at once. You disable the argument by either unchecking it in the scheme editor or deleting the argument entry.

Flipped Interfaces (OS X)

Under OS X, you can easily flip your interface to test right-to-left layout without changing system languages. Set both `AppleTextDirection` and `NSForceRightToLeftWritingDirection` to `YES` in your scheme's launch arguments (see Figure 5-12).

Figure 5-12   Flipping text directions tests deployment for right-to-left language locales.

These arguments leave your development language intact; they don't change the locale. Instead, they allow you to see how your interface reacts to left/right flipping for deployment to locations like Saudi Arabia or Israel.

Here is where you find any problems with left/leading or right/trailing confusion. Left and right always refer to the physical left and right edges of the screen. You use those constraints to place items users have physically dragged into place. Leading and trailing refer to logical interface flow. You use them to place views in a way that a user's eyes naturally scans. A right-to-left writing direction only affects leading and trailing constraints. Right and left constraints remain unaffected.

Flipped Interfaces (iOS)

iOS supports two right-to-left languages at this time: Arabic and Hebrew. If you want to test interface flipping, add either an `ar.lproj` or `He.lproj` localization to your project and test the interface under that language.

The following instructions walk you through the language selection process. These steps are designed to work in iOS 7, regardless of the currently selected language so that you don't get stuck in Japanese or French, unable to find your way back to English. Please note these steps have changed since iOS 6.

This walkthrough assumes that you're testing on the simulator, but the same steps apply to device testing:

1. If you are running an application, press Command+Shift+H (Hardware > Home) or press the Home button.

2. Choose Settings (a silver icon with a series of geared wheels that usually appears on the first page of simulator icons).

3. Choose General. This is on the main settings page on iPhones, and it is in the left column on tablets. It shows a smaller version of the geared icon and should be easy to spot when you're scrolling up and down the main page.

4. Choose International. This one can be difficult to spot. In iOS 7, it usually appears in the third group from the bottom. From the bottom of the screen, going up, you find a single item section with Reset. Above that you find iTunes Wi-Fi Sync, VPN, and Profiles. (If you're on the simulator, this group may not appear.) The final item in the group above that is International. Select it. (On iOS 6, this is the third item from the top in General settings. It appears in the middle of the second group of options.)

Figure 5-13 shows the location of International in iOS 7.

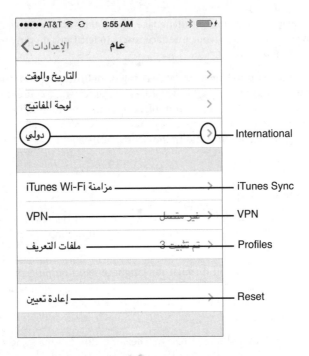

Figure 5-13   Locate the International option in the General settings.

5. In International settings, choose the first item in the first group (see Figure 5-14). This option enables you to choose a specific language.

Figure 5-14   Choose the first item to pick a new language.

6. Choose any language from the pop-up. Each language appears in its localized format, so you'll easily be able to spot English. Tap the top-right button (see Figure 5-15) to confirm your change. The screen goes black, and the device updates to match your choice. Click the top-left button to cancel.

Figure 5-15   The top-right button is Done. Cancel is at the top left.

Once you apply a right-to-left language in iOS settings, you can test left/leading or right/trailing constraints and ensure that they work as designed.

> **Note**
>
> If you do not include a language-approriate *lproj* for your application, the app reverts to English layout regardless of system settings.

Profiling Cocoa Layout

Instruments offers an OS X–only Cocoa Layout profiling tool. You attach it just as you would any other tool, like leak monitoring or memory allocation tracing. Chose Product > Profile and select the Cocoa Layout template (see Figure 5-16).

Figure 5-16   The Cocoa Layout template profiles Auto Layout.

Instruments tracks your layout, showing where and when constraints are added to or removed from views and when constants are modified. You can see this in Figure 5-17, which shows an ongoing session.

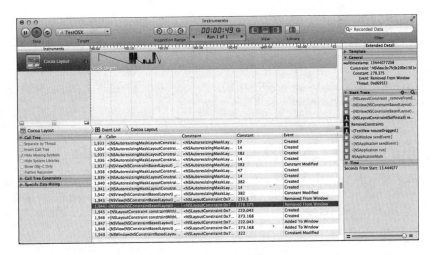

Figure 5-17   A Cocoa Layout session monitors constraint changes within your interface.

Several constraints were affected when I rapidly moved items around and resized the window, forcing the interface to update. You see this reflected in the trace. Constraint-related events appear in the stack trace on the right-hand side. These are instances of my self-install utilities removing my constraints from the system during drags. The profiler tracks all constraints participating in Auto Layout, including Autosizing and content size items.

To be honest, this tool has limited utility, at least in its current incarnation. I'm curious to see where Apple goes with it, especially if and when it makes the leap to iOS.

Auto Layout Rules of Debugging

Here's a summary of the debugging rules mentioned earlier in this chapter. This list is by no means exhaustive:

- When you see autoresizing constraints listed in your console output, check your `translatesAutoresizingMaskIntoConstraints` properties. You may have forgotten to switch this setting off for one or more of your views.

- Required constraints must not contradict each other. Two required constraints cannot ask Auto Layout to do inconsistent things at the same time. Try removing constraints or adjusting priorities to resolve a conflict.

- Every logged constraint tells you what it does. The better you understand your logs, the more easily you can identify constraints and connect them to your coding.

- When creating layouts using items instead of formats, *rigorously check your math*. It's way too easy to flip the sign of your constant. And, if you can, just use formats.

- Content compression resistance and content hugging are first-class players in Auto Layout. Their priorities can and will overrule layout constraints. Don't forget to review these values when debugging your layouts.

- When debugging, you must consider all constraints that your view participates in, not just the ones installed directly to the view itself. Constraint references may reside in any ancestor view and positioning references will *always* reside in ancestor views.

- Common indications of underconstrained layout include missing views, partially displayed views, and random positions.

Exercises

After reading this chapter, test your knowledge with these exercises:

1. IB finds Auto Layout issues at design time and compile time. Why worry about runtime and the console?

2. What role do multipliers play in constraints?

3. An image view appears clipped, showing only about half its vertical content. What might be wrong?

4. A visual constraint leaves 20 vertical points between `item1` and `item2` (`V:[item1]-20-[item2]`). What sign is the constant in the constraint produced by this format? Why? If you multiply the constant by –1, what happens to the layout?

5. IB reports a fully satisfied, unambiguous layout. At runtime, one or more views express ambiguity. Why might this be?

6. A view appears properly placed until you test your application using an Arabic localization. In Arabic, the view placement is flipped horizontally. Why might this be?

Conclusions

This chapter introduces many ways you can inspect, understand, and correct the constraints that shape your interface. Here are a few final thoughts:

- Tags and identifiers are your friends, not your enemies. Use whatever resources you can to help understand and label each view and constraint. The more you understand your interface, the better you will debug it. As you will discover in Chapter 6, tagging constraint groups can be *wicked useful*.

- Just because IB adds a constraint at your request doesn't make that layout *right*. *Unambiguous* does not necessarily equate to *correct*. Trim away any constraint that doesn't fit your interface vision and adjust the ones that remain to match your design goals. The largest part of the debugging process is tracking down what items are standing between you and a well-functioning app.

- Design incrementally. You'll get a lot less grief at the console when fewer things are breaking at any time.

- Don't be afraid of conflicting constraints. Adding multiple rules that cover the same ground is *fine*. Just adjust the priorities so that your interfaces express the behaviors you want without killing Auto Layout.

Building with Auto Layout

Designing for Auto Layout changes the way you build interfaces. It's a descriptive system that steps away from exact metrics like frames and centers. You focus on expressing relationships between views, describing how items follow one another onscreen. You uncover the natural relationships in your design and detail them through constraint-based rules.

In return, your interfaces gain flexibility. Auto Layout articulates many more conditions than "allow this view to stretch" and "pin this edge." Its design vocabulary leapfrogs past Autosizing's springs and struts to provide a more nimble and serious visual construction language.

This chapter introduces the expressiveness of Auto Layout design, spotlighting its underlying philosophy and offering examples that showcase its features.

Basic Principles of Auto Layout

Exact measures, such as widths, heights, origins, and centers, are the hallmark of traditional layout. Before Auto Layout, you'd create a view, set its frame, tweak its resizing mask, and add it to a parent. Under Auto Layout, the focus shifts toward relationships. You build in a new way, describing the way views relate to each other. Here are a few points to keep in mind about Auto Layout:

- **Auto Layout is declarative**—You add rules to the system to express interface layout. The runtime system implements those rules on your behalf.

- **Auto Layout minimizes calculation**—You specify the layout, not the points and pixels.

- **Auto Layout design is indirect, but it's also very flexible**—Views require fewer updates for changed window geometries, and they decompose more readily into maintainable layout components.

- **Auto Layout is driven by geometry**—Its basic language terms are natural geometric properties such as edges, centers, and sizes.

- **Auto Layout focuses on relationships**—You relate view layouts to each other using geometric equalities and inequalities, shifting from absolute terms to relative ones.

- **Auto Layout allows and even encourages conflicting rules**—Prioritized rules are an essential component of Auto Layout. They enable you to add low-priority fallback conditions and high-priority boundary limits to build sophisticated interfaces.

- **Auto Layout expresses natural content**—Intrinsic view content drives sizing and alignment, offering content a key role in layout.

- **Auto Layout seeks optimal solutions**—It determines the best layout it can, given the rules you supply and variably sized contents and containers.

- **Auto Layout is distributed**—Its naturally decomposed layouts support clean implementation, with few dependencies between components.

Layout Libraries

Two common challenges in day-to-day development are addressed by building layout libraries: redundancy and density. By creating libraries of reusable code, you help fight these two natural obstacles.

Auto Layout is *redundant*—exceedingly so. You often perform the same tasks over and over again: Center this view, stretch that view to its parent, or lay out these views in a row or column. Layouts you create for one app often apply to others. There's no reason you shouldn't reuse code you've already debugged and refined in multiple projects.

Auto Layout code in its most natural form is *dense*, verbose bordering on illegible. Consider the code in Example 6-1. These method calls do little more than create a view, size it (100×80 points), and center it in its superview. This snippet highlights common frustrations in working directly with constraint calls: difficulties with inspection, validation, and self-documentation. That's an awful lot of code for doing so little, especially for such simple layout.

Example 6-1   **Auto Layout Code Density**

```
UIView *childView = [[UIView alloc] initWithFrame:CGRectZero];
[parentView addSubview:childView];

// Prepare for Auto Layout
childView.translatesAutoresizingMaskIntoConstraints = NO;

// Width is 100
constraint = [NSLayoutConstraint
    constraintWithItem:childView
    attribute:NSLayoutAttributeWidth
    relatedBy:NSLayoutRelationEqual
    toItem:nil
    attribute:NSLayoutAttributeNotAnAttribute
```

```
    multiplier:1
    constant:100];
[parentView addConstraint:constraint];

// Height is 80
constraint = [NSLayoutConstraint
    constraintWithItem:childView
    attribute:NSLayoutAttributeHeight
    relatedBy:NSLayoutRelationEqual
    toItem:nil
    attribute:NSLayoutAttributeNotAnAttribute
    multiplier:1
    constant:80];
[parentView addConstraint:constraint];

// Center X
constraint = [NSLayoutConstraint
    constraintWithItem:childView
    attribute:NSLayoutAttributeCenterX
    relatedBy:NSLayoutRelationEqual
    toItem:parentView
    attribute:NSLayoutAttributeCenterX
    multiplier:1
    constant:0];
[parentView addConstraint:constraint];

// Center Y
constraint = [NSLayoutConstraint
    constraintWithItem:childView
    attribute:NSLayoutAttributeCenterY
    relatedBy:NSLayoutRelationEqual
    toItem:parentView
    attribute:NSLayoutAttributeCenterY
    multiplier:1
    constant:0];
[parentView addConstraint:constraint];
```

Building Libraries

Many developers build libraries of constraint actions. These libraries transform Auto Layout from impenetrable to an essential development tool. Contrast Example 6-1 with Example 6-2. The two are functionally equivalent, performing exactly the same tasks, but the latter leverages a library of macro definitions. It's short, it's easy to follow, and it's essentially self-documenting.

Example 6-2   **Simple Macros**

```
UIView *childView = [[UIView alloc] initWithFrame:CGRectZero];
[parentView addSubview:childView];
PREPCONSTRAINTS(childView);
CONSTRAIN_SIZE(childView, 100, 80);
CENTER(childView);
```

Many constraint expressions are just one-line calls. Macros provide a good match to these. Often, constraints simply relate a view to its superview, or two views to each other, lining up centers or edges with optional offsets. These requests are easily encapsulated, exposing a simple parameter or two.

Although Example 6-2 is much simpler to read and understand than Example 6-1, it's also more limited. These macros install constraints at a single priority and don't expose those constraints for any form of annotation or grouping. In other words, these macros best provide a solution for super-simple layouts. The approach quickly shows its limitations for any sophisticated design.

Example 6-3 may not be as readable as Example 6-2, but it adds priority and annotation features for controlled layout. The macro calls in this example enable finer design expression.

Example 6-3   **Nuanced Macros**

```
UIView *childView = [[UIView alloc] initWithFrame:CGRectZero];
[parentView addSubview:childView];
PREPCONSTRAINTS(childView);
INSTALL_CONSTRAINTS(1000, @"Centering",
    CONSTRAINTS_CENTERING(childView));
INSTALL_CONSTRAINTS(750, @"Sizing",
    CONSTRAINTS_SETTING_SIZE(childView, 100, 80));
```

Macros aren't mandatory. If macros aren't your thing, use Objective-C. Example 6-4 shifts away from macros, implementing layout through functions. Like the examples that precede it, these calls create a view, size it to 100×80, and center it in its parent. This example falls somewhere between Examples 6-2 and 6-3 in terms of complexity and readability. These particular functions support priorities but not annotation—although you could easily build calls that do.

Example 6-4   **Functions**

```
UIView *childView = [[UIView alloc] initWithFrame:CGRectZero];
[parentView addSubview:childView];
childView.translatesAutoresizingMaskIntoConstraints = NO;
CenterViewInParent(childView, 100);
ConstrainViewSize(childView, CGSizeMake(100, 80), 750);
```

Functions offer clear advantages over macros, especially when tasks become more complex than a single line or two. They combine standard programming with portability. They can be called from any class. This enables you to develop a layout library independent of any specific view or app implementations.

Example 6-5 implements the same sizing and centering features you've seen so far, but this time with methods. Because methods are less portable than functions, the methods in Example 6-5 have been added to a view class category, allowing calls from any view subclass. Method calls are far more self-documenting than function calls. They fit in better with day-to-day Objective-C best practices. They offer the standard go-to for most development.

On the negative side, this particular solution carries with it all the standard risks for implementing categories. You must namespace your categories and their members carefully to guard against future development by Apple. A too-obvious method or category name may eventually conflict with Apple-supplied libraries.

> **Note**
>
> The examples in this book do not use developer-specific prefixes, but I encourage you to do so in your own code. I've chosen readability over practicality for my book examples.

Example 6-5 **Methods**

```
UIView *childView = [[UIView alloc] initWithFrame:CGRectZero];
[parentView addSubview:childView];
childView.translatesAutoresizingMaskIntoConstraints = NO;

NSArray *constraints;
constraints = [UIView constraintsCenteringViewInParent:childView
    withPriority:1000];
[parentView addConstraints:constraints];

constraints = [UIView constraintsSettingSize:CGSizeMake(100, 80)
    forView:childView withPriority:750];
[parentView addConstraints:constraints];
```

I have bundled up many common layout tasks into various sets of functions, methods, and macros for my own development work. You will likely want to do the same. Building constraint utility libraries offers several advantages:

- Library calls greatly improve readability, transforming boilerplate layout into instantly recognizable components.

- Library calls expose streamlined parameters. You can tell at a glance what the layout is supposed to do, and you can tweak arguments as needed.

- Libraries minimize complexity. You leverage already-established relationships such as view-to-superview parenting or leading-to-trailing edge placement to reduce the information you need to supply.

- Libraries enable you to debug once and use the fruits of that labor as often as needed.

You decide what kind of libraries you want to build: macros, functions, methods, class categories, or a hybrid that leverages some or all of these. Regardless of your implementation approach, consider your answers to the following questions before you build your solutions:

- **Should your libraries return constraint instances?** If so, how will you install them? If not, how will you handle priorities?

- **Do you need to set priorities directly (recommended), or can you live with convenience calls that handle that for you?** Ask yourself if you'll encounter any critical edge conditions that need priorities? If not, it's perfectly okay to let your library place items in rows and columns or center your views using standard, fixed priorities.

- **Will you need to group or annotate the constraints you build?** If you have constraints specific to landscape or portrait layout, or if you want to tag constraints for easy retrieval and updating, how will your library support building these groups?

When programming, I find myself using all the approaches shown in these examples. There are times you need to build constraints by hand, times you can rely on cookie-cutter layout for quick and reliable solutions, and times you need a little more finesse. No matter what approach you use, and no matter how you build your libraries, you will benefit. Investing time in layout libraries means shifting your attention from implementation details to the greater design story when it comes to building apps.

Planning Interfaces

When laying out interfaces, you should always be evaluating design requirements. Consider the following topics. The answers to the questions these raise help establish the rules you build in Auto Layout:

- **Evaluate your geometry**—Will your app geometry change? If so, when will it change, and why? For example, on OS X, you can create user-resizable windows. On iOS, geometry varies by device, including tablets and 3.5-inch and 4-inch handsets. Does your app support multiple orientations? On iOS in particular, interfaces regularly flip from landscape to portrait and back. Enumerate your geometries before strategizing your interface.

- **Detail your edge conditions**—What edge conditions will your views encounter? Edge conditions include extremes of permitted size or location, multiple views competing for the same space, and literal edge conditions where, for example, a view hits the edge of a superview or window. Do user interactions cause these conditions, or are they due to device or window limitations? Brainstorm as many edge conditions as you can.

- **Explore your conflicts**—Use edge conditions as a basis for exploring conflicting rules. When a view hits its superview's edge, should the parent resize? Or should it resist the view, forcing it to stay inside its current bounds? Are there natural boundaries that views should not cross? If so, what should happen? List these conflicts and explain why they could occur. Then focus on how you plan to resolve them, specifying which views should win and why.

- **Enumerate fallbacks**—Fallbacks establish the minimum ways your interface should behave in the absence of highly prioritized rules. What kind of backup system can you develop to support your primary graphical user interface (GUI) so that items have a natural place to return to? List as many fallback rules as you can. "My view should always be at least this big" and "all views should at a minimum appear within their parent's bounds" and "if there's no other rule controlling this view, it should return to this position" all describe robust defaults you can implement at low priorities.

- **Find natural groupings**—The more you cluster your interface, the better you can transform your app into modules. Natural groupings allow you to divide interface elements into fixed low-maintenance components. Find elements with tightly coupled layout requirements and encapsulate them wherever possible.

- **Explore grouped layouts**—Groups enable you to perform more holistic layouts than individual views. Consider possible geometries with respect to your groupings. Does a side-by-side landscape layout translate to a top-down portrait layout? Or would you need to decompose further to accommodate the layout's geometry? Reevaluate your edge conditions and your conflicts, using the groups as primary actors instead of views. Do the rules need to change?

- **Prioritize your rules**—When surveying your layout, what rules are most important in your interface? Categorize the interface rules you've developed to describe which ones have the most sway. What are things that *must* happen? And what are just things you'd *like* to happen? What rules can "break"? And when will they do so? Understanding the deep story of your interface helps you translate the importance of rules into constraint priorities.

- **Consider content**—Don't forget that rules aren't limited to layout constraints. Consider the contribution of content hugging and compression resistance, as discussed in Chapter 2, "Constraints." For example, descriptive labels often have high resistance priorities, enabling your interface to remain understandable. Review the features that influence content sizes, such as font choices and image assets, and bring them into your design consideration.

Building for Modularity

The more modular your interface, the more easily it integrates with Auto Layout. Figure 6-1 shows an interface screen consisting of a pair of simple panes: a settings pane and a credits pane. These panes display in a variety of device orientations and geometries. Both panes were created in Interface Builder (IB) and are instantiated by the primary view controller.

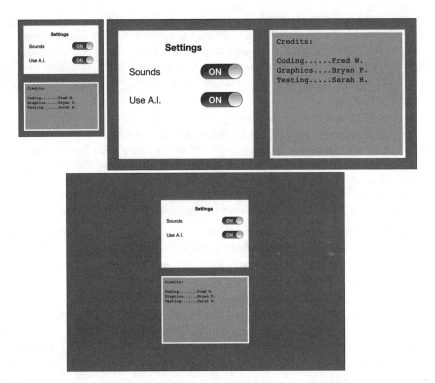

Figure 6-1   Designing modular interfaces pays off in Auto Layout. This app supports iPhone 3.5-inch (top left), iPhone 4-inch (top right), and iPad (bottom) using component-based layout. This sample does not use separate nibs for iPad and iPhone families, although it easily could.

Here's the code that loads the two views from their nib files:

```
// Load Settings View
settingsView = [[[UINib nibWithNibName:@"Settings"
    bundle:[NSBundle mainBundle]]
    instantiateWithOwner:self options:0] lastObject];

// Load Credits View
creditsView = [[[UINib nibWithNibName:@"Credits"
    bundle:[NSBundle mainBundle]]
    instantiateWithOwner:self options:0] lastObject];

// Add to the view controller
for (UIView *view in @[settingsView, creditsView])
{
    [self.view addSubview:view];
    view.translatesAutoresizingMaskIntoConstraints = NO;
}
```

Assigning the owner, as this example does, allows IB-assigned outlets and actions to properly connect. The two switches in the settings view are live; they call back to the view controller when toggled.

This sample interface needs to work in at least six scenarios, specifically landscape and portrait orientations on 3.5-inch iPhones, 4-inch iPhones, and iPads. Apple's iOS device family might grow even further in the future.

The modular design and loading used for this example provide layout flexibility. Instead of concentrating on the minutia of switches, labels, and text, Listing 6-1 handles each pane as a coherent component. Depending on the view geometry, it builds left/right or top/down placement. This greatly simplifies the design task.

Listing 6-1   **Geometry-Driven Layout**

```
if (IS_IPAD)
{
    // Align centers horizontally
    for (UIView *view in @[settingsView, creditsView])
        CENTER_H(view);

    // Build column
    CONSTRAIN(@"V:|-[spacerTop(==spacerBottom)]\
        [settingsView(==creditsView)]-30-[creditsView][spacerBottom]-|",
        settingsView, creditsView, spacerTop, spacerBottom);

    // Constrain widths
    CONSTRAIN_WIDTH(settingsView, 320);
    MATCH_WIDTH(settingsView, creditsView);
    CONSTRAIN_HEIGHT(settingsView, 240);
    MATCH_HEIGHT(settingsView, creditsView);
}
else if (layoutIsPortrait)
{
    // Stretch horizontally
    for (UIView *view in @[settingsView, creditsView])
        STRETCH_H(view, AQUA_INDENT);

    // Build column
    CONSTRAIN(@"V:|-[spacerTop(==spacerBottom)]\
        [settingsView(==creditsView)]-30-[creditsView][spacerBottom]-|",
        settingsView, creditsView, spacerTop, spacerBottom);
}
else
{
    // Stretch vertically
```

```
    for (UIView *view in @[settingsView, creditsView])
        STRETCH_V(view, AQUA_INDENT);

    // Build row
    CONSTRAIN(@"H:|-[spacerLeft(==spacerRight)]\
        [settingsView(==creditsView)]-30-[creditsView][spacerRight]-|",
        settingsView, creditsView, spacerLeft, spacerRight);
}
```

This example considers just three scenarios: iPad, portrait iPhone family, and horizontal iPhone family. For the iPad, it builds a column, squeezes its size, and centers it all horizontally. The portrait layout is much the same, except instead of squeezing views, it stretches them toward each edge. The landscape layout builds a row and stretches vertically.

As you can see in the code, there's relatively little design to consider because the settings and credits views hide the details of their internals. The more you decompose your views into modular elements, the simpler and cleaner your layout becomes.

> **Note**
>
> Several examples in this chapter, including the code you just saw, use spacer padding, which enables you to float complex layouts into the center of views. You'll read more about this trick in Chapter 7, "Layout Solutions."

Updating Constraints

When devices rotate and windows resize, view constraints may become invalid. You update constraints in the `updateConstraints` (`UIView` and `NSView`) and/or `updateViewConstraints` (`UIViewController`) methods. The code you saw in Listing 6-1 properly belongs in an `updateViewConstraints` implementation. These implementations follow a certain flow:

1. Call `super` (for example, `[super updateViewConstraints]`). Never forget this step.

2. Clean away any invalid constraints. You may also remove valid constraints entangled with the invalid ones in order to start off with a clean slate for your updated layout.

3. Add constraints to express your fresh layout.

Listing 6-2 shows an incredibly trivial example of this. It expresses an interface with a single view that's aligned center-top for portrait orientation and center-right for landscape. It enumerates each of the required steps, starting by calling the superclass implementation of `updateViewConstraints`.

Next, it removes constraints that reference the sample view from its superview ancestry. This catches any constraints that set the view's position. It leaves alone any constraints installed directly onto the view, so its size remains unaffected by the updated layout. If this view had been loaded from IB, the way the ones in Listing 6-1 were, limiting the constraint search to superviews would have similarly preserved the layout of each view's children.

Finally, it reestablishes the view layout, aligning the view in accordance with the current device orientation—portrait or landscape.

Listing 6-2   **Updating View Constraints**

```
- (void) updateViewConstraints
{
    // Always call super
    [super updateViewConstraints];

    // Remove constraints referencing exampleView
    // These methods were introduced in Chapters 2 and 5
    for (NSLayoutConstraint *constraint in
        exampleView.referencingConstraintsInSuperviews) // C05
        [constraint remove]; // C02

    // Re-establish position constraints using
    // self-explanatory layout macros
    BOOL layoutIsPortrait =
        UIDeviceOrientationIsPortrait(self.interfaceOrientation);
    if (layoutIsPortrait)
    {
        ALIGN_CENTERTOP(exampleView, AQUA_INDENT);
    }
    else
    {
        ALIGN_CENTERRIGHT(exampleView, AQUA_INDENT);
    }
}
```

Calling Updates and Animating Changes

When working with views, you call `setNeedsUpdateConstraints` (`setNeedsUpdate Constraints:` on OS X) to indicate that a view needs attention at the next layout pass. With view controllers, you call the `updateViewConstraints` method directly, generally when setting up (`viewWillAppear:`) and responding to rotation callbacks.

Listing 6-3 demonstrates how you might do this in iOS, using an approach that does not transfer to OS X. This solution animates the layout update during reorientation, using the reorientation animation timing. This coordinates the two updates, so they finish simultaneously and draw little attention to the updates. The views slide around a bit onscreen, but the entire view is rotating already, so the updates don't really draw much attention.

On iOS, you animate constraint updates by embedding a call to `layoutIfNeeded` inside an animation block, as in Listing 6-3. Always make sure to call `layoutIfNeeded` on the parent, as is done in this example. This call forces subview layouts and enables the animation to include those updates. If you skip the call, the changes will jump from the before values to the after ones without a smooth transition.

Listing 6-3   **Animating Constraint Updates During Rotation**

```
- (void) willAnimateRotationToInterfaceOrientation:
    (UIInterfaceOrientation)toInterfaceOrientation
    duration:(NSTimeInterval)duration
{
    [UIView animateWithDuration:duration animations:^{
        [self updateViewConstraints];
        [self.view layoutIfNeeded];
    }];
}
```

Animating Constraint Changes on OS X

OS X constraint animation uses a slightly different approach, based on the `NSAnimatablePropertyContainer` protocol. Instead of directly changing a constraint's constant, you perform the change on the `animator` proxy. The `animator` proxy executes the animation steps for the updated property. Here's an example of an OS X method that collects views into a vertical stack, demonstrating a basic constraint animation approach:

```
- (IBAction)stackViews:(id)sender
{
    [NSAnimationContext beginGrouping];
    NSAnimationContext.currentContext.duration = 0.3f;
    for (int i = 0; i < views.count; i++)
    {
        // Retrieve position constraints
        NSArray *constraints = [self.view
            constraintsNamed:@"Dragging Position Constraint"
            matchingView:views[i]];

        // Find the horizontal one, and update its constant
        for (NSLayoutConstraint *constraint in constraints)
        {
            CGFloat c = IS_HORIZONTAL_ATTRIBUTE(
                constraint.firstAttribute) ? 0 : 100 * i;
            [constraint.animator setConstant:c];
        }
    }
    [NSAnimationContext endGrouping];
}
```

Fading Changes

Listing 6-4 offers a distinct approach to the challenge of updating constraints during device rotation. It fades away the old layout, updates constraints during the rotation, and fades the new layout back in afterward.

I have reservations about this solution. First, it tends to flash. Second, it takes approximately twice as long to execute as Listing 6-3. However, it provides a strong visual approach. You fade out, reorganize content, and then fade back in. The advantage is that you don't see views scrabbling around the screen either jumping (without animation) or sliding (with animation) to their new position. The fades provide natural bookends to the update process.

Listing 6-4   **Fading Constraint Updates In and Out**

```
- (void)willRotateToInterfaceOrientation:
    (UIInterfaceOrientation)toInterfaceOrientation
    duration:(NSTimeInterval)duration
{
    // Fade away old layout
    [UIView animateWithDuration:duration animations:^{
        for (UIView *view in @[settingsView, creditsView])
            view.alpha = 0.0f;
    }];
}

- (void) didRotateFromInterfaceOrientation:
    (UIInterfaceOrientation)fromInterfaceOrientation
{
    // Update the layout for the new orientation
    [self updateViewConstraints];
    [self.view layoutIfNeeded];

    // Fade in the new layout
    [UIView animateWithDuration:0.3f animations:^{
        for (UIView *view in @[settingsView, creditsView])
            view.alpha = 1.0f;
    }];
}
```

> **Note**
>
> I removed the discussion of orientation-specific text layout that appeared here in the first edition of this book. Under iOS 7, labels reflow without specific layout widths. Further, labels now support dynamic text updates to respond to user-generated setting changes.

Designing for Edge Conditions

Figure 6-2 shows a custom control used for locking and unlocking the interface. Users drag the slider thumb from the left to the right in order to open the lock. If the thumb goes past the 75% mark, the unlock succeeds, sending out delegate notifications and removing itself from the screen.

Figure 6-2   Constraints limit the thumb's travel to within its parent track.

This view consists of four items: a gray backsplash, a lock image, a track image (the horizontal rounded rectangle), and a thumb image (the light circle in the track). This control is built entirely with constraints, both for layout and user interaction. Because constraint constants are easily updated and animated, they provide an excellent solution for many direct manipulation elements.

Listing 6-5 implements rules that constrain the user-maneuverable thumb. The rules it establishes are as follows:

- The thumb lies vertically inside its parent. This rule is mandated with a required (1,000) priority, so nothing is going to change that placement without breaking the interface.

- The thumb must not reach the horizontal edges of its parent. Constraints impose a forced gap between the thumb and the start and end of its superview. The gap amounts to half the thumb image width. These rules form absolute boundaries and are required with a 1,000 priority.

- Rules place the thumb at the leading edge of its parent with a 500 priority. Because of the edge constraints already described, it cannot *reach* that edge, so it just gets as close as it can. This placement constraint is named (via the THUMB_POSITION_TAG) for easy reference and updating during user interaction.

Listing 6-5   **Building Edge Conditions**

```
// Layout Thumb Constraints

// Center the thumb vertically on its parent
centerViewY(thumbView, 1000);

// Do not allow the thumb to reach the horizontal edges
CGFloat thumbInset = thumbView.image.size.width / 2;
for (NSString *format in @[
    @"H:|-(>=inset)-[view]",
    @"H:[view]-(>=inset)-|",
    ])
{
    NSArray *constraints = [NSLayoutConstraint
        constraintsWithVisualFormat:format
        options:NSLayoutFormatAlignAllCenterY
        metrics:@{@"inset":@(thumbInset)}
        views:@{@"view":thumbView}];
    for (NSLayoutConstraint *constraint in constraints)
        [constraint install:1000];
}

// Add an initial position constraint
constraint = CONSTRAINT_POSITION_LEADING(thumbView, 0);
constraint.nametag = THUMB_POSITION_TAG;
[constraint install:500];
```

Because these initial constraints clearly define edge rules, there's little left to implement in the control tracking methods. Listing 6-6 shows how simply the constraints respond to user touches.

In Listing 6-6, the tracking method first checks the touch to see if it has strayed. If so, it resets the thumb position back to 0 and cancels tracking. With its low priority, the thumb position constraint cannot reach 0, but the thumb returns as close as is allowed. The animation block gracefully moves the thumb back into place.

If the tracking continues, the thumb's position updates to match the user's touch in the parent view. This code doesn't worry whether that touch reaches the ends of the parent, nor does it consider the touch's Y-position. Higher-priority constraints take care of those details. The "don't go too far left/right" constraints overrule the "slide left and right as you will" constraint, so the thumb position accommodates both the user's touch and the boundary conditions.

Make sure you test the sample project in this chapter's repository to get a sense of this behavior using real-world touches.

Listing 6-6   **Balancing Touches with Constraints**

```
- (BOOL)continueTrackingWithTouch:(UITouch *)touch
    withEvent:(UIEvent *)event
{
    // Strayed too far out?
    CGPoint touchPoint = [touch locationInView:self];
    CGRect largeTrack = CGRectInset(trackView.frame, -20.0f, -20.0f);
    if (!CGRectContainsPoint(largeTrack, touchPoint))
    {
        // Reset on failed attempt
        [UIView animateWithDuration:0.2f animations:^(){
            NSLayoutConstraint *constraint =
                [trackView constraintNamed:THUMB_POSITION_TAG];
            constraint.constant = 0;
            [trackView layoutIfNeeded];
        }];
        return NO;
    }

    // Track the user movement by updating the thumb
    touchPoint = [touch locationInView:trackView];
    [UIView animateWithDuration:0.1f animations:^(){
        NSLayoutConstraint *constraint =
            [trackView constraintNamed:THUMB_POSITION_TAG];
        constraint.constant = touchPoint.x;
        [trackView layoutIfNeeded];
    }];
    return YES;
}
```

Building a View Drawer

Figure 6-3 shows a drawer that users can drag open and closed. In its basic implementation, it provides another example of edge conditions. In this case, the drawer cannot rise any higher than the position shown in the left image or any lower than the position shown on the right. The handle remains visible at all times.

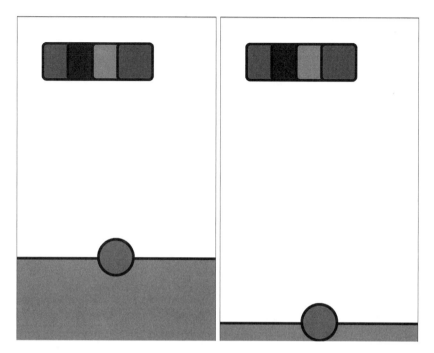

Figure 6-3   Users drag the bottom drawer open (left) and closed (right) by manipulating the circular handle. The drawer cannot open any farther or close beyond the minimum position that shows the entire handle.

As with the lock control, this behavior is set through a pair of constraints that establish the minimum and maximum positions of the drawer's top edge. The handle view manages a lower-priority constraint that matches the drawer's offset to the user's touch. So far, this implementation is not very different from the lock.

The more interesting situation involves the draggable items shown at the top of the view. There are four of them in this implementation. Users can move them anywhere onscreen, including into the drawer. They are subviews of the view controller's view.

Once they're moved "into" the drawer, however, the drawer view takes over their management. As Figure 6-4 shows, items in the drawer are always uniformly placed from left to right. Users can drag them back to the main area or can slide the drawer shut to hide them. Their placement remains fixed to the drawer.

This behavior is implemented through a trio of methods. Items dragged to or out of the drawer are added to and removed from its set of managed views. Other classes can query the drawer to ask if it currently takes responsibility for a given view:

```
- (void) removeView: (UIView *) view;
- (void) addView: (UIView *) view;
- (BOOL) managesViewLayout: (UIView *) view;
```

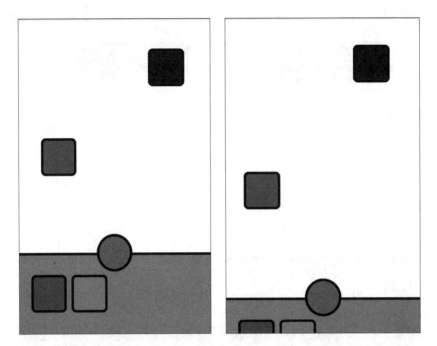

Figure 6-4   The drawer controls the placement of the views it manages (left), creating a fixed layout that moves with the drawer (right).

Critically, the drawer needs a way to reference any external constraints that set the view's position. When the drawer takes over, it must remove these constraints and replace them with its own. It does so using an array of competing constraint names:

```
@property (nonatomic, retain) NSArray *competingPositionNames;
```

In turn, it publishes the names it uses to position its views so other classes can take over management when the drawer relinquishes them:

```
+ (NSArray *) originatedPositionNames;
```

Listing 6-7 shows the implementation of the three management methods. As you can see, these involve nothing more than adding to and removing items from a view array and then calling `setNeedsUpdateConstraints`. The actual layout work takes place in the `updateConstraints` method.

Listing 6-7   Adding and Relinquishing View Management

```
// Is the view's layout managed by the drawer?
- (BOOL) managesViewLayout: (UIView *) view
{
```

```
    return [views containsObject:view];
}

// Remove view from drawer management
- (void) removeView: (UIView *) view
{
    [views removeObject:view];

    // Animate any changes
    [UIView animateWithDuration:0.3f animations:^{
        [self setNeedsUpdateConstraints];
        [self.window layoutIfNeeded];
    }];
}

// Add view to drawer management
- (void) addView: (UIView *) view
{
    if (!views)
        views = [NSMutableArray array];
    [views removeObject:view];
    [views addObject:view];

    // Animate any changes
    [UIView animateWithDuration:0.3f animations:^{
        [self setNeedsUpdateConstraints];
        [self.window layoutIfNeeded];
    }];
}
```

Building the Drawer Layout

The updateConstraints method is where you evaluate and update constraint setup. You call setNeedsUpdateConstraints whenever your current layout becomes invalid, as happens in the drawer's addView: and removeView: methods. Listing 6-8 shows the actual method that implements the drawer's layout.

It consists of two layout sections, which lay out the entire drawer. The first section establishes maximum and minimum boundaries that limit the drawer's travel both up and down in its parent. Notice that the drawer does not "squish." Its bottom edge is not tied to any point, so the entire drawer travels up and down, ensuring that any view shown inside it remains a fixed distance from its top and bottom.

The second section lays out the managed views. This section starts by removing existing position constraints as well as any constraints managed externally for each of the drawer's items. This creates a fresh palette for new constraints.

The layout itself consists of pinning the first item to the leading edge, centering the views vertically in the drawer, and creating a row spacing each item out. These rules create a well-behaved layout.

Note that these items are the drawer's siblings and not its children. The views still belong to the main view controller's view. This allows the views to be dragged back out without having to be reparented. It's only the view layout that the drawer manages. The handle, incidentally, is also a sibling, allowing it to accept touches on its entire extent without clipping. Touches on the handle outside the drawer's primary frame are recognized. Constraints tie the handle to the drawer, allowing the two to act in concert as a single unit.

Listing 6-8 **Laying Out the Drawer**

```
- (void) updateConstraints
{
    [super updateConstraints];

    NSLayoutConstraint *constraint;

    // MinMax Layout
    // Remove prior constraints
    for (NSLayoutConstraint *constraint in
        [self constraintsNamed:MINMAX_NAME])
        [constraint remove];

    // Maximum Ascent
    constraint = [NSLayoutConstraint
        constraintWithItem:self
        attribute:NSLayoutAttributeBottom
        relatedBy:NSLayoutRelationGreaterThanOrEqual
        toItem:self.superview
        attribute:NSLayoutAttributeBottom
        multiplier:1 constant:0];
    constraint.nametag = MINMAX_NAME;
    [constraint install:750];

    // Minimum Ascent
    constraint = [NSLayoutConstraint
        constraintWithItem:self
        attribute:NSLayoutAttributeTop
        relatedBy:NSLayoutRelationLessThanOrEqual
        toItem:self.superview
        attribute:NSLayoutAttributeBottom
        multiplier:1
        constant: - _handle.bounds.size.height / 2.0f];
    constraint.nametag = MINMAX_NAME;
    [constraint install:1000];
```

```objc
// View layout
for (UIView *view in views)
{
    // Remove prior constraints
    for (NSLayoutConstraint *constraint in
        [view constraintsNamed:LINE_BUILDING_NAME
            matchingView:view])
        [constraint remove];

    // Remove competing constraints
    for (NSString *name in _competingPositionNames)
        for (NSLayoutConstraint *constraint in
            [view constraintsNamed:name matchingView:view])
            [constraint remove];
}

if (views.count)
{
    // Pin the first view to the drawer's leading edge
    UIView *view = views[0];

    constraint = [NSLayoutConstraint
        constraintWithItem:view
        attribute:NSLayoutAttributeLeading
        relatedBy:NSLayoutRelationEqual
        toItem:self
        attribute:NSLayoutAttributeLeading multiplier:1
        constant:AQUA_INDENT];
    constraint.nametag = LINE_BUILDING_NAME;
    [constraint install:LayoutPriorityFixedWindowSize + 2];
}

for (UIView *view in views)
{
    // Center each view vertically in the holder drawer
    constraint = [NSLayoutConstraint
        constraintWithItem:view
        attribute:NSLayoutAttributeCenterY
        relatedBy:NSLayoutRelationEqual
        toItem:self
        attribute:NSLayoutAttributeCenterY
        multiplier:1 constant:0];
    [constraint install:LayoutPriorityFixedWindowSize + 2];
    constraint.nametag = LINE_BUILDING_NAME;
}
```

```
    // Layout the views as a line
    buildLine(views, NSLayoutFormatAlignAllCenterY,
        LayoutPriorityFixedWindowSize + 2);
}
```

Managing Layout for Dragged Views

Listing 6-8's layout intentionally "breaks" whenever a user drags any item, forcing an update. If a view is dragged out of the middle of the drawer, any views to its right will animate to fill that space as the view moves away. Notifications produced by the dragged objects enable this behavior. Listing 6-9 shows the updates for the start and end of the drag.

Views that leave the drawer return to external layout management. Views that remain in the drawer by the end, however, are re-added. Because dragged views always lose their position in line, they animate to the trailing end when placed back into the drawer.

Listing 6-9   **Updating Drawer Layout**

```
// Check the start of drag
[[NSNotificationCenter defaultCenter]
    addObserverForName:DRAG_START_NOTIFICATION_NAME
    object:nil queue:[NSOperationQueue mainQueue]
    usingBlock:^(NSNotification *note)
{
    // Remove dragged objects from the drawer
    UIView *view = note.object;
    [holder removeView:view];
}];

// Check the end of drag
[[NSNotificationCenter defaultCenter]
    addObserverForName:DRAG_END_NOTIFICATION_NAME
    object:nil queue:[NSOperationQueue mainQueue]
    usingBlock:^(NSNotification *note)
{
    // Test dragged objects for position, adding
    // to the drawer when overlapped
    UIView *view = note.object;
    if (CGRectIntersectsRect(view.frame, holder.frame))
        [holder addView:view];
    else
        [holder removeView:view];
}];
```

Dragged Views

The final piece of this implementation lies in the views that users drag around the screen. These consist of standard UIView instances. They host a pan gesture recognizer and a well-defined set of constraints. Listing 6-10 shows the methods that power view movement.

The moveToPosition: method acts like a position-dependent updateConstraints implementation. It removes previous location constraints and establishes ones that match the new position. Unlike updateConstraints, it's called far more often, specifically whenever the pan gesture recognizer updates. Instead of handling an entire layout, it just updates the view's position.

Listing 6-10 reveals the notifications that powered Listing 6-9. The gesture recognizer sends off notifications when the recognizer begins (UIGestureRecognizerStateBegan) and ends (UIGestureRecognizerStateEnded). These notifications enable the checks used in Listing 6-9, allowing views to enter and leave the drawer's management.

Listing 6-10 **Moving Views via Gesture Recognizers**

```
- (void) moveToPosition: (CGPoint) position
{
    NSArray *array;

    // Remove previous location constraints for view
    array = [self.superview constraintsNamed:POSITIONING_NAME
        matchingView:self];
    for (NSLayoutConstraint *constraint in array)
        [constraint remove];

    // Remove participation from competing position groups
    for (NSString *name in _competingPositionNames)
    {
        array = [self.superview constraintsNamed:name
            matchingView:self];
        for (NSLayoutConstraint *constraint in array)
            [constraint remove];
    }

    // Create new constraints and add them
    array = constraintsPositioningView(self, position);
    for (NSLayoutConstraint *constraint in array)
    {
        constraint.nametag = POSITIONING_NAME;
        [constraint install:LayoutPriorityFixedWindowSize + 1];
    }
}
```

```
- (void) handlePan: (UIPanGestureRecognizer *) uigr
{
    // Store offset and announce drag
    if (uigr.state == UIGestureRecognizerStateBegan)
    {
        origin = self.frame.origin;
        [self notify:DRAG_START_NOTIFICATION_NAME];
    }

    // Perform movement
    CGPoint translation =
        [uigr translationInView:self.superview];
    CGPoint destination = CGPointMake(origin.x + translation.x,
        origin.y + translation.y);
    [self moveToPosition:destination];

    // Check for end / announcement
    if (uigr.state == UIGestureRecognizerStateEnded)
        [self notify:DRAG_END_NOTIFICATION_NAME];
}
```

Window Boundaries

To wrap up this chapter, I wanted to add an OS X-specific example because window sizing offers a good match to both edge conditions and rule balancing. Figure 6-5 shows an app whose window size depends on the placement of the views within it.

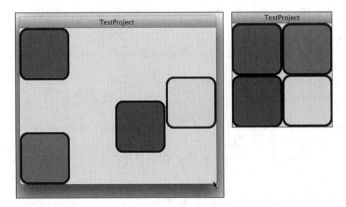

Figure 6-5   In this application, the window's size is set by the draggable views that inhabit it.

Note the cursor at the bottom right of the image on the left. It is not a window-sizing cursor (a double-headed arrow) because you cannot directly resize this window. Instead, sizing follows subview placement due to the app's limiting constraints.

This content view expresses competing constraints. It must fully show all the views that lie within it. It also wants to shrink as small as possible. The result is a window that "hugs" its content's subviews, no matter how they're positioned.

Listing 6-11 shows the hugging part of the rules. Its constraints attempt to scale the window down to nothing, to a size of (0,0). These rules use a fixed window size priority, using the standard NSLayoutPriorityWindowSizeStayPut constraint level. Unless this is overruled, the window wants to get as small as possible.

Listing 6-11   **Window Constraints Limiting Its Size**

```
// Request zero content size at a fixed window priority
_view = _window.contentView;
constrainViewSize(_view, CGSizeMake(0, 0),
    NSLayoutPriorityWindowSizeStayPut);
```

On the other side of things are the views themselves, which are created in Listing 6-12. They consist of user-draggable squares with a size fixed at a required priority (1,000). The constrainToSuperview method first introduced in Chapter 4, "Visual Formats," establishes that the views must stay within the superview. Together, the methods mandate fixed-sized views that lie entirely within their parent.

Listing 6-12   **Constraints Preventing View Clipping**

```
TestView *view = [TestView randomView];
[self.view addSubview:view];
constrainToSuperview(view, 100, LayoutPriorityRequired);
[view enableDragging:YES];
```

Listing 6-13 explains the rest of the story. In it, you see the methods that implement view dragging. Each time the view moves, position constraints set the new position at a priority of NSLayoutPriorityWindowSizeStayPut + 1. Between the fixed size, the need to stay within the parent view, and the priority level for the position, view-specific rules will always win out over the parent's "size to (0,0)" constraints. Although the parent shrinks as far as it possibly can, the content views always win out, forcing the edges further and further away as the views move out. The result is a window that hugs its content but allows that content to resize it as needed.

Listing 6-13   **Draggable Views Overruling Window Sizing**

```
- (void) mouseDragged:(NSEvent *) event
{
    if (!allowDragging) return;

    CGPoint pt = [event locationInWindow];
    CGFloat dx = pt.x - touchPoint.x;
    CGFloat dy = pt.y - touchPoint.y;

    // Find the destination point and move to it
    CGPoint destination = CGPointMake(origin.x + dx,
        (self.superview.frame.size.height - self.frame.size.height)
        - (origin.y + dy));
    [self moveToPosition:destination];
}

- (void) moveToPosition: (CGPoint) position
{
    NSArray *array;

    // Remove previous location for view
    array = [self.superview
        constraintsNamed:@"Dragging Position Constraint"
        matchingView:self];
    for (NSLayoutConstraint *constraint in array)
        [constraint remove];

    // Create new constraints and add them
    array = constraintsPositioningView(self, position);

    // The increased priority enables window resizing
    // If you want a different result, e.g. no resizing,
    // adjust the priority downwards
    for (NSLayoutConstraint *constraint in array)
    {
        constraint.nametag =  @"Dragging Position Constraint";
        [constraint install: NSLayoutPriorityWindowSizeStayPut + 1];
    }
}
```

Exercises

After reading this chapter, test your knowledge with these exercises:

1. A view has two constraints. One, at a priority of 300, says the view should hug the superview's top edge. Another, at a priority of 301, says the view should center vertically within the superview. What is the outcome of these two rules?

2. A view has two constraints. One, at a priority of 300, says to place the view's vertical center at the superview's top edge. Another, at a priority of 301, says the view must be at least 50 points away from the superview's top edge. What is the likely outcome of these two rules?

3. Figure 6-1 demonstrated modular layout, where the view was decomposed into two children. If you used Autosizing to place content into the child views, would you disable `translatesAutoresizingMaskIntoConstraints`? If so, when? If not, why not?

4. When might you add Auto Layout rules between siblings instead of using parent–child relationships? Why does the drawer example in this chapter use a sibling handle?

5. How do the window-sizing examples in Figure 6-5 relate to iOS?

6. When can you skip implementing `updateViewConstraints` and `updateConstraints`?

Conclusions

Success with Auto Layout design often depends on how hard you think about the problem *before* coding your solutions. You can save yourself headaches by carefully evaluating edge conditions, conflicts, and priorities on paper before you open Xcode. Here are a few final thoughts to carry out of this chapter:

- I cannot overstate the utility of building and using constraint libraries. The nature of Auto Layout means you can build these once and reuse them a lot. Although you can't (and shouldn't) pre-guess all the constraints you will use in your development, you can certainly cover the bases for many common layout elements.

- Concision is the hallmark of a well-designed interface. If your code is growing large and complicated, step back and try to find the fundamental principles that *should* be guiding your layout and express them via constraints. When you let higher-priority edge conditions rule over your lower-priority general behavior, lines of code shrink dramatically.

- As you can tell in this chapter, I am a fan of labeling constraints. This practice enables you to find, tweak, remove, or replace constraints with a minimum of coding and fuss. It is also a form of self-annotation, explaining the constraint's role within the interface. If this approach doesn't work for you, consider building outlet collections or array properties that group functionally related constraints.

- Auto Layout benefits from early planning in a way you don't encounter with springs and struts. If you are used to quick IB prototyping, you should schedule in extra time for layout analysis. Although Auto Layout requires an extra investment in strategy, the interfaces you create can be stronger, more nimble, and more reliable.

- Whenever possible, decompose your interface. Don't forget that any self-contained view that lays out its subviews with Auto Layout should implement the `requiresConstraintBasedLayout` class method and return `YES`.

Layout Solutions

The previous chapters in this book have focused on know-how and philosophy. This chapter introduces solutions. You'll read about a variety of real-world challenges and how Auto Layout provides practical answers for day-to-day development work. The topics are a grab bag, showcasing requests developers commonly make.

Table Cells

Despite rumors to the contrary, Auto Layout isn't the enemy of table cells. Figure 7-1 shows an application built around a constraint-based table. Each cell item, including the track title, album art, price button, and playback indicator, is positioned and sized using Auto Layout rules. You see an example of the playback indicator on the fourth row of the table. The cell layout design was built in code using a custom table view cell subclass.

Developers who are new to Auto Layout often encounter issues attempting to combine constraints with table view cells. If you're experiencing assertion failures related to Auto Layout, like the following, step back and reevaluate your approach:

```
2013-02-01 18:55:49.125 HelloWorld[506:c07] *** Assertion failure in -[CustomCell
layoutSublayersOfLayer:], /SourceCache/UIKit_Sim/UIKit-2380.17/UIView.m:5776
2013-02-01 18:55:49.126 HelloWorld[506:c07] *** Terminating app due to uncaught
exception 'NSInternalInconsistencyException', reason: 'Auto Layout still required
after executing -layoutSubviews. CustomCell's implementation of -layoutSubviews needs
to call super.'
```

The success of constraint-based cells depends on two things. First, follow standard Auto Layout best practices for constraint layout and updates. Second, you need to limit your custom subviews to the cell's contentView; don't add the subviews directly to the cell itself. Otherwise, treat Auto Layout cells as you would those built with Autosizing.

Listing 7-1 shows the key methods behind the table in Figure 7-1. Here are several points to keep in mind for your own implementations:

Figure 7-1   This table's cells were built using Auto Layout.

- **Create a custom cell class**—It works best when you start fresh. It is better to subclass `UITableViewCell` than to add Auto Layout–based subviews to standard cells.

- **Implement `requiresConstraintBasedLayout:`**—Return `YES` from this class method, as your cell depends on Auto Layout.

- **Add subviews**—Listing 7-1 creates and adds its subviews in the class initializer, ending a method by calling `setNeedsUpdateConstraints`. It performs no layout; it just returns the newly initialized cell instance.

- **Centralize your layout**—Establish `updateConstraints` in the usual manner. Start by calling the superclass's implementation. Remove any stale or invalid constraints. Finally, lay out the view.

Listing 7-1   **Building Auto Layout Cells**

```
// Require Auto Layout
+ (BOOL) requiresConstraintBasedLayout
{
    return YES;
}
```

```
// Lay out the view
- (void) updateConstraints
{
    // Always call super
    [super updateConstraints];

    // Clean up stale or invalid constraints
    for (UIView *view in self.contentView.subviews)
    {
        NSArray *constraints = [self.contentView
            constraintsReferencingView:view];
        for (NSLayoutConstraint *constraint in constraints)
            [constraint remove];
    }

    // Lay out Track Label
    HUG(customLabel, 750);
    ALIGN_CENTER(customLabel);

    // Lay out Album Image
    HUG(customImageView, 750);
    ALIGN_CENTERRIGHT(customImageView, 8);

    // Lay out Buy Button
    HUG(_buyButton, 750);
    ALIGN_CENTERLEFT(_buyButton, AQUA_SPACE);

    // Lay out Playback Progress
    LAYOUT_V(progressImageView, 4, _buyButton);
    CONSTRAIN_SIZE(progressImageView, 20, 20);
}

// Initialize a new cell instance
- (instancetype) initWithStyle:(UITableViewCellStyle)style
    reuseIdentifier:(NSString *)reuseIdentifier
{
    self = [super initWithStyle:style
        reuseIdentifier:reuseIdentifier];
    if (!self) return self;

    // Add general styling
    self.contentView.backgroundColor = AQUA_COLOR;
    self.selectionStyle = UITableViewCellSelectionStyleNone;

    // Add Track Label
    customLabel = [[UILabel alloc] init];
    customLabel.numberOfLines = 0; // Enable wrapping
```

```
    customLabel.textAlignment = NSTextAlignmentCenter;
    customLabel.preferredMaxLayoutWidth = 150;
    [self.contentView addSubview:customLabel];
    PREPCONSTRAINTS(customLabel);

    // Add Album Image View
    customImageView = [[UIImageView alloc] init];
    [self.contentView addSubview:customImageView];
    PREPCONSTRAINTS(customImageView);

    // Add Buy Button
    _buyButton = [UIButton buttonWithType:UIButtonTypeRoundedRect];
    [self.contentView addSubview:_buyButton];
    PREPCONSTRAINTS(_buyButton);

    // Add Progress Image View
    progressImageView = [[UIImageView alloc] init];
    [self.contentView addSubview:progressImageView];
    PREPCONSTRAINTS(progressImageView);

    // Mark for refresh
    [self setNeedsUpdateConstraints];
    return self;
}
```

Auto Layout and Multiple-Height Table Cells

Tables with multiple-height cells, as in Figure 7-2, present an Auto Layout challenge. That's because cells generally live outside a parent view until the very last second. The common trick that enables you to calculate layout size (`systemLayoutSizeFittingSize:`) doesn't necessarily work with cell views.

Consider calculating cell heights more traditionally, as in Listing 7-2, even when your cells are built using Auto Layout. While there are many approaches that get you to the same place, sadly the fitting size typically causes internal consistency errors.

Listing 7-2   Calculating Cell Heights

```
+ (CGFloat) heightForString: (NSAttributedString *) aString
    inTableView: (UITableView *) tableView
{
    CGRect r = [aString boundingRectWithSize:
            CGSizeMake(tableView.bounds.size.width -
                4 * AQUA_INDENT, CGFLOAT_MAX)
        options:NSStringDrawingUsesLineFragmentOrigin
        context:nil];
```

```
    r.size.height += 4 * AQUA_INDENT;
    aString.nametag = @(r.size.height).stringValue;
    return r.size.height;
}

- (CGFloat) tableView:(UITableView *)tableView
    heightForRowAtIndexPath:(NSIndexPath *)indexPath
{
    NSAttributedString *aString = array[indexPath.row];
    if (aString.nametag)
        return [aString.nametag floatValue];
    return [CustomTableViewCell heightForString:aString inTableView:tableView];
}
```

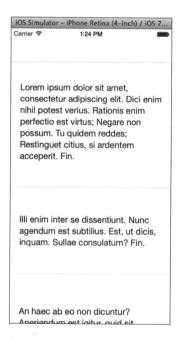

Figure 7-2   Constraint-based cells with varying heights.

Preserving Image Aspect

A view's content mode may not preserve its natural image aspect. That's because content modes control the way a view presents its content when the view's size changes. A content mode, such as UIViewContentModeScaleToFill, allows content to completely fill a view but offers no guarantees about *how* that content gets scaled.

Auto Layout offers an easy way to mandate a natural image aspect. Install a constraint that relates a view's width to its height, using the native aspect as the multiplier. Listing 7-3 demonstrates this approach.

In Listing 7-3, the `addImageView:` method loads a `UIImage` instance. It uses the image's `size` property to build a natural aspect by dividing its width by its height. The method builds a constraint to preserve this aspect and installs it at a high priority. This is one of the rare instances where a legal constraint relates items in one axis (width, which is horizontal) to items in the other axis (height, which is vertical).

The method then lowers the compression resistance priority, enabling the image view to resize more readily. It finishes by adding an arbitrary scaling mode, enabling the content to fill whatever space is available.

All together, the rules work to establish image views that are readily resized by Auto Layout but that maintain their view's intrinsic aspect. The left image in Figure 7-3 shows the results built by Listing 7-3.

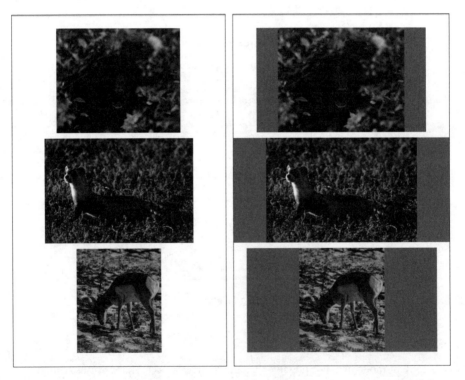

Figure 7-3   Left: Despite scaling, each view maintains the natural aspect of the image it presents. Right: View extent isn't affected by applying an aspect-fitting content mode.

Public domain images courtesy of the National Park Service

You might wonder why Listing 7-3 doesn't just use `UIViewContentModeScaleAspectFit`. This content mode displays an entire image, scaling it to fit the size of the view and maintaining the intrinsic aspect ratio. The right image in Figure 7-3 demonstrates the answer.

Unlike the constrained aspects built by Listing 7-3, content modes don't affect view layout. The true extents of each view, highlighted here by the solid backsplash (in blue if you're reading this book in a color e-reader), do not naturally follow the intrinsic content. Adding an aspect-limiting constraint forces the view size to match its content, regardless of its scale.

Listing 7-3   **Using Constraints to Mandate Aspect**

```
- (void) addImageView: (NSString *) source
{
    NSLayoutConstraint *constraint;

    // Load the image into a new image view
    UIImage *image = [UIImage imageNamed:source];
    UIImageView *imageView = [[UIImageView alloc] initWithImage:image];
    [self.view addSubview:imageView];
    PREPCONSTRAINTS(imageView);

    // Limit aspect at high priority
    CGFloat naturalAspect =
        image.size.width / image.size.height;
    constraint = [NSLayoutConstraint
        constraintWithItem:imageView
        attribute:NSLayoutAttributeWidth
        relatedBy:NSLayoutRelationEqual
        toItem:imageView
        attribute:NSLayoutAttributeHeight
        multiplier:naturalAspect
        constant:0];
    [constraint install:1000];

    // Lower down compression resistance priority
    RESIST(imageView, 250);

    // Enable arbitrary image scaling
    imageView.contentMode = UIViewContentModeScaleToFill;

    [views addObject:imageView];
}
```

Accordion Sizing

Figure 7-4 demonstrates a common layout pattern. You create a line of views that stretch from one edge to the other, vertically or horizontally. Each view occupies the same extent percentage, regardless of the amount of available space. To fit, the views must stretch or contract in unison, much as the folds of an accordion do, to provide consistent sizing for each element.

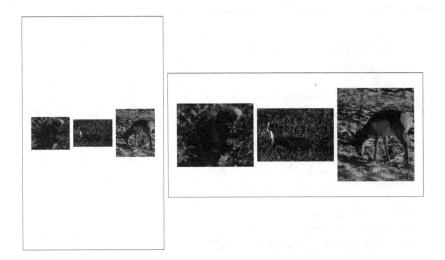

Figure 7-4   Accordion-style constraints allow the images to stretch proportionally while ensuring that each view occupies the same horizontal space. Although the portrait orientation on the left offers less room to work with than the landscape orientation on the right, the relationships between each image remain constant.

Public domain images courtesvy of the National Park Service

It is remarkably easy to implement this pattern using visual formats. Listing 7-4 shows that all you have to do is create a format that places one item after another and that matches each successive view to the first.

All the remaining space is fixed: between the superview and the first and last items and between each pair of views. These spacing rules remove any ambiguity and allow the views to resize in concert.

Listing 7-4   **Matching Multiple View Widths**

```
- (void) loadView
{
    self.view = [[UIView alloc] init];
    self.view.backgroundColor = [UIColor whiteColor];

    views = [NSMutableArray array];
```

```
    [self addImageView:@"bear.jpg"]; // Listing 7-3
    [self addImageView:@"ferret.jpg"];
    [self addImageView:@"pronghorn.jpg"];


    NSArray *constraints = [NSLayoutConstraint
        constraintsWithVisualFormat:
            @"H:|-[view1]-[view2(==view1)]-[view3(==view2)]-|"
        options:NSLayoutFormatAlignAllCenterY
        metrics:nil
        views:@{
            @"view1":views[0],
            @"view2":views[1],
            @"view3":views[2]}];
    for (NSLayoutConstraint *constraint in constraints)
        [constraint install:750];

    // Align first view to remove placement ambiguity
    CENTER_V(views[0]);
}
```

Scroll Views

In an ideal world, scroll views would integrate seamlessly with Auto Layout. They'd provide a public ready-to-use `contentView`, whose children could be laid out using standard Auto Layout rules. In this utopia, `contentView` would tightly couple to the scroll view's `contentSize`, enabling you to tie that size to constraints.

In such a scenario, you'd be able to express rules like the following:

```
contentView.width = scrollView.width * views.count
contentView.height = scrollView.height
```

These rules request a content size expressed as multiples of the parent scroll view's width. They also match the content to the parent's height. This setup would be perfect for creating a paged layout for some *N* number of views, such as in a scrolling album of photographs.

If this were to be implemented, changes in the scroll view's geometry would automatically update the content view and its size. Sadly, this scenario doesn't exist. Apple provides no public `UIScrollView` content views. You can't set a scroll view's `contentSize` property in constraints. Nor can you directly tie a child view's sizing to the parent's bounds.

Apple's May 2013 Technical Note TN2154 discusses these limits and offers two solutions. First, you can use a pure Auto Layout approach, but there are a couple special rules you must follow. Second, you can mix and match Auto Layout with Autosizing to bypass those limitations.

Scroll Views and Pure Auto Layout

Although scroll views work directly with Auto Layout, they do so in a frustrating and counter-intuitive way. Your subviews must stretch to all four edges of the scroll view parent and create sizing that does not rely on the scroll view parent.

The following examples showcase the difficulty of the pure Auto Layout approach:

- Say you want to add a grid backsplash similar to the one introduced in Chapter 5, "Debugging Constraints," (refer to Figure 5-4). Although these child views stretch to all four parent edges, they rely on sizing themselves by multiplying the parent's width and height. You cannot do that. You end up with zero-sized subviews.

- You build a small image view and center it in the parent. The image view provides an intrinsic content size, so it does not rely on the scroll view for its sizing. However, your layout does not reach from edge to edge. You end up with a "frozen" scroll view that fails to respond to user touches.

Although scroll views *technically* work with pure Auto Layout, a hybrid approach is much more practical.

Hybrid Solution

Fortunately, it's relatively easy to bypass the pure Auto Layout issues by creating a custom content view. Table 7-1 examines the layout tree for a content view solution, showcasing the Auto Layout gap that you fill with this solution.

Table 7-1   Locating the Scroll View Layout Gap

Parent	Child	Notes
Primary view	Scroll view or scroll view subclass	UIScrollView is well behaved in Auto Layout. Place the view and add its sizing and positioning rules. Manually manage the scroll view's contentSize.
Scroll view of some class	Content view	Content view is not a standard feature. Add your own subview using Autosizing and match the scroll view's contentSize.
Content view	Custom views	Use Auto Layout to manage the placement and sizing of child views added to your custom content view.

Although you can add your own content view to a UIScrollView instance—for example, in loadView or viewDidLoad—it's easier to build a compliant subclass, as in Listing 7-5. This AutoLayoutScrollView class is constraint ready, automatically passing along subviews to its custom content view. This way, when the content size changes, the content view updates its frame, allowing the subviews to respond accordingly.

Listing 7-5   **An Auto Layout–Ready Scroll View Subclass**

```
@interface AutoLayoutScrollView : UIScrollView
@property (nonatomic, readonly) UIView *customContentView;
@end


@implementation AutoLayoutScrollView
- (instancetype) initWithFrame:(CGRect)frame
{
    if (!(self = [super initWithFrame:frame])) return self;

    // Create custom content view using Autosizing
    _customContentView = [[UIView alloc]
        initWithFrame: (CGRect){.size=frame.size}];
    [self addSubview:_customContentView];

    return self;
}

// Override addSubview: so new views are added
// to the content view

- (void) addSubview:(UIView *)view
{
    if (view != _customContentView)
        [_customContentView addSubview:view];
    else
        [super addSubview:_customContentView];
}

// When the content size changes, adjust the
// custom content view as well

- (void) setContentSize:(CGSize)contentSize
{
    _customContentView.frame =
        (CGRect){.size = contentSize};
    [super setContentSize:contentSize];
}
@end
```

Building a Paged Image Scroll View

Listing 7-5 shows a way to incorporate Auto Layout into scroll views, allowing layout to update as the content size changes. A more interesting challenge for developers is a scroll view whose content size updates with respect to the scroll view's frame. Although it may sound wacky to couple content size with the parent's frame size, there's a compelling use case for this approach.

Figure 7-5 shows a scroll view whose paged content is laid out using Auto Layout. This particular example consists of five picture pages. A page view indicator, powered by the scroll view's delegate, keeps track of the current image. The size of the scroll view, and thus the size of each image, is determined by the device characteristics and orientation.

Figure 7-5   Auto Layout controls the paged scroll view layout.
Public domain image courtesy of the National Park Service

When its frame changes (you can key-value observe the scroll view's bounds), the scroll view adjusts its content size. Since this class inherits from Listing 7-5, the constraints guiding the layout of the child views adjust, matching each view to the scroll view's new width.

When you add new content, the scroll view updates its constraints, invalidating the old layout. Listing 7-6 introduces the updateConstraints method that does this. It lays out the new row of views and adjusts the paged content offset.

Paged scroll views may suffer from Auto Layout's best approximations, although this issue seems to be greatly diminished in iOS 7. With Auto Layout, a view that is 200.5 points across is very close to one that is 200 points across. You don't sweat the difference. Unfortunately, scroll views *require* layout precision. When paging, each set of data must be exactly the same width, or you will see artifacts near the page edges. Auto Layout cannot guarantee such precision.

Listing 7-6   **Building a Scroll View's Contents with Auto Layout**

```objc
// Update view layout and adjust content view
- (void) updateConstraints
{
    [super updateConstraints];

    if (!views.count)
        return;

    // Clean up previous constraints
    for (UIView *view in views)
    {
        NSArray *constraints =
            [view referencingConstraintsInSuperviews];
        for (NSLayoutConstraint *constraint in constraints)
            [constraint remove];
    }

    for (UIView *view in views)
    {
        // Center each view vertically
        CENTER_V(view);

        // Match each to the scroll view width
        INSTALL_CONSTRAINTS(500, nil,
            CONSTRAINT_MATCHING_WIDTH(view, self));
    }

    // Lay out the views in a horizontal row with flush alignment
    // These use routines from Chapter 4
    BuildLineWithSpacing(views,
        NSLayoutFormatAlignAllCenterY, @"", 750);
    Pin(views[0], @"H:|[view]");
    Pin([views lastObject], @"H:[view]|");

    // Update content size and page offset
    [self updateContentSize];
    [self setContentOffset:CGPointMake(
        (CGFloat) _pageNumber * self.frame.size.width, 0)];
}

// Update layout after adding a new child view
- (void) addView:(UIView *)view
{
    if (!views)
```

```
    views = [NSMutableArray array];
[views addObject:view];

// Add new child to the content view
[self.pagedContentView addSubview:view];
PREPCONSTRAINTS(view);

// Request fresh layout
[self setNeedsUpdateConstraints];
}
```

Centering View Groups

You might assume that with Auto Layout, you must anchor your content to a side when laying out views. That's because Auto Layout does not directly offer buffering to enable your content to float to the middle. You can work around this limitation to achieve the effect you want, as Figure 7-6 demonstrates. The secret lies in adding managed spacers around your content.

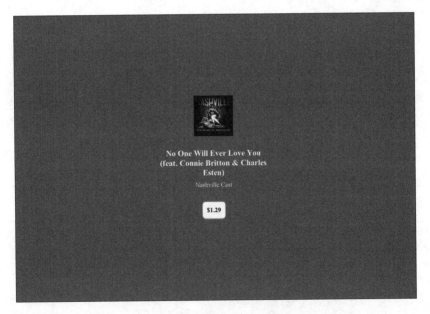

Figure 7-6   Buffering enables complex content to float to the middle of views.

You create spacers by adding generic views to your content. Spacers enable you to establish Auto Layout rules that create buffers and mandate floating layouts. This approach targets groups of views; it's meaningless for single views. You can always center a single view in its parent by equating centerX attributes.

Views, by default, are invisible. With clear backgrounds, you don't need to explicitly hide a view or apply a zeroed alpha level. Newly created views are otherwise nonfunctional and will not track user interaction. They provide an efficient, lightweight layout solution that's invisible to users and that doesn't interfere with application functionality.

These buffers push content to the center by adding rules that state "leave an equal amount of space above and below (or to the left and right) of these items." To make this approach work, you add two spacer views per axis for each group of views you want to float. Listing 7-7 shows an example of this.

In Figure 7-6, there are four spacers to manage. For more complex layouts, the spacer count grows accordingly. Make sure you consider ways to refer to your spacers for possible layout updates. You might tag them, collect them into outlet collections (yes, this approach works in Interface Builder [IB]), add them to arrays, and so forth.

You'll find a more general discussion of using spacers in Chapter 4, "Visual Formats."

Listing 7-7   **Adding Spacer Views**

```
// Create equal-sized spacers to float the view vertically
void FloatViewsV(VIEW_CLASS *firstView,
    VIEW_CLASS *lastView, NSUInteger priority)
{
    if (!firstView.superview) return;
    if (!lastView.superview) return;

    VIEW_CLASS *nca =
        [firstView nearestCommonAncestor:lastView];
    if (!nca) return;

    // If the common ancestor is the first view,
    // move one level up to accommodate the spacer
    if (nca == firstView)
        nca = firstView.superview;

    // Create and install spacers
    VIEW_CLASS *spacer1 = [[VIEW_CLASS alloc] init];
    VIEW_CLASS *spacer2 = [[VIEW_CLASS alloc] init];
    [nca addSubview:spacer1];
    [nca addSubview:spacer2];
    PREPCONSTRAINTS(spacer1);
    PREPCONSTRAINTS(spacer2);

    for (VIEW_CLASS *view in @[spacer1, spacer2])
        view.nametag = @"SpacerView";
```

```
    // Add spacers to leading and trailing
    // See the layout functions from Chapter 4
    BuildLineWithSpacing(@[spacer1, firstView],
        NSLayoutFormatAlignAllCenterX, @"", priority);
    BuildLineWithSpacing(@[lastView, spacer2],
        NSLayoutFormatAlignAllCenterX, @"", priority);

    // Hug edges, match sizes
    AlignView(spacer1, NSLayoutAttributeTop, 0, priority);
    AlignView(spacer2, NSLayoutAttributeBottom, 0, priority);
    MatchSizeV(spacer1, spacer2, priority);
}
```

Custom Multipliers and Random Positions

Constants are the only constraint property that you can update after you create and install a layout constraint. Here's what Apple has to say on the matter:

> Unlike the other properties, the constant may be modified after constraint creation. Setting the constant on an existing constraint performs much better than removing the constraint and adding a new one that's just like the old but for having a new constant.

Some constraints, however, depend on custom multipliers. Unlike constants, which refer specifically to exact point offsets, multipliers enable you to create relational attributes more in keeping with Auto Layout philosophy. For example, you can position a view a certain percentage across its parent without knowing that parent's size. Or you can size a view to be some factor of its parent's size, such as half as big or one-third as big. These relations enable you to avoid specific points and pixels.

Listing 7-8 demonstrates a multiplier-based layout. It establishes a (somewhat) random view position, as shown in Figure 7-7. This method places the view's center for each axis at a random location from 0% to 100% along its parent. To implement this placement, you need to remove any previous placement constraint entirely rather than update it in place, the way you would with constants.

This approach doesn't force views to remain onscreen. A placement at 0% would leave the left or top half of the view beyond the parent's edge. The same happens at 100% for the right or bottom half. To counteract this, you can use some sort of layout limiter, such as the limitToSuperview: method, to constrain the view inward. This has a somewhat negative effect on your random distribution near the edges.

As an alternative that doesn't suffer from parent edge cases, you could use buffers above and below or to the left and right of each view, adjusting their sizes proportionally to random values. I don't recommend this approach. It requires four extra views per placement, and the math is ugly.

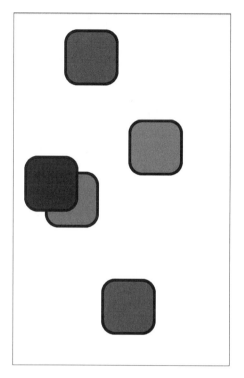

Figure 7-7   These views were positioned using random values for constraint multipliers.

Listing 7-8   **Establishing Random Positions Using Constraints**

```
- (void) setRandomPosition: (UIView *) view
{
    CGFloat randomX = (double) random() / (double) LONG_MAX;
    CGFloat randomY = (double) random() / (double) LONG_MAX;

    // Remove previous position entirely
    NSArray *constraints =
        [view constraintsNamed:@"View Position"
            matchingView:view];
    [self.view removeConstraints:constraints];

    // Establish new constraints
    NSLayoutConstraint *constraint;

    // Horizontal
    constraint = [NSLayoutConstraint
        constraintWithItem:view
```

```
            attribute:NSLayoutAttributeCenterX
            relatedBy:NSLayoutRelationEqual
            toItem:view.superview
            attribute:NSLayoutAttributeTrailing
            multiplier:randomX
            constant:0];
    constraint.nametag = @"View Position";
    [constraint install:500];

    // Vertical
    constraint = [NSLayoutConstraint
        constraintWithItem:view
        attribute:NSLayoutAttributeCenterY
        relatedBy:NSLayoutRelationEqual
        toItem:view.superview
        attribute:NSLayoutAttributeBottom
        multiplier:randomY
        constant:0];
    constraint.nametag = @"View Position";
    [constraint install:500];
}

- (void) limitToSuperview: (UIView *) view withInset: (CGFloat) inset
{
    if (!view || !view.superview)
        return;

    NSDictionary *bindings =
        NSDictionaryOfVariableBindings(view);
    NSDictionary *metrics = @{@"inset":@(inset)};

    for (NSString *format in @[
        @"H:|->=inset-[view]",
        @"H:[view]->=inset-|",
        @"V:|->=inset-[view]",
        @"V:[view]->=inset-|"])
    {
        NSArray *constraints = [NSLayoutConstraint
            constraintsWithVisualFormat:format options:0
            metrics:metrics views:bindings];
        [self.view addConstraints:constraints];
    }
}
```

Building Grids

Figure 7-8 shows a simple grid pattern that is common in Auto Layout projects. It's built from rows made up of labels, switches, and buttons. You can easily build similar layouts in your own projects. You generate arrays of views (in this case, labels, switches, and buttons) and apply rules that establish a proper grid. Listing 7-9 demonstrates how this layout was built.

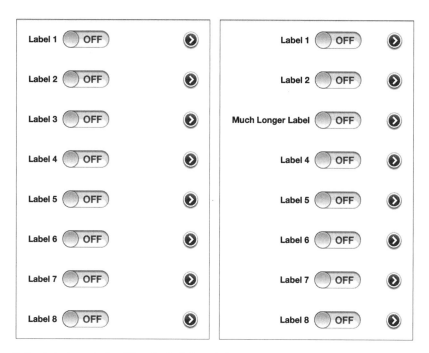

Figure 7-8   Auto Layout simplifies the building of view grids. Both of these layouts were built using the code in Listing 7-9. In the right image, the string `"Much Longer Label"` was manually assigned to the third label.

For vertical designs, start by considering how rows should be built. In this example, each label sits a fixed distance from a switch, and a disclosure button lies a fixed distance from the trailing edge. The behavior of Label 3 demonstrates the flexibility inherent in this layout.

Choose a row alignment. On the whole, the `centerY` spacing used in Figure 7-8 produces good-looking results, but you are not limited to this. If you prefer to align the tops, the bottoms, or (if on OS X, since the option is not yet supported on iOS) baselines, you may do so.

As Listing 7-9 demonstrates, it's easiest to build each row in the loop that creates your views. After establishing and storing views, you create the row that lays out those items. Every iteration adds a new row.

Each row in Figure 7-8 was built using two formats. The first of these installs at a high priority. It creates the two fixed relationships: between the label and the switch and between the button and the parent's edge. The second format installs at a low priority. It attempts to move the labels as close to the leading edge as possible:

```
@"H:|-(>=20)-[label]-[switch]-(>=0)-[button]-|"
@"H:|-[label]"
```

The second format explains where the label *wants* to be, even though the first set of rules prevents it from getting too close (it must stay 20 points away). Without this second rule, the label and switch placements are ambiguous. They tend to float away from the left edge.

So why do the labels and switches line up, even when the third label drastically changes its size? Strong constraints keep the switches aligned, matching their leading edges to each other.

Always identify the tallest items in each row. In the case of Figure 7-8, the tallest items are the switches. The tallest objects should always command your vertical layout, forming the basis for how each row follows the next. Listing 7-9 builds an aligned column of switches, pinning the first and last items to the top and bottom of the parent view.

This approach forms a reliable basis for most of the grid layout you'll encounter. You should separate the row creation from the column placement and stitch them together in a way that respects the physical height of each view.

Listing 7-9   Establishing Grids Using Auto Layout

```objc
- (void) loadView
{
    self.view = [[UIView alloc] init];
    self.view.backgroundColor = [UIColor whiteColor];

    buttons = [NSMutableArray array];
    switches = [NSMutableArray array];
    labels = [NSMutableArray array];

    for (int i = 0; i < 8; i++)
    {
        UILabel *l = [self createLabel];
        l.text = [NSString stringWithFormat:@"Label %d", i+1];
        l.translatesAutoresizingMaskIntoConstraints = NO;
        l.tag = i;
        [self.view addSubview:l];
        [labels addObject:l];

        UISwitch *s = [[UISwitch alloc] init];
        s.tag = i;
        s.translatesAutoresizingMaskIntoConstraints = NO;
        [self.view addSubview:s];
```

```
    [switches addObject:s];

    UIButton *b = [UIButton buttonWithType:
        UIButtonTypeDetailDisclosure];
    b.tag = i;
    b.translatesAutoresizingMaskIntoConstraints = NO;
    [self.view addSubview:b];
    [buttons addObject:b];

    // Layout each row
    NSArray *constraints = [NSLayoutConstraint
        constraintsWithVisualFormat:
            @"H:|-(>=20)-[l]-[s]-(>=0)-[b]-|"
        options:NSLayoutFormatAlignAllCenterY
        metrics:nil
        views:NSDictionaryOfVariableBindings(l, s, b)];
    [self.view addConstraints:constraints];

    // Pin each label to the left using a low priority
    pinWithPriority(l, @"H:|-[view]", nil, 300);
}

// [labels[2] setText:@"Much Longer Label"];

// Build vertical column of switches
pseudoDistributeWithSpacers(self.view, switches,
    NSLayoutFormatAlignAllLeading, 500);
pin(buttons[0], @"V:|-[view]");
pin([buttons lastObject], @"V:[view]-|");
}
```

Making Room for the Keyboard

Constraints offer the perfect match to keyboards, enabling you to use constants and animation to adjust text views around their appearance and disappearance. Developer Steven Hepting first introduced me to the idea of adding a dedicated keyboard spacing view rather than using other approaches, like content insets. This is a clever idea, as you see in Listing 7-10. It enables you to add to the bottom of your layout a view whose sole purpose is to listen for and manage keyboard events. This implementation is fully hardware aware and properly adjusts for optional input accessory views.

The `installToView:` class method offers the preferred entry point. The following snippet demonstrates how you might create and use a spacer in your own application.

```
// Create a spacer
KeyboardSpacingView *spacer =
    [KeyboardSpacingView installToView:self.view];

// Place the spacer under the text view.
CONSTRAIN(@"V:|[textView][spacer]|", textView, spacer);
```

Listing 7-10 Creating a Dedicated Keyboard Spacer

```
@implementation KeyboardSpacingView
{
    NSLayoutConstraint *heightConstraint;
}

// Listen for keyboard
- (void) establishNotificationHandlers
{
    // Listen for keyboard appearance
    [[NSNotificationCenter defaultCenter]
        addObserverForName:UIKeyboardWillShowNotification
        object:nil queue:[NSOperationQueue mainQueue]
        usingBlock:^(NSNotification *note)
    {
        // Fetch keyboard frame
        NSDictionary *userInfo = note.userInfo;
        CGFloat duration =
            [userInfo[UIKeyboardAnimationDurationUserInfoKey]
                floatValue];
        CGRect keyboardEndFrame = [self.superview
            convertRect:[userInfo[UIKeyboardFrameEndUserInfoKey]
                CGRectValue] fromView:self.window];

        // Adjust to window
        CGRect windowFrame = [self.superview
            convertRect:self.window.frame fromView:self.window];
        CGFloat heightOffset =
            (windowFrame.size.height - keyboardEndFrame.origin.y) -
                self.superview.frame.origin.y;

        // Update and animate height constraint
        heightConstraint.constant = heightOffset;
        [UIView animateWithDuration:duration animations:^{
            [self.superview layoutIfNeeded];}];
    }];
```

```objc
    // Listen for keyboard exit
    [[NSNotificationCenter defaultCenter]
        addObserverForName:UIKeyboardWillHideNotification
        object:nil queue:[NSOperationQueue mainQueue]
        usingBlock:^(NSNotification *note)
    {
        // Reset to zero
        NSDictionary *userInfo = note.userInfo;
        CGFloat duration =
            [userInfo[UIKeyboardAnimationDurationUserInfoKey]
                floatValue];
        heightConstraint.constant = 0;
        [UIView animateWithDuration:duration animations:^{
            [self.superview layoutIfNeeded];}];
    }];
}

// Stretch sides and bottom to superview
- (void) layoutView
{
    self.translatesAutoresizingMaskIntoConstraints = NO;
    if (!self.superview) return;

    for (NSString *constraintString in
        @[@"H:|[view]|", @"V:[view]|"])
    {
        NSArray *constraints = [NSLayoutConstraint
            constraintsWithVisualFormat:constraintString
            options:0 metrics:nil views:@{@"view":self}];
        [self.superview addConstraints:constraints];
    }

    heightConstraint = [NSLayoutConstraint
        constraintWithItem:self attribute:NSLayoutAttributeHeight
        relatedBy:NSLayoutRelationEqual toItem:nil
        attribute:NSLayoutAttributeNotAnAttribute
        multiplier:1.0f constant:0.0f];
    [self addConstraint:heightConstraint];
}

+ (instancetype) installToView: (UIView *) parent
{
    if (!parent) return nil;
    KeyboardSpacingView *view = [[self alloc] init];
    [parent addSubview:view];
```

```
    [view layoutView];
    [view establishNotificationHandlers];
    return view;
}
@end
```

Inserting Views at Runtime

Updating a layout to insert views can prove challenging. Consider Figure 7-9. It shows a line of views before and after a new view is inserted in the middle. To add that new view, you must replace the existing constraints between the left and right views. The lines in the figure represent the current constraint set.

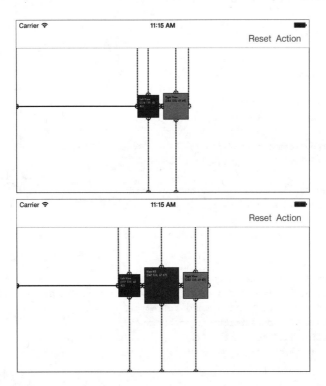

Figure 7-9   Adding new views requires that you locate and replace existing constraints.

Listing 7-11 extends the constraint matching approach first introduced in Chapter 2, "Constraints," to return an array of view-to-view constraints. Each item in the array references both views passed to the method.

Listing 7-11   **View-to-View Constraint Matching**

```
- (NSArray *) constraintsReferencingView: (VIEW_CLASS *) firstView
    andView: (VIEW_CLASS *) secondView
{
    NSArray *firstArray = [self constraintsReferencingView:firstView];

    NSMutableArray *array = [NSMutableArray array];
    for (NSLayoutConstraint *constraint in firstArray)
    {
        if ([constraint refersToView:secondView])
            [array addObject:constraint];
    }

    return array;
}
```

Fetching this array enables you to remove view-to-view constraint items and assign a new layout. Here's how the layout in Figure 7-9 transitions from the first screen shot to the second:

```
// Remove view-to-view constraints
NSArray *constraints =
    [self.view constraintsReferencingView:v1 andView:v2];
RemoveConstraints(constraints);

// Establish new layout rules
BuildLine(@[v1, newView, v2],
    NSLayoutFormatAlignAllCenterY, 500);

// Animate the results into place
[UIView animateWithDuration:0.3f animations:^{
    [self.view layoutIfNeeded];}];
```

To provide the smoothest animation, I set newView's initial frame to match either the left (v1) or right (v2) view's frame.

Adding iOS Frame and Constraint Overlays

Although OS X offers a way to visualize frames and overlays (as you saw in Chapter 5, in Figure 5-9), iOS provides no equivalent functionality. As I found this an extremely valuable debugging tool, I built my own solution, which you saw illustrating the example in Figure 7-9. This implementation appears in the ConstraintUtilities-Description file in the book's github repository, as the VisualLayoutHint category for UIView. It involves nothing more than drawing onto view layers and consists of a lot of tedious drawing tasks that relate little (if at all) to actual constraint development.

When this implementation is enabled, a display link timer updates the constraint and view drawings, so you can use this implementation in direct manipulation interfaces as well as static layouts. To enable the functionality, call `toggleVisualLayoutHints` on your main view controller view in `viewDidAppear:`, making sure to toggle again as the view disappears.

Motion Effects, Dynamic Text, and Containers

Before concluding this chapter, I want to offer a few final notes about iOS technologies and Auto Layout.

Auto Layout views work seamlessly with iOS 7's new motion effects and dynamic text. For motion effects, you can add behaviors to your views without worrying about any frame tweaking. iOS implements motion effects using layer transforms. They happily coexist with constraint-based layout.

With dynamic text, add an observer for `UIContentSizeCategoryDidChangeNotification`. In your handler, update layouts for top-level views, typically with `layoutIfNeeded`. Support for text updates is already built right into `UITextView` and `UILabel` for you. If all you're doing is updating these elements, let iOS do the work on your behalf.

When using Auto Layout with container views, be sure to reestablish view-to-parent constraints in `didMoveToParentViewController:`. iOS 7 automatically disposes layout constraints when you remove a view from its parent. When you add the view back to a parent, if you're using Auto Layout rather than Autosizing, you need to add those constraints back in.

Adding test colors to your view controller backgrounds can help you spot re-parenting errors, where child controllers have not fully and properly laid out with respect to their containers. Most typically, you'll see the background still laid out for a previous orientation.

Exercises

After reading this chapter, test your knowledge with these exercises:

1. How can you duplicate Listing 7-7's spacer solution in IB?

2. How do you set view aspect in IB?

3. Can you use the keyboard spacer from Listing 7-10 in IB?

4. How do you use the hybrid scroller strategy from Listing 7-5 in IB?

Conclusions

This chapter presents solutions for many Auto Layout challenges that commonly come up in forums, chat rooms, and e-mail lists. It provides concrete examples of implementing practical answers to those challenges. Here are a few final thoughts to take from this chapter:

- Leverage Auto Layout's power whenever you can. But be aware that not every technology is ready for it. When you're working with scroll views, use hybrid layout. With table cells, consider traditional content calculation for cell heights.

- Any design feature offered through IB, such as the layout of table view cells, has a code-based equivalent. On the whole, code-based solutions always offer at least as much expressiveness as IB.

- Let geometry guide the way as you build your constraints. As several of the solutions in this chapter show, finding relatable properties within your views can greatly simplify your final layout. Whether you're matching view sizes for accordion-style layout or equating negative spaces for view buffering, Auto Layout offers many more solutions than you might think.

- Even though these features are not emphasized in documentation, Auto Layout works beautifully with direct manipulation and animation. Any adjustment you make to a constraint constant can be performed in an animation block with `layoutIfNeeded`. Note that Auto Layout does not respond to `UIView` transforms. If you scale a view using transforms rather than constraint rules, other views will not move out of the way.

A

Answers to Exercises

Chapter 1

1. A label is constrained with 8-point offsets from its superview's leading and trailing edges. It is 22 points high. Is this label's layout ambiguous? If so, how can you remove the ambiguity?

   The layout is ambiguous. The label is missing a vertical position. Remove the ambiguity by setting a y position, such as by centering the label vertically in its superview or offsetting it a fixed amount from its superview's top edge.

2. You create a system-style button and assign it the title Continue. The button's center is constrained to a point (150, 150) from its superview's top and leading edges. Is this view's layout ambiguous? If so, how can you remove the ambiguity?

   The layout is not ambiguous. The view's height and width are established by the button's title. The button expresses an intrinsic content size, based on the words in its title and the system font settings.

3. In `viewWillAppear:` you create a new test view and add it to your view controller:

   ```
   UIView *testView = [[UIView alloc]
       initWithFrame:CGRectMake(50, 50, 100, 30)];
   view.backgroundColor = [UIColor blueColor];
   [self.view addSubview:view];
   view.translatesAutoresizingMaskIntoConstraints = NO;
   ```

   After these lines, you add constraints that center the test view within its superview. What size will the view be when the app runs? Why?

   The view will probably be zero sized at runtime. Although you established an initial frame, Auto Layout does not use the frame property for layout. It has no rules beyond the one that performs the centering to lay out the view. Since `UIView` instances do not express an intrinsic content size, this view will likely default to zero.

4. A 54-by-54-point image consists of a 50-by-50-point square, with a drop shadow offset 4 points to the right and 4 points down. (a) Show code that assigns alignment insets to this image. (b) When the image is added to an image view and center-aligned to its superview on both axes, what geometric point within the image lies at the center of the superview?

```
UIImage *image = [[UIImage imageNamed:@"sample.png"]
    imageWithAlignmentRectInsets:UIEdgeInsetsMake(0, 0, 4, 4)];
```

The center point should correspond to (25, 25) on the adjusted image.

5. You add a button to your view and constrain it to stretch from side to side at a priority of 500. Will it stretch? Why or why not?

The button will stretch. The button's default content hugging priority is 250. The constraint that stretches it has a priority of 500. The higher priority wins, and the button stretches at runtime.

Chapter 2

1. Can you build an NSContentSizeLayoutConstraint by hand? How and why do these constraints appear in Auto Layout?

You cannot build this by hand. This is not a public class, and you should not interact with it directly from code. This constraint derives from a view's intrinsic content size. Most system-supplied controls and image views express intrinsic content sizes. You can build your own methods to define a content size for your custom views.

2. What happens at runtime when two conflicting rules have exactly the same priority?

Auto Layout automatically breaks one rule or the other at runtime. This almost never ends in a visually pleasing interface layout.

3. Why use layout priorities like 251 and 249 in preference to ones like 257 and 243?

You rarely if ever need to express a cascade of priorities. A single-digit offset from standard values (250 is Auto Layout's predefined "low" priority) indicates a priority that's set with respect to that standard. Using one-off values makes your code more understandable at a glance. In the (rare) event that you need a second reference priority, use 252 or 248. This maintains the relative distance rule and ties that number to the standard priority it's set with relation to.

4. Why might you use views without intrinsic content size?

Many views without intrinsic content size play roles in your interface. From backdrops to content spacers, unadorned or invisible views help establish important areas within your layout, even without direct content of their own.

5. What happens if you install a constraint between a view and its superview on the child view?

The application terminates with an uncaught exception: "Unable to install constraint on view. Does the constraint reference something from outside the subtree of the view? That's illegal." This is not the user experience you should be aiming for. Make sure you install constraints to the nearest common ancestor between the two views.

6. What is the difference between constraining View A's width to twice the size of View B's width and constraining View B's width to half of View A's width? What happens if you install both constraints?

The two constraint rules produce identical results. Since the constraints do not contradict each other, you may safely install both. Auto Layout is not sensitive to redundant rules.

7. In Figure 2-6, where would you install a constraint between (a) View 1 and View 3? (b) Between View 1 and View 2? (c) Between View 2 and View 3? (d) Between View 2 and View 4? (e) If you add a button as a subview to View 2, where do you install a constraint between that button and View 1? (f) Between that button and View 2?

(a) View 3. (b) View 3. (c) View 3. (d) You cannot install a constraint because View 4 is in a different window from View 2, and they do not share a hierarchy. (e) View 3. (f) View 2.

8. You create View A and add a subview, View B. You add constraints that center View B in its superview and size View B to 100 points by 100 points. (a) Is View B's layout ambiguous? (b) How many items are stored in View A's `constraints` array? (c) How many items are stored in View B's `constraints` array?

You remove View B from its superview. (d) After this, how many constraints are stored in View A's constraints array? (e) How many constraints are stored in View B's array?

(a) The layout is not ambiguous. View B has a fixed position and size. (b) View A stores two constraints, specifically the center position constraints. (c) View B stores two constraints, specifically the height and width constraints. This follows the principle of installing to the closest common ancestor. Constraints that affect only one view install to the view itself. (d) After you remove View B, View A's two constraints are automatically removed. View A stores zero constraints in its array. (e) View B continues to store both size constraints, so the answer is two.

Chapter 3

1. Add three buttons to your view. Add constraints so the three buttons remain centered within the view, regardless of orientation and platform, with fixed offsets (see Figure 3-39).

Follow these steps to add the three buttons and keep them centered in the view:

  a. Select Button 2. In the Align pop-up, check Horizontal Center in Container and Vertical Center in Container. Click Add and Update Frames.

  b. Select Button 1 and then Button 2. In the Pin pop-up, check Vertical Spacing and set the constant to 8. Click Add and Update Frames.

    c. Select Button 2 and then Button 3. In the Pin pop-up, check Vertical Spacing and set the constant to 8. Click Add and Update Frames. Alternately, use the Editor > Pin > Vertical Spacing option.

    d. Select all three buttons. In the Align pop-up, check Horizontal Centers. Click Add and Update Frames.

2. Add a view with a colorful background color to a view controller. Constrain it so it's inset on each side by 40 points, regardless of orientation (see Figure 3-40).

Select the view. In the Pin pop-up, enable all four bars at the top and set each spacing value to 40 (see Figure A-1). Click Add and Update Frames. The top bar sets a constraint between the view and the top layout guide, which is where the 40-point inset starts.

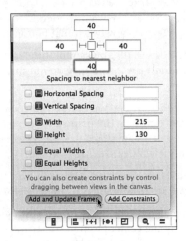

Figure A-1   Stretch a view with an inset.

3. Add three views to a new view controller (see the top image in Figure 3-41). Using IB alone, create a constraint system, as in the middle image in Figure 3-41, that when applied by updating frames produces the equally sized results you see in the bottom image in Figure 3-41.

Follow these steps to add the three views and apply the constraints specified:

    a. Select all three views. Choose Editor > Pin > Widths Equally.

    b. Select all three views. Choose Editor > Pin > Heights Equally.

    c. Select all three views. Choose Editor > Align > Horizontal Center in Container.

    d. Select View 1 and View 2. Choose Editor > Pin > Vertical Spacing.

    e. Select the new constraint and edit its constant to 0.

    f. Repeat steps d and e for Views 2 and 3.

g. Select View 1. Pin Leading Space, Trailing Space, and Top Space to the superview. Edit each constant to 0.

h. Select View 3. Pin Bottom Space to the superview. Edit the constant to 0.

i. Update the frames in the controller and save and use a preview pane to test the view.

4. Create a table that consists of left-aligned labels and two buttons in a row on the right (see Figure 3-42). Add constraints so the label and buttons remain properly aligned in every orientation, with all three items centered vertically.

Follow these steps to create this table, with three items centered vertically:

a. Select the label. Pin it to the left with a standard offset and align it vertically in the container.

b. Select the info button. Pin it to the right with a standard offset and align it vertically in the container.

c. Select the add button. Align it vertically in the container.

d. Ctrl+drag from the Add button to the Info button. Set the horizontal offset. Edit the offset to use standard spacing.

e. Update the frames in the cell. Save and test the view.

Chapter 4

1. How many constraints does the format @"H:[view1]-[view2]" produce? How many constraints does it produce if the options parameter is NSLayoutFormatAlignAllBaseline?

The format produces at least one constraint, relating the trailing edge of View 1 to the leading edge of View 2. It may produce more constraints if you pass a nonzero option to the options parameter. If you pass NSLayoutFormatAlignAllBaseline, the format produces two constraints. The second constraint aligns the two baselines.

2. How many constraints does the format @"H:[view1]" produce? How many constraints does it produce if the options parameter is NSLayoutFormatAlignAllTop?

The format produces no constraints, whether you pass 0 or any other options parameters. Although this format mentions view1, it does not request that any constraints be built.

3. Your format string is @"H:[view1]-[view2]". (a) You pass NSDictionaryOf VariableBindings(view1, view2, view3, view4, view5) to the views parameter. What happens? (b) You pass NSDictionaryOfVariableBindings(view1, view3) to the views parameter. What happens?

a. You produce the same constraint or constraints you did in question 2. The extra items in the bindings dictionary do not affect the result.

b. You raise an exception: "view2 is not a key in the views dictionary".

4. How do you request a set of views to align both on the top and on the bottom?

Pass an OR'ed mask of `NSLayoutFormatAlignAllTop` | `NSLayoutFormatAlignAllBottom` to the options parameter for a horizontal format.

5. How do you request a bottom alignment for a vertical format string, such as `@"V:[view1][view2]"`?

You do not. Alignment requests must be orthogonal to the layout axis.

6. What result does the visual format `@"H:|-(50@100)-[view1(==320@200)]-(50@300)-|"` produce on a screen that is 320 points wide? On a screen 480 points wide?

On a screen that is 320 points wide, the view stretches flush from the left side and goes 270 points to the right. It stops 50 points before the right side. The space to the right has a higher priority (300) than either the view sizing request (200) or the left spacing request (100). See the left image in Figure A-2.

On a 480-point-wide screen, the view starts at an inset of 110 points from the left. The 320-point spacing request, prioritized at 200, overrules the left inset request, prioritized at 100. See the right image in Figure A-2.

Figure A-2   Balancing priorities.

7. How wide will this view be: `@"H:[view(>=20,<=10)]"`?

Auto Layout will be unable to satisfy both constraint requests at once. It will randomly break one of these rules. The only thing you can say with some confidence is that the view will not be between 10 and 20 points wide.

8. Describe the results the constraint `@"H:|-(-20)-[view1(==50)]"` produces.

The view's height is constrained to 50 points. It's placed 20 points above the top of the view. Only the bottom 30 points of the view extend within its superview.

Chapter 5

1. IB finds Auto Layout issues at design time and compile time. Why worry about runtime and the console?

The console plays its most important role for constraints built in code and constraints that implement edge conditions and rule prioritization. For simple interfaces, you can often fully debug your GUI before runtime.

2. What role do multipliers play in constraints?

Multipliers are not included in IB. In code, multipliers provide a way to describe a portion of a view's extent. Use them to describe a view that covers only part of its superview or to place a view with respect to a proportion of its superview's leading or bottom edge. For example, you might place a view one-third of the way along its superview and extending half its width using multipliers.

3. An image view appears clipped, showing only about half its vertical content. What might be wrong?

Most likely, the view's compression resistance is low, allowing the clip to occur. Check the view's content mode, intrinsic size, and any developer-applied size constraints to see how to work around this limitation.

4. A visual constraint leaves 20 vertical points between `item1` and `item2` (`V:[item1]-20-[item2]`). What sign is the constant in the constraint produced by this format? Why? If you multiply the constant by –1, what happens to the layout?

The sign depends on how Auto Layout creates the constraints from this format. If the first item is `item1` and the second is `item2`, the sign is negative. If the two are assigned in the opposite order, the sign is positive. It really doesn't matter since the constraint describes the same condition: 20 points between the bottom edge of `item1` and the top edge of `item2`.

If you multiply the constant by –1, the two views will overlap by 20 points instead of space by 20 points. Auto Layout allows you to modify constants, even in installed constraints.

5. IB reports a fully satisfied, unambiguous layout. At runtime, one or more views express ambiguity. Why might this be?

If you mark any IB constraint as a placeholder, it is automatically removed on your behalf at runtime. This leaves an ambiguous set of constraints. This feature is meant for you to supply your own custom constraints. If you forget to do so, your views will be underconstrained.

6. A view appears properly placed until you test your application using an Arabic localization. In Arabic, the view placement is flipped horizontally. Why might this be?

Right-to-left (RTL) localizations only affect leading and trailing attributes. If you use left and right attributes, their positions do not flip.

Chapter 6

1. A view has two constraints. One, at a priority of 300, says the view should hug the superview's top edge. Another, at a priority of 301, says the view should center vertically within the superview. What is the likely outcome of these two rules?

The view will stretch from top to bottom to fulfill both rules.

2. A view has two constraints. One, at a priority of 300, says to place the view's vertical center at the superview's top edge. Another, at a priority of 301, says the view must be at least 50 points away from the superview's top edge. What is the likely outcome of these two rules?

The view will move as close as it can to the top but approach no closer than 50 points away.

3. Figure 6-1 demonstrated modular layout, where the view was decomposed into two children. If you used Autosizing to place content into the child views, would you disable `translatesAutoresizingMaskIntoConstraints`? If so, when? If not, why not?

Any view that participates directly (that is, is referenced as a `firstItem` or `secondItem` of a constraint) in Auto Layout must disable its translation property. Since the two child views are positioned using Auto Layout, their translation property must be disabled.

Within the two children, each content subview is laid out using Autosizing. `translatesAutoresizingMaskIntoConstraints` remains enabled for these.

4. When might you add Auto Layout rules between siblings instead of using parent–child relationships? Why does the drawer example in this chapter use a sibling handle?

Sibling relationships enable you to provide touch responses for all items, without worrying about view clipping or the edge of the responder area of the superview. In the drawer example, the handle was tied to the drawer by constraints but independently managed its presentation and touch responses.

5. How do the window-sizing examples in Figure 6-5 relate to iOS?

For the most part, they do not. `NSLayoutPriorityDragThatCanResizeWindow` and the other window-specific layout priorities are not defined on iOS. That said, you can use this approach on tablets to divide screen areas between two competing sections. Tablet space splitting is about as close as iOS currently gets to windowing.

6. When can you skip implementing `updateViewConstraints` and `updateConstraints`?

   If there are no circumstances where your layout will change and invalidate the current constraint set, you do not need to implement these update methods. You see this with simple layouts that easily adapt to portrait and landscape presentation. For example, a view with three centered buttons (for example, Load Game, New Game, and Credits) does not require orientation-specific design tweaks.

Chapter 7

1. How can you duplicate Listing 7-7's spacer solution in IB?

   Add two spacer views and, for convenience, give them a background color. Constrain them to the left and right (or top and bottom) and match their widths (or heights) to each other. Pin the horizontal (vertical) spaces between the first spacer and the first view and between the last view and the last spacer. Edit the constants to zero. Finish by reverting the two views' background colors to clear.

2. How do you set view aspect in IB?

   You cannot perform any multiplier-dependent tasks, including setting aspect, in IB. Use code instead.

3. Can you use the keyboard spacer from Listing 7-10 in IB?

   Yes, but you have to modify the code a little bit. Follow these steps:

   a. In Listing 7-10, the height constraint is an instance variable. Adjust this to a class property so you can assign a constraint from IB and update code references from `heightConstraint` to `_heightConstraint`.

   b. Add a plain view to the IB editor. Set its class to `KeyboardSpacingView` by using the Identity Inspector.

   c. Pin it to the bottom of the superview and stretch it horizontally. Add a text view above it and pin the vertical space between the two, adjusting the constant to 0. Add a new height constraint to the view and set its constant to 0. Assign the constraint to the class property.

   d. Make sure you call `establishNotificationHandlers` in `viewDidLoad` so the view responds to keyboard events.

4. How do you use the hybrid scroller strategy from Listing 7-5 in IB?

   The easiest way is to create a separate xib file and lay out the scroll view contents there. Create the scroll view in your normal storyboard and set its class to `AutoLayoutScrollView`. At runtime, load the content view from the xib file and add it to the scroll view's `customContentView`.

Index

D

K-L

W-X-Y-Z

    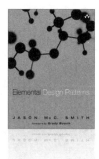

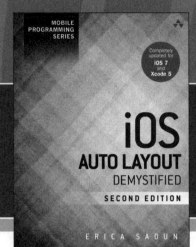

FREE
Online Edition

Your purchase of *iOS Auto Layout Demystified* includes access to a free online edition for 45 days through the **Safari Books Online** subscription service. Nearly every Addison-Wesley Professional book is available online through **Safari Books Online**, along with over thousands of books and videos from publishers such as Cisco Press, Exam Cram, IBM Press, O'Reilly Media, Prentice Hall, Que, Sams, and VMware Press.

Safari Books Online is a digital library providing searchable, on-demand access to thousands of technology, digital media, and professional development books and videos from leading publishers. With one monthly or yearly subscription price, you get unlimited access to learning tools and information on topics including mobile app and software development, tips and tricks on using your favorite gadgets, networking, project management, graphic design, and much more.

Activate your FREE Online Edition at
informit.com/safarifree

STEP 1: Enter the coupon code: HSIDWFA.

STEP 2: New Safari users, complete the brief registration form.
Safari subscribers, just log in.

If you have difficulty registering on Safari or accessing the online edition,
please e-mail customer-service@safaribooksonline.com